THE TYGER
THE LAMB
AND
THE TERRIBLE DESART

THE TYGER
THE LAMB
AND
THE TERRIBLE DESART

Songs of Innocence and of Experience in its times and circumstance
Including facsimiles of two copies

Stanley Gardner

cygnus arts

London **Cygnus Arts**
Madison & Teaneck **Fairleigh Dickinson University Press**

Published in the United Kingdom
by Cygnus Arts, a division of Golden Cockerel Press
16 Barter Street
London
WC1A 2AH

Published in the United States of America
by Fairleigh Dickinson University Press
Associated University Presses
440 Forsgate Drive
Cranbury
NJ 08512

First published 1998

ISBN 1 900541 35 1
ISBN 0 8386 3566 0

BRITISH LIBRARY CATALOGUING-IN-PUBLICATION DATA

A catalogue record for this book is available from the British Library

LIBRARY OF CONGRESS CATALOGUING-IN-PUBLICATION DATA

Gardner, Stanley
 The Tyger, the lamb, and the terrible desart : Songs of innocence and of experience in its times and circumstance :
including facsimiles of two copies / Stanley Gardner.
  p. cm.
 Includes bibliographical references and indexes.
 ISBN 0-8386-3566-0 (alk. paper)
 1. Blake, William, 1757–1827—Contemporary England. 2. Poets. English—18th century—Biography.   I. Title
 [DNLM: 1. Blake, William, 1757–1827. Songs of innocence and of experience.]
PR4144.S63G37   1998
821'.7—DC21   97–48277
                                                                                                                      CIP

Printed and bound in Kranj, Slovenia, by Gorenjski Tisk

To my sister

Shelagh Wilkinson

Contents

The Songs of Innocence and of Experience

To chart the historic background to Blake's *Songs*, we go back to the previous century, when Isaac Newton put in control of his universe 'a divine power', fashioned expressly on that which authorised England's social system. The security of status and privilege in Blake's aggrandising century was reflected in the cosmos, sacrosanct and scientific. Yet, rattling the gridlocked framework, and first recognised in Newton's day by Samuel Pepys, was King Mob. He was still potent enough to whoop the hearse of his darling, Queen Caroline, through the streets, as Blake was moving to his last lodging from his rooms over 'Tyburn's bloody river'. King Mob's was the longest reign of any sovereign.

Against the running tumult of the mob, an inbred and cultivated subservience sustained imperial commerce. It was a commerce which filtered down to children's books, where the income was so gratifying that even the trouble with France failed to disturb a profitable francophile tone, in books aimed at children of 'the better sort'. For the rest, it meant licensing, even more profitably managed. Neither tone was ever matched by Blake, who saw only the suffering contingent with the perpetuation of dutiful humility and polite good breeding.

There is little or nothing about 'sources' here, since, when we seem to recognise them, Blake always turned them. So *Emblems*, Francis Quarles's book of versified and illustrated piety, came out as early as 1635. Having fostered countless up-dated imitations, it was still reprinted, to be folded into the hands of children by aunts with propriety in mind, two hundred years later. An apparently infallible pattern for Blake's initial commercial intention, as a source of Innocence finally achieved it is a non-starter. But it lies there among the perpetuated detritus of eighteenth- century thinking—a stale circumstance, among so many more potent which transformed the book in Blake's mind, from a business undertaking into a vision of social cohesion.

It was a vision so potent, that in his last hours, Blake worked with clear delight on a little 'calling card' for George Cumberland, which became a reflection of Innocence recalled from "ancient time". It "would have been more finished if WB had lived" beyond the evening of 12 August 1827.

Personal biography, rather than relationships, comes into this book only as it touches Innocence and Experience. So, crucially through his early years, Blake's parents tacitly and unwittingly gave direction to his future as an artist, a recusant and a poet. By keeping the child to read and draw at home, they spared him both from the linguistic polish all school-teachers applied to their putative poets, and from being 'brought into some sense of religion and duty'. So Blake grew up thinking his poetry in the vernacular, and with an undirected sense of divinity and duty. Then, in line with eighteenth-century dexterity in turning a legal requirement to commercial advantage, it seems Blake's apprenticeship with Basire brought him, not only self-confidence, frustration and interesting contacts, but also relief to think his own poetic thoughts in peace. Round this off with his irritation in the Royal Academy, and two near misses with authority, and we can see the youth riding towards both tribulation and accomplishment, and towards the triumphant uniqueness of the *Songs*.

The most consistent and creative motivators of both Innocence and Experience were the familiar people around Blake, whom we may now come to know more closely. Among these, alongside the schoolmistress who spied for the Home Office, the master sweep, in church while his son climbed the flues, the solicitous nanny, the under-bred, parents, the dropped infant rescued from 'saddling the spit' and even the exemplary nurses, the most potent were the most vulnerable—those forlorn children he knew so intimately, rescued from St James's Workhouse by his neighbours across a few years of unacknowledged enlightenment.

As he printed copy after copy of the *Songs* across the years, varying each copy to meet a new idea or the taste of a buyer, the brevity of their rescue in *Innocence* was often recalled, while the victims of *Experience* were never far from his mind.

Readers will draw their own converging parallels through history to our contemporary reflections of *Experience*. But the unfulfilled challenge of its 'contrary', the selfless concord of *Innocence*, is more disturbing to contemplate, as it lies bound discretely in the pages of a masterpiece.

The second part of a book is usually a supplement. Here, in varying degrees of immediacy, it is the focus of all that has gone before. Further, the two copies of the *Songs*, facsimiled side by side, here offer the reader the chance to match Blake's engraving, as the constant basis of all the copies he individually coloured, alongside one of these copies.

The black and white facsimile is based on the copy printed, soon after Blake died, by Frederick Tatham from the original copper plates that somehow had slipped into his hands. Tatham's pagination differs wildly from any Blake set himself, and has no authority. It has seemed reasonable here to align these engravings alongside their finished colouring. Both facsimiles then conveniently follow Blake's own most familiar sequence, that commonly followed today.

Without the generosity and determination of Thomas Yoseloff, the founder of Associated University Presses, the book would never have appeared—certainly not in its present form. The inclusion of the two facsimiles, plain engraving and a finished copy, is entirely owed to his sustained initiative. We are then particularly indebted to the Widener Collection, Harvard University, for permission to facsimile their *Songs of Innocence and of Experience* copy I; and to the Houghton Library at Harvard for permission to reproduce their black and white engraved copy b. As the bulk of the original plates is now lost, the latter is the closest we can come to the *Songs*, as they were engraved by Blake before he variously coloured them to the end of his life.

Writing a book means building on the expertise and goodwill of many people, too easily taken for granted. I have had generous help from the following libraries: The Bodleian Library, The British Library, Colchester Public Library, the University of Essex Library and Westminster City Library. My reliance on the work of so many authorities on Blake and his times is evident from the notes. Particularly I am indebted to G. E. Bentley for his personal help and his essential publications; and to the illuminating work of D. V. Erdman, Robert N. Essick, M. D. George, Humphrey Jennings, M. G. Jones, J. R. Pafford, Michael Phillips and Samuel F. Pickering; and to the contributors to the *Kent County History*, the *Surrey County History* and *The Survey of London*. The spectacular eleven volume edition of *The Diary of Samuel Pepys*, by Robert Latham and William Matthews, brings the embryonic decades of Blake's century into intimate focus. And then there is the *Oxford English Dictionary*—invariably revealing and indispensable.

Sir Peter Parker's interest has been an unfailing support, since we first discussed the project many years ago. Ms Alison Shell, Curator of Rare Books at the British Architectural Library, gave me generous help in relation to the problems chimney boys faced above the hearths of Blake's neighbours, and with the flow of the two Tyburns. Richard Milward's complete knowledge of Wimbledon local history has been an on-going enlightenment. My daughter, Mary R. Gardner, has given all the help I have asked for with the illustrations, and incidentally brought to light the intriguing link between Holy Trinity, Wimbledon, and the foundation of The Waifs and Strays. This link between continuing child care and Wimbledon Common stretches back towards Blake's lifetime. Now nationwide, it is The Children's Society.

Was its origin in that small community south of the Thames a coincidence difficult to credit? Or do we have a continuum?

PART 1
THE TIMES AND CIRCUMSTANCE

Figure 1. SECTION OF THE PLAN OF THE CITIES OF LONDON AND WESTMINSTER ... BY R. H.[ORWOOD]. (1792–99). *Reprinted with permission of The British Library.*

This section of the *Plan of the Cities of London and Westminster* (1792–99) covers the locality of Blake's homes in Broad Street and Poland Street.

From Oxford Street (the wide street across the top of the plan), it could take a full hour for a coach to reach St James through the chaos that was Swallow Street (now the line of Regent Street).

Blake's birthplace, 28 Broad Street (now Broadwick Street), was on the corner of Broad Street and Marshall Street. No. 27, where he later set up the print shop, was next door. The houses, four floors and comfortabled, backed on to the St James's burial ground. Blake's brother, John, it was said, spent nine years as a ginger bread baker at no. 29, directly across the street.

"St James's Infirm[ar]y" is the cartographer's euphemism for the workhouse. Its entrance is marked in Poland Street, the Polish Ambassador's residence being next door at no. 49. In 1785 Blake moved to no. 28, opposite the side entrance to the Pantheon, now the site of Marks and Spencer's in Oxford Street. His garden backed on to the timber yard.

From Broad Street, a walk through Carnaby Market would bring him him as a young man to deliver haberdashery to the King Street school, adjacent to M. Foubert Passage, now Foubert Place, off Regent Street. King Street is Kingly Street now.

Thomas Butts, Blake's patron, occupied a house with an elegant garden in Great Marlborough Street, behind the Pantheon. Butts's close neighbour, Joshua Brookes the anatomist, kept a menagerie of wild animals.

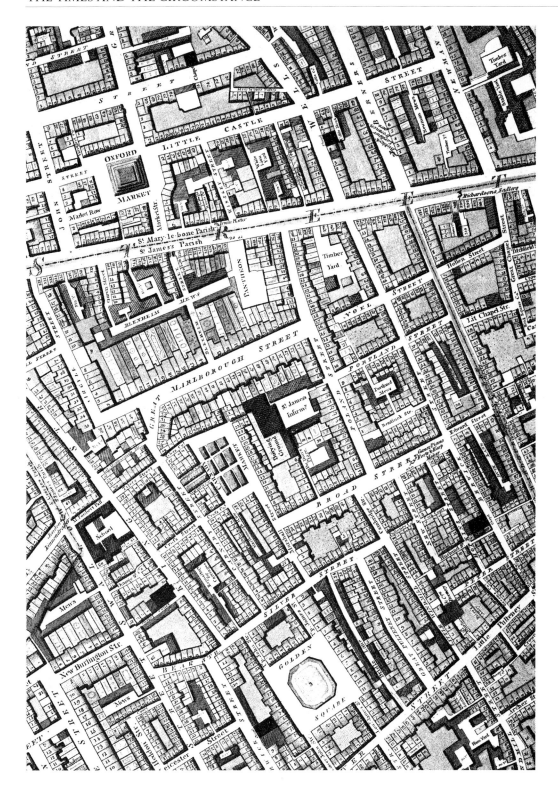

From Counter to Academy

Monday, 28 November 1757: William Blake came into the world in a room above the family's hosiery and haberdashery shop at 28 Broad Street, now Broadwick Street, a short walk southeast of what is now Oxford Circus. The house had been his mother's family home when she was Catherine Harmitage. The address was variously given as Broad Street, Carnaby Market, to be almost precise; or Broad Street, Golden Square, for respect, when James Blake advertised his business.

From this house, spacious enough to accommodate the family in a manner far better than most for its day, Blake knew the lifestyles of the city round him in all their inevitable extremes. On errands as a boy with haberdashery along Marshall Street for the superior ladies of Golden Square, Blake walked into a world of brittle and cosmopolitan delicacy, sustained by privilege and dressed in indifference. The Square and the surrounding streets were much favoured by artists as Blake grew up, including, most notably, Angelica Kauffmann. Established as a portrait painter in Italy as a child, by the time she was twenty-six and Blake was ten, Kauffmann was working for a time from Golden Square, and caught up disastrously with an adventurer, the 'Count de Horn'. With her pretty mythological and classical paintings and heady life-style, she typified the people Blake brushed against as a boy, in their "handsome and uniform buildings" overlooking the private grass plots and gravel walks.

The Square was then "very neat, though small, containing about two acres". The neatness did not last. By the end of the century, the two acres were unkempt as fashion moved out, making room for the likes of Ralph Nickleby. Soon "the first and second floors" were "let to single gentlemen", who "took boarders besides". But the two acres still retained a dejected cosmopolitan air around the sad statue of George II, now "the guardian genius of a little wilderness of shrubs". He is still there today, with only two houses left from his reign, numbers 11 and 21. Next door but one was number 23, the embassy fired by the mob Blake was mixed up with in 1780. The iron railings that fenced in the old privacy were fed into the war effort in the 1940s. The Westminster Paving Act, passed when Blake was five years old, had made walking the square more pleasant. But it was slow to bring improvements elsewhere. Open cellars and coal holes still invited a fall, though less night soil blocked the kennels, and refuse was at least dumped in the fields across Oxford Street, or carted to Battle Bridge, Pancras. But nothing for Blake alleviated the distress of an errand round the corner across Carnaby Market, where "the ox in the slaughterhouse" moaned under the knives of men and women who shared their rookery with the creatures they butchered. Blake was dead before this shambles was cleared away.

Hours before a child's working day finished as midnight approached, some eighteen times a month from sunset on moonless nights, James Blake Senior no doubt filled his statutory lamp with fish blubber oil (got from the vestry of St James's church, Piccadilly), lit the cotton twist at his stove, and hung the can outside his shop. One way its smoke blew towards the rookeries. The other way, going left up Poland Street, was another world which Blake came to savour as he grew older.

Here, early in 1772, a few months before Blake was apprenticed, the peerage opened the Pantheon, built over the previous two years at a cost of £60,000 (£6m today), on the corner of Oxford Street.[1] To reach it, Blake walked past the residence of the Polish ambassador, whose fish blubber oil illuminated the families locked out of the workhouse next door. Twenty yards up the road, the ladies of the town paraded in the brilliance of the light from the Pantheon, "20,000 lamps burning at once, ranged in curious devices, and reflected from an immense number of looking-glasses"[2] At this time, ladies who lacked virtue, as well as status and wealth, were "exempted from admission" without the recommendation of a peeress; not a peer, but a peeress. It was a rule which Blake saw relaxed for the oldest of commercial reasons a dozen years later, when he lived opposite the side entrance (see page 81 below).

But perhaps none of these vivid juxtapositions was as pervasive in Blake's everyday living, as was the 'breath' of the dead. Number 28 Broad Street stood on land anciently titled Pest House Close. It had been only twenty years before Blake was born that the pesthouse itself was moved out to Paddington (Blake's "mournful ever-weeping Paddington") and the Close opened up for the speculators. Part of the Close was left undeveloped as an extension of the adjacent burial ground, known evocatively as Pawlett's Garden. The ground was declared full even before the houses in Broad Street were built. Yet poor-holes were still dug for decades in Pawlett's Garden. These, an Address to Parliament reported two years after the Pantheon's doors opened,

are pits capable of holding three or four coffins abreast and about seven in depth; are always kept open till they are full, then the tops covered over with earth; and another pit about the same size is dug on the side of it, leaving the sides of the former coffins always open.

The disgrace was so common that it is strange that the report needed to be so explicit. The offence to Broad Street and other neighbours from

1. A few steps east of the present Oxford Circus.

2. William Hutton, *A Journey from Birmingham to London* (1785), quoted in Humphrey Jennings, *Pandæmonium 1660–1866* (London: André Deutsch, 1985), p. 84. The book presents an irresistible sequence of extracts clarifying the two centuries.

Pawlett's Garden persisted, "especially in sultry seasons and after rain".[3] It was thirty years before the grave diggers from Blake's parish were filling a fresh burial ground beside the Hampstead Road at St Pancras. Meanwhile he lived on the "circumambient air" of Pawlett's Garden, from his first breath until after he married. Yet the dereliction of the dead goes without mention in his writing while the dereliction of the living, who were privileged to go "to bed with the dead" in the workhouse, or haunted the night along Poland Street, was never far from his transforming pen. Never was a poet less self-concerned.

On the second Sunday after he was born, William was baptised in the reassuring elegance of the parish church of St James, Piccadilly. As he was taken to church, the infant made a symbolic journey across the social landscape of the eighteenth century, which was to possess his imagination all his life. Round Golden Square, it was a short walk down Swallow Street, straight into his parish church. Around him here were not only "the palaces of the greatest men", but also, in adjacent alleys, the ubiquitous cellars and garrets of the Piccadilly poor, luxurious alongside the unspeakable slums of St James's Market, as near to the church as was Burlington House itself.

By coming into the world at 28 Broad Street, William had chosen his parents well. Nothing distinctive in their lives has come down to us, but a successful parent is not always distinguished in history—rather often otherwise. Most profitable to the child was a stable and considerate home in a dangerous and vindictive century.

The social pecking order at the time among people who worked or begged for their bread was this: housekeeper, lodger, decayed housekeeper, settled poor, casual poor, destitute, criminal poor. William's father was a housekeeper. Finding yourself in that advantageous state was one thing; maintaining it against the eighteenth century's vagaries of injury, death, misfortune and miscalculation was something else—a distinctive, if unrecorded, triumph. Not least of the threats to commercial comfort was the outbreak of peace, in a managed sequence of profitable wars. Then all business was seasonal, and out-of-season ruin was commonplace. Without land and title, the effective insurance against ruin lay in belonging to one of the close-knit merchant families who ruled the city of commerce. Borne upward on the status quo, wealth rose and settled in the corporate purses. At this height, the only fatal threat was a disastrous gamble, and even that was seldom irrecoverable, given supportive connections.

When necessity drove, anyone turned a hand to selling something. Competition was universal. One woman in South Street, Hanover Square, kept a stall in which to eat, sleep and run her stocking mending business, while along the pavement the bankers, attorneys and directors could ask a

3. See M. Dorothy George, *London Life in the Eighteenth Century* (Harmondsworth: Penguin Books, 1987, 1st. ed. 1925), p. 345.

four-figure fee for apprenticeships and so keep the accounts within their family circles.

Misfortune struck lesser mortals every day. Francis Place gave a detailed account of his family's repetitive calamities. While his father was the contemporary social equal of Blake's father, their lives were unrecognisably different. A master baker, he lost and rebuilt his business twice, putting his family periodically on the street. He vanished for years, then turned up home unannounced. The one-time master baker then ran a sponging house in the Marshalsea prison, until the Act of 1779 ruined that business, which he had to sell for what it would fetch. He then turned innkeeper at the King's Arms in Arundel Street, lost all in a state lottery, and, beaten at last by circumstance, retired to a room in the Fleet prison, while his wife kept going by taking in washing.[4] The point his son was making in fixing the family record was not its drama of profit and loss, but its sheer common-and-garden ordinariness.

Against all this, James Blake, Sr, sustained a comfortable family concern in hosiery, haberdashery and, doubtless, the usual associated cosmetics, across four decades. When he died in 1784, he left his son and heir with a business competent enough to gain a parish contract. James Blake, Jr, four years older than William, kept the firm going, if in gradual decline in common with the vicinity, until he retired as late as 1812. To fend off chance and adversity so long across the eighteenth century was no slight family achievement.

Not only was William's home life consistently secure and undisturbed by ill-fortune, it was also supportive. His parents were apparently of an independent turn of mind. His father was "well to do, of moderate desires, moderate Enjoyments & of substantial Worth,' [and] by his Son's description, a lenient & affectionate Father, always more ready to encourage than to chide."[5] In an age when the rod was more readily offered than a reward, this is convincing testimony. It is surely impossible to join in identifying this gentle dealer in frills and face creams as the model for Blake's future and omnipresent Father, the progenitor of oppression.

Blake himself wrote when he was fifty, that he had "not lost any of his life since he was five years old without incessant labour & study."[6] To begin with, the labour was no doubt shop work and running errands. In the normal way of things, children from infancy joined the whole family in running a small business. Given that shop hours stretched from seven in the morning to near midnight, no help could be spared.

Haberdashers took in apprentices at very different levels, at fees ranging from hundreds of pounds for professional training, down to five pounds and less for workhouse drudges, almost invariably exploited. There was the apprentice aged thirteen, thrashed to death by Mrs Meteyard in her

4. George, *London Life*, pp. 302–4.
5. Frederick Tatham, in G. E. Bentley, *Blake Records* (London: Oxford University Press, 1969), p. 508.
6. David V. Erdman, ed., *The Complete Poetry and Prose of William Blake* (New York: Doubleday, 1988), p. 736.

haberdashery stall in Bruton Street, off Hanover Square. For once, exceptionally, the law squared matters and hanged the owner.[7] Against this, there was Misocapelus, the "second son of a country gentleman by the daughter of a wealthy citizen of London", whose 'letter' Dr Samuel Johnson printed in *The Rambler* on Saturday 27 April 1751. In Misocapelus, among the lace and cosmetics, we may read what might have been for Master William Blake.

Misocapelus's mother was accustomed to "the precincts of Cornhill", and the "civilities paid her at the companies' feasts by men, of whom some are now made aldermen, some have fined for sheriffs, and none are worth less than forty thousand pounds". She often spoke of her father and

the heaps of gold which he used on Saturday night to toss about with a shovel; the extent of his warehouse, and the strength of his doors; and when she relaxed her imagination with lower subjects, described the furniture of their country-house, or repeated the wit of the clerks and porters.

Her second son, "impatient to enter into a path which led to such honour and felicity", and, following his grandfather's maxim

that a young man seldom makes much money, who is out of his time before two-and-twenty . . . was transplanted to town, and, with great satisfaction to myself, bound to a haberdasher . . . By his instructions I learned in a few weeks to handle a yard with great dexterity, to wind tape neatly upon the ends of my fingers, and to make up parcels with exact frugality of paper and thread; and soon caught from my fellow apprentices the true grace of a counter-bow, the careless air with which a small pair of scales is to be held between the fingers, and the vigour and sprightliness with which the box, after the riband has been cut, is returned to its place . . . Applying all my powers to the knowledge of my trade, I was quickly master of all that could be known, became a critic in small wares, contrived new variations of figures, and new mixtures of colours, and was sometimes consulted by the weavers, when they projected fashions for the ensuing spring.

Returning home in the fourth year of his apprenticeship, the correspondent was uneasy to find that the country ladies despised his mother as a cit who had hurried him "into a state of meanness and ignominy". He continues:

I returned, however, to my master, and busied myself among thread, and silks, and laces . . . but I had now lost any felicity in contemplating the exact disposition of my powdered curls, the equal plaits of my ruffs, or the glossy blackness of my shoes; nor heard with my former elevation those compliments which ladies sometimes condescended to pay me upon my readiness in twisting paper, or counting the change. The term Young Man, with which I was sometimes honoured, as I carried a parcel to the door of a coach, tortured my imagination.

7. George, *London Life*, p. 228. The shopkeeper's daughter was also hanged. Again the proximity of different social classes is evident in the address.

A danger to trade, Misocapelus was discharged from the counter to the warehouse. However, in the sixth year of his "servitude", his elder brother, as was right and proper, "died of drunken joy, for having run down a fox that had baffled all the packs in the province. I was now heir, and with the hearty consent of my master commenced gentleman".

Young William Blake's release from being "young-man'd" was less elevating, but even less probable, and maybe no less approved by the management. Far from being compelled into family service as a quasi-haberdasher's apprentice, the boy "was privately encouraged by his mother" in such "insubstantial vanities" as drawing everything around him on "the backs of all the shop bills, and made sketches on the counter".[8] When he was ten his parents helped the "insubstantial vanities" along by putting him to "the preparatory school for juvenile artists then in vogue", conducted by Henry Pars, who had "gone into the juvenile Art-Academy line" in "the great room" of a house "on the left hand side of the Strand, as you go citywards, just at the eastern corner of Castle Court: a house and court demolished when Agar Street and King William Street were made".[9] Here the young Blake

soon attained the art of drawing from casts in plaster of various antiques. His father bought for him the Gladiator, the Hercules, the Venus de Medicis, and various heads, hands, and feet. The same indulgent parent soon supplied him with money to buy prints; when he immediately began his collection, frequenting the shops of the print-dealers, and the sales of the auctioneers. Langford called him his little connoisseur; and often knocked down to him a cheap lot, with friendly precipitation. He copied Raphael and Michael Angelo, Martin Hemskerck and Albert Durer [sic], Julio Romano, and the rest of the historic class, neglecting to buy any other prints, however celebrated. His choice was for the most part "contemned by his youthful companions, who were accustomed to laugh at what they called his mechanical taste.[10]

Such copying exercises as he experienced under Mr Pars were always much approved by Blake. At the end of the century, he discounted the opinion of Sir Joshua Reynolds in a note, punctuated in his personal way: "To learn the Language of Art Copy for Ever. is My Rule".[11] After two years "learning the language of art", Blake was back home helping in the shop and, apart from his time with Henry Pars, "never was sent to school".

It was some time around 1787, when his mind was turning to the relief-etching of Songs of Innocence, that he wrote these four lines in the Notebook which had belonged to his dead brother:

You say their Pictures well Painted be
And yet they are Blockheads you all agree

8. Alan Cunningham, Lives of the Most Eminent British Painters (1830), in Bentley, Blake Records, p. 477.

9. Alexander Gilchrist, The Life of William Blake, edited by W. Graham Robertson (London: The Bodley Head, 1907), p. 9.

10. B. H. Malkin, A Father's Memoirs of His Child (1806), in Bentley, Blake Records, p. 422.

11. Erdman, ed., Poetry and Prose, p. 636.

> *Thank God I never was sent to school*
> *To learn to admire the works of a Fool,*

and then altered the last line to read: "To be Flogd into following the Style of a Fool."[12] Clearly the two years copying antiques with Mr Pars did not count as a flogging in good taste; and the lines do not refer to his argumentative time at the Royal Academy, to which he "never was sent", but went himself. However Henry Pars' training was usually "preparatory to the Academy of Painting and Sculpture in St Martin's Lane", a follow-up Blake avoided.[13] The reference must be either to this escape, or to the expense which saved him from a 'flogging' in good taste, at the hands of 'a painter of Eminence', and saw him apprenticed to an engraver instead. The first line makes clear that Blake is not referring to his missing conventional schooling, and that the second thought about being "Flogd" is metaphoric, not physical.

Blake's lack of formal schooling was much deplored by his contemporaries, if picturesquely justified. Five years after Blake's death, while still profiting from selling the works he had acquired and burning what offended him, Frederick Tatham wrote of his friend: "like the Arabian Horse, he is said to have so hated a Blow that his Father thought it most prudent to withhold from him the liability of receiving punishment. He picked up his Education as well as he could." Crabb Robinson had made the last point in 1811—that Blake "early gave himself up to his own guidance, or rather, misguidance".[14]

In fact, we may see Blake's lack of an eighteenth-century education as a distinct advantage, given his parentage. Blake's early biographers record that his father was a dissenter, having changed his mind since William was baptised in some Anglican splendour. The boy clearly thought for himself. His mother was attentive. He was fully literate at an early age and read intensely and widely, across the previous centuries, and in contemporary poetry. Both literacy and literature can only have derived from his home, augmented by books he must have found as an apprentice in the house of James Basire. But even by the age of fourteen, before he joined Basire, he was reportedly writing verse of original quality.

The parents' neglect of a proper education for their son was as important as their independent-minded encouragement. Whatever the school he might have attended, the beginning of formal learning was simple—the implanting in the young, by boredom and the birch, of what Defoe called 'the Great Law of Subordination'. To start with, it would have been a hornbook school somewhat superior to that run by the local Dame Lurch.[15] Later, appropriately for the son of a householder of James Blake's status, it would have been a private academy, or one of the Free Grammar Schools,

12. David V. Erdman, ed., *The Notebook of William Blake, A Photographic and Typographic Facsimile*, (London: Oxford University Press, 1973), N. 42.

13. Gilchrist, *Life of Blake*, p. 9.

14. Bentley, *Blake Records*, pp. 510 and 448.

15. See 'The Little Vagabond'.

established for scholars to be "taught and instructed in the art of grammar for ever". The grammar school might well have been endowed "to nominate a sufficient scholar to the Masters and Seniors" of a college in the Universities of Oxford or Cambridge. This was another intellectual discipline Blake missed, for good or ill, through his parents' independent turn of mind.

A grammar school would have given the boy a drilling in the old classics, a method that was temporarily losing favour to private venture competition, promoted mainly by speculative clergymen with eyes on ambitious parents. The vogue was for a 'liberal' schooling, that is, encyclopædian aspirations and the indoctrination of urbanity and the sophisticated tricks of manners, in an age adept at self-seeking and time-serving—not that the daily grind of rote learning was spared, whatever the programme. Some private academies offered 'servile' instruction in commerce, military science, surveying and navigation; others advertised 'liberal' studies— natural or experimental philosophy (science), the globes (geography), chronology (history) and the like, all promoted at vastly ranging fees. The instruction was sciolistic at best, supplemented with a peripatetic gloss of dancing, music and French. It was a fashion that publishers of children's books were quick to feed, as we shall see.

Blake's parents were judiciously unimpressed and would do better for the child at home. Private tuition was common among the gentility, though in Broad Street it was of necessity unpaid and parental. By denying their son immersion in some stultifying and pretentious pool of learning, Blake's parents unwittingly shaped him for an uncomfortable future. He responded spectacularly.

Whichever schoolmaster might have taken on moulding Blake's mind would have lengthened the day with compulsory versification, both in translation from the classics and in original 'effusions'. In this respect, little had changed, since *The Spectator* reported, on 21 February 1712, that "nothing is more usual than to see forty or fifty boys of several ages, temper and inclinations, ranged together in the same class…all to be made poets…alike. They are all obliged to have the same capacity, to bring in the same tale of verse."

By parental indulgence, again Blake was denied the poetic good manners schoolmasters impressed upon children, from times pre-Milton to post-Keats. He lacked coaching in 'correct' diction. Having escaped a metrical flogging, Blake went on too naturally to write, in the vernacular we still speak today, poetry that was so often 'unsuitable': *Experience.*

Underpinning all, pupils were interminably "in the first place, directed to religion, and that as professed by the Church of England", unless the academy dissented. A little older, having perhaps been "taught to read, they proceed to the study of the Holy Scriptures". Once more, Blake avoided this saturation, from infancy to adolescence, in appropriated religion. Above all, perhaps, he missed the implacable lead into the Bible. So he remained his own Christian to the end of his days and, while all deplored his errant upbringing, as those who knew him time and again insisted, "through life, his Bible was every thing with him", and "His greatest pleasure was derived from the Bible—a work ever in his hand, and which he often assiduously consulted in several languages". Tatham recorded it as "a remarkable fact, that among the Volumes bequeathed by Mrs Blake to the Author of this Sketch, the most thumbed from use are his Bible & those books in other languages." Alongside this, Blake's friends acknowledged "how highly he reverenced the Almighty".[16] Without the perspective of hindsight, they could hardly recognise that such lifelong reverence might owe something to a want of schooling directed to sustain "the moral and religious advantages of Society", as the newspaper saw them—so fundamental to the interests of its readers.[17] Defoe's Great Law was a pragmatic sanction Blake was never taught by rote, and never respected.

When Blake was fifteen, "his love of Art increasing", "a painter of Eminence" was approached to take him as pupil. But the huge premium required led Blake to decline, "as he thought it would be an injustice to his brothers and sisters". The use of the word 'pupil' implied a tutorial commitment beyond even professional apprenticing. Blake's considerateness sounds typical; but it measures the status of the family business, that such a premium could even be discussed. It would have been nothing like the thousand guineas required in the closed shops of banking and shipping, but it could have run into hundreds. Blake & Son, Haberdashers and Hosiers, was no petty stall. Blake "himself proposed Engraving as being less expensive & sufficiently eligible for his future avocations",[18] and his father was shrewd and cautious in his choice of the master engraver to whom his son was apprenticed on 4 August 1772.

James Basire "was a superior, liberal-minded man, ingenuous and upright",[19] an artist and engraver to the Society of Antiquaries with long-standing family credentials. So the firm at 31 Great Queen Street, Lincoln's Inn Fields, was established in respectability. Basire's fee was fifty guineas, which covered the apprentice's keep and his training in industry as a journeyman engraver. Though Basire came to use his brilliant apprentice professionally, the training was not registered as professional. Nevertheless, through the door from the workshop, Blake was surrounded by counters and shelves of books and prints, and he was in touch day by day with discriminating and learned customers. Blake never forgot the day Goldsmith walked into the shop.

After two years, Basire sent his apprentice on continuous visits to Westminster Abbey, where, Malkin records,

16. J. T. Smith and Frederick Tatham in Bentley, *Blake Records*, p. 458, p. 467, pp. 526–7.

17. *The Observer*, 4 December 1791.

18. Tatham in Bentley, *Blake Records*, pp. 510–11.

19. Gilchrist, *Life of Blake*, p. 14.

he was employed in making drawings from old buildings and monuments, and occasionally, especially in winter, in engraving from those drawings. This occupation led him to an acquaintance with those neglected works of art, called Gothic monuments. There he found a treasure, which he knew how to value. He saw the simple and plain road to the style of art at which he aimed, unentangled by the intricate windings of modern practice.[20]

Basire's motive was to use Blake's skill to fulfil his engagement "to Engrave a Work for the Antiquarian Society". Blake found himself under instructions to draw for whole days among "the Monuments of Kings & Queens in Westminster Abbey".[21] The apprentice's drawings, "ever attentive to the delicacies & timorous lineaments of the Gothic Handling", and the fact that they he could be used profitably, led his master to consider the opinionated apprentice "an acquisition of no mean capacity".[22]

These long days in Westminster Abbey, and "other Churches in and about London",[23] were a unique experience, at the same time profound and resistible, as Blake's subsequent work shows. Among the banners of decrepit pride, he was copying the features of medieval tyrants and their episcopal accomplices—and the activity most revered in his prescribed drawings was warfare. There was nothing of medieval romance hanging in the "the gloomth of abbeys and cathedrals" for the gifted apprentice.[24] Against this, the months Blake spent free from the workshop and the Basire household, where privacy for an apprentice would hardly exist, must have facilitated his early versifying in more than one way.

These long spells of directed labour among the tombs and monuments lead us to speculate on how much time Blake in fact spent in Basire's house. Under the indenture his master was to find him "Meat, Drink, Apparel, Lodging, and all other Necessaries".[25] We do not know how closely these terms were met by Basire, and the exceptional responsibility he loaded on his brilliant apprentice begs a question. It matters how Basire might have defined 'exceptional' to his own advantage, given the ample scope the practice of the time afforded him. The weeks Blake spent among dead monarchs were hardly the norm for an engraver's apprentice but this was simply Basire's personal adjustment to the system of apprenticing, progressively and privately manipulated through the eighteenth century.

The most agreeable and profitable arrangement all round was seen to be out-door apprenticing. By 1772, the very year Blake joined the Basire establishment, a past apprentice to the King's printer, no less, testified that "a very fatal and unhappy practice has taken place in London and Westminster and which has been followed up in the country, of taking what is called out-door apprentices."[26] In little time it easily became "a very common custom", and, like many common customs then profitably adopted, righteously and ineffectually deplored.

20. Bentley, *Blake Records*, p. 422.

21. Frederick Tatham in Bentley, *Blake Records*, p. 511.

22. Ibid., p. 512.

23. Ibid., p. 511.

24. See David Bindman, 'Blake's Imagination and the History of England' in *William Blake, Essays in Honour of Sir Geoffrey Keynes*, edited by Morton Paley and Michael Phillips (London: Oxford University Press, 1973), ending in an authoritative summary, p. 49.

25. Bentley, *Blake Records*, p. 10.

26. George, *London Life*, pp. 268–69, and pp. 382–4.

With the growth of this convenient move towards non-residential apprenticing—less expensive for parents, less tiresome for masters—went (inevitably in the century) a gratuitous relaxation of the rule of residence. By 1775, Jonas Hanway was writing that "there is but a small number of masters in these days who can or will keep their apprentices within doors in the evening, when their shops are shut".[27]

It was, of course, the riotous, even murderous, conduct of apprentices on the streets that led to criticism of masters who relaxed their discipline. There is no evidence that Basire was in the slightest way negligent as a master. But he had in Blake the apprentice least likely to riot should he be released from supervision. At the same time, Tatham's assertion of Blake's stubborn involvement in "frequent quarrels" among the boys at Basire's house "concerning intellectual argument" rings true.[28]

One justification for sending Blake off to sketch medieval monuments must have been that Basire knew him to be well ahead of instruction. His presence in a workshop, bored with skills he had long mastered and stirring up "intellectual argument", must have been tiresome. The haberdashery shop was some half mile west of Basire's house, on the way to the Abbey. Given the contemporary attitude to apprenticing, it seems inevitable that Blake made more than occasional visits home. Indeed it is reasonable to assume that it was congenial all round, if he curtailed his evening walk at 28 Broad Street, after days locked in the Abbey. Apprentices invariably dossed down under the shop counter, in a garret or in the workshop, never in rooms of their own. Evenings away from provocation, and the chance of his own bed in Broad Street, must have been easy for the apprentice to take. No-one could have minded much; and nobody need have recorded it as 'exceptional', under the relaxing rules of the current apprenticeship game.

While his absorption with "Gothic Handling" "gathered to itself impressions that were never forgotten", it had limited effect on the verse of his youth. Circumstances suggest that the verses in *Poetical Sketches* were written more often at home. It must have been easier there than at 31 Great Queen Street, in between raising arguments in the print shop. Then it is not true that Blake's imagination, in Tatham's exalted phrasing, "ever after wandered in a cloister, or clothing itself in the dark Stole of mural sanctity, it dwelt amidst the Druid terrors".[29] Compelling as the daily confinement may have been among the residue of medieval oppression, the robust company he characterises in *An Island in the Moon*, together with an unprecedented social rescue, clearly erased it all from his mind in the 1780s.

Though he acquired from Basire no more than "the mechanical part of Art, even of the engraver's art", Blake came out as a journeyman engraver

27. Jonas Hanway, *Citizen's Monitor* (1780), p. 57.
28. Bentley, *Blake Records*, p. 511.
29. Ibid., p. 512.

with ideas to take him beyond life as an artisan. He had, after all, been entrusted with drawing for the Master's commission to engrave the illustrations for a book no less weighty than Richard Gough's *Sepulchral Monuments in Great Britain*. He recollected later in life that from his early days he had objectively "cultivated the two arts, Painting & Engraving", since, in an engraving, "no other Artist can reach the original Spirit so well as the Painter himself".[30]

So the journeyman extended his scope by getting a recommendation from an approved artist, submitting successfully an anatomical drawing with detailed notes, and gaining admission to the Antique School of the Royal Academy of Arts in its new quarters in Somerset Place, the Strand. On 8 October 1779, he was registered as a student in engraving, a discipline lately and reluctantly acknowledged by the Academicians, since painters profited from engravers. On the same day the Academy admitted a sculptor and several painters, one aged fourteen and perhaps about to be "flogd" in the way Blake avoided. George Moser, the first Keeper at the Academy, in charge of students, had formerly run the school in St Martin's Lane, which as a junior Blake had dodged. Moser, well into his seventies when he caught up with Blake, was revered by Reynolds as "the Father of the present race of artists". It was a paternity that Blake secretly raged to disown. Moser died in 1783, the year after Blake's favourite brother, Robert, entered the Academy.

30. Erdman, ed., *Poetry and Prose*, p. 567. Blake's 'apprenticeship' in Republican Art at the time is covered by David Erdman in chapter 3 of his *Blake: Prophet Against Empire* (New York: Dover, 1977, 3rd ed.).

CHAPTER TWO

Indiscreet Involvements

There are stories of Blake's resisting what he saw as intellectual intimidation at the Academy, where engravers were disciplined as painters. George Moser was a fine enamel painter and medallist, eccentric, popular among students, and proud to have entertained Queen Charlotte to a long chat in her native German when she invited herself into his apartment. He was also a stickler, often too close to Blake for comfort. And Moser was not the only one. Blake even expressed his lifelong indignation at having been instructed by the President, Reynolds himself, "to work with less extravagance and more simplicity, and to correct his drawing".[1]

The friction Blake's manner could generate comes well through the recollection of his student days, which he noted decades later in the margin of Reynolds's *Works*. No doubt it was the proximity of Reynolds' paintings that roused the memory of George Moser:

I was once looking over the Prints from Raphael & Michael Angel[o] in the Library of the Royal Academy Moser came to me & said You should not Study these old Hard Stiff & Dry Unfinishd Works of Art. Stay a little & I will shew you what you should Study. He then went & took down Le Bruns & Rubens's Galleries How I did secretly Rage. I also spoke my mind [a line Blake thought judicious to delete] I said to Moser, These things that you call Finishd are not Even Begun how can they then, be Finishd? The Man who does not know The Beginning, never can know the End of Art.[2]

About this time Blake was "frequently passing his evenings in drawing and designing" in the company of John Flaxman, Thomas Stothard and George Cumberland. It was the beginning of long friendships. Flaxman, frail of body and gentle of mind, had entered the Academy in 1769, and was rarely without work as a sculptor for the rest of his life, though much of his income came from his delicate designs for Wedgwood. He married in 1782, the same year as Blake, and they met often in the late 1780s. His monumental sculptures, of considerable grace, may be seen in Chichester Cathedral and Westminster Abbey. By 1810 he held the Chair of Sculpture at the Academy, and by 1817, the year his wife Nancy wrote her name in a copy of Blake's *Songs*, Blake had engraved many of Flaxman's designs. Despite the disparity in their circumstances, their friendship survived difficulties and differences, and Flaxman was buying Blake's work to the end of his life. He died the year before Blake himself.

1. Gilchrist, *Life of Blake*, p. 286.
2. Erdman, ed., *Poetry and Prose*, p. 639. Gilchrist, *Life of Blake*, p. 30.

Early in Thomas Stothard's life, the eighteenth century dealt him the familiar shifts of fortune that Blake had missed. His father died before the boy began his apprenticeship to a pattern-drawer, who then cleared the way for the apprentice by dying before the indenture was out. The apprentice stayed home with the pattern-drawer's widow, who encouraged him in the designs he left lying round the place. Stothard was rescued from a lifetime of pattern drawing among textiles by another turn of fortune, when his sketches were picked up by a publisher who called on the widow. An instant commission was the first of three thousand or so designs Stothard produced in his lifetime, some of them engraved by Blake, still on the ground, as it were, while fortune propelled his friend skyward. By 1794, the year *Songs of Experience* was printed and ignored, Thomas Stothard was a Royal Academician. By 1813, when Blake was labouring in obscurity, Stothard was Academy Librarian.

Blake's friendships ranged across the social spectrum. George Cumberland, the third companion of these years who also remained a friend throughout Blake's life, was of a different cut. Though his branch of the family had come heavily down in the world in a way typical of the times, he was still of consequential stock. His mother was the daughter of Richard Bentley, the avaricious collector of ecclesiastical preferments, Royal Librarian at the Court of St James, and litigious Master of Trinity, Cambridge. His father, a money-lender who died when George was nineteen, was the grandson of Richard Cumberland, Bishop of Peterborough and respondent of Hobbes. His cousin was another Richard Cumberland, who slipped into a fellowship at Trinity by the door of divine right. He then lost £4,500 of his own money in a farcical undercover mission to Spain, as Secretary to the Board of Trade. This disaster behind him, Richard retired to invent other dramatic farces. Immortality was conferred upon him by Sheridan—he remains Sir Fretful Plagiary in *The Critic*.

George Cumberland, so different from Blake in temperament and lapsed connections, shared his family's wayward streak. In 1780 he was making his way in art work for an assurance company, until a windfall legacy of £300 a year projected him into a life of modest independence. He had the talent to enjoy it. He turned his mind, among much else, to a string of inventions, to liberating trade, and to the reformation of prostitutes. At the same time, having travelled indulgently, he always returned to London as required, to enjoy the unabashed accommodation of the wife of his landlord, and to collect his dividends.

George Cumberland (indirectly) and Thomas Stothard (directly) were both associated with Blake at the time, in escapades that could have been dangerous. On Wednesday, 7 June 1780, Cumberland wrote that he had spent most of the previous Sunday night balanced on a wall,

near the Romish chapel in Moor fields witnessing scenes wh[ich] made my heart bleed …
the Mob encouraged by Magistrates and protected by troops—with the most orderly
injustice destroying the property of inocent [sic] individuals.[3]

He had been watching the Gordon Riots, which on the Tuesday had
involved Blake. This was not a rabble, but an eighteenth-century mob at
work. It was a phenomenon Blake lived with most of his life and which
helped to shape his thinking. It is not that he condoned the violence, but
he instinctively knew what motivated it. The frustrations and aspirations
of the rioters to an extent shaped his thinking, and in this respect the
nature of the mob is more relevant than Blake's reported involvement on a
June day in 1780.

The mob invented itself a century before Blake knew it, and from the
beginning, through the tumult of decades, no aspect of it changed very
much. Longevity was a main feature, the mob's influence seemingly irrepressible. This being so, we can even let Samuel Pepys define it for us, as he
watched the mob roll into history.

Mob: the first date the dictionary gives to the word is 1688. Earlier on,
Pepys had recorded the activity without using the word. Rioting apprentices were a spectacle worth a visit, but no more than a mention, so
common were their affrays, then and through the next century. Coal
heavers marching, or the mutinies of seamen reacting to misery, injustice,
or the withholding of rations or pinch-gut money, were easily put aside
with exemplary jailing and hanging, as formally as the passing of months.
As Pepys remarked: "31 August 1663: the City-Marshall and his men did lay
hold of two or three of the chief of the companies that were in the mutiny
the other day and sent them to prison. I home to dinner".[4] Even in the first
days of the Restoration, when there was the noise of guns "over against
Somerset House", and he "saw the Foot face the Horse and beat them back"
in the Strand, "bawling and calling in the street for a free Parliament and
money", Pepys went on without comment to "a sport called Selling of a
Horse for a Dish of Eggs and Herrings". Since the intervention in politics
was military, it had a familiar, official stamp. It seemed little worse when
"30 or 40 prentices of the City" ganged up with the foot-soldiers. Pepys
went off "to Priors, the Renish wine-house, and there had a pint or two of
wine and a dish of Anchovies" (2–3 February 1660).

Four years later it was different, when a riot of seventeenth-century
seamen, applauded by their wives, mutated into an eighteenth-century
mob:

4 June 1667: The City is troubled at their [the trainbands'] being put upon duty:
summoned in one hour and discharged two hours after and then again summoned two

3. Bentley, *Blake Records*, p. 18.

4. Quotations from Pepys are from
the magnificent transcription of
the *The Diary of Samuel Pepys* in 11
volumes, by R. C. Latham and W.
Matthews, (London: G. Bell &
Sons, 1970–83), and are located by
dates.

hours after that, to their great charge as well as trouble; and Pelling the pothecary tells me the world says all over that less charge then what the kingdom is put to, of one kind or other, by this business, would have set out all our great ships. It is said they did in open streets yesterday, at Westminster, cry, "A Parliament! a Parliament!"; and do believe it will cost blood.

It did cost blood. The cry was the same, but the voice had changed. The mob turned on the house of the Lord Chancellor, cut down his trees, broke the windows, "and a Gibbet either set up before or painted upon his gate, and these words writ – 'Three sights to be seen; Dun-kirke, Tanger, and a barren Queen' ".

When Pepys dined this June day there was talk "very sorowfully of the posture of the times", and that:

people do make nothing of talking treason in the streets openly: as, that we are bought and sold and governed by Papists and that we are betrayed by people about the King and shall be delivered up to the French, and I know not what.

Thoughts at dinner that night were sombre, concerning prophesies of "the burning of the city", and even of "a greater desolation".

In March the next year the mob was out in force round Poplar and Moorfields. The nature of the disorder, "the posture of the times", constituted a new and serious threat to the establishment. On 24 March 1668, "the apprehensions which this did give to all the people at Court" meant "all the soldiers, horse and foot, to be in armes". Drawn by the excitement of an affray, Pepys himself is away to Lincoln's Inn Fields as of old, to see the apprentices in action. But the spectacle takes a menacing turn. Authority dissolves in panic, with the fields "full of soldiers all in a body, and my Lord Craven commanding of them, and riding up and down to give orders like a madman".

Later, when some who were "pulling down bawdy-houses" were brought by the guard to Whitehall, the bystanders found no "fault with them, but rather of the soldiers for hindering them". Then a Justice of the Peace explained to the King, that: "he had been endeavouring to suppress this tumult, but could not; and that imprisoning some in the new prison at Clerkenwell, the rest did come and break open the prison and release them". The next day Pepys wrote the coda:

But here it was said how these idle fellows have had the confidence to say that they did ill in contenting themselves in pulling down the little bawdy-houses and did not go and pull down the great bawdy-house at Whitehall. And some of them last night had a word among them, and it was "Reformation and Reducement!" This doth make the courtiers ill at ease to see this spirit among people, though they think this matter will not come to much; but it speaks people's mind. And they do say that there are men of understanding among them, that have been in Cromwell's army; but how true that is I know not.

Exemplified vividly in these so casual yet incisive records we have the initial elements that characterised the mob for the next century—with one change, precisely as Blake himself was to know them during his life.

By his time, the mob had the status of antiquity. Updated only to accommodate empire, gin and commercial oligarchy, the first principles remained: the rumour ("how true that is I know not"), the violence against property, "No Popery!", the opening of prisons, the menace to the establishment beyond the breach of order, the official helpless panic, the resentment at martial intervention, the equivocation of the military, the disengaged background of mass support, the outraged sense of betrayal, the catchphrase "Reformation and Reducement!", treason shouted in the streets. The roots went down a hundred years—reformative, reactionary, jealous of rights invaded in charters, though never revolutionary. And then, crucially, two things: the mob "speaks people's mind", and yet is grossly manipulable by "men of understanding", at times "among them".

Above all others, Pepys knew that in the mob, it was these last two elements that would erase from the next century the courtly self-deception he recorded. As ever, how grievously, historically mistaken was Whitehall's initial reaction: "this matter will not come to much".

By 1715, under the Riot Act, a congregation of twelve had become an insurrection punishable by hanging. But the mob survived the Act. It survived both the gallows at the end of Oxford Street, and the plot of earth alongside, marked conveniently on contemporary maps as "the Field where the Soldiers are shot"; many for not dutifully shooting the mobsters.

It is noticeable that Pepys neither sounded so sure that it would "not come to much" nor felt so queasily "ill at ease" as the courtiers. He knew "the people's will" more familiarly than did they, and his class was not so essentially threatened. Neither was Blake's, when a mob that Pepys would still have recognised was moving round Broad Street a century later. It drew Blake on 6 June 1780, as hypnotically as it had drawn Samuel Pepys. Much had changed, yet so much remained the same, and the mob had so spoken "people's mind", that its unthinkable, brutally fought aspirations were distilled in politics by radicals like Horne Tooke, and in familiar tragedy by Blake in the lines of *Experience*. The impertinent claims of the Little Vagabond and the "mind-forg'd manacles" along the "charter'd Thames" subsume a century of wrong.[5]

When George Cumberland wrote that he had spent the best part of the

5. That Blake knew Horne Tooke seems likely. See Bentley, *Blake Records*, p. 77, n. 1, and p. 318, n. 2. Horne Tooke lived in Wimbledon, and, tantalisingly, (Richard Milward tells me) rented his house to one of the hundreds of Blake's namesakes in the county.

previous Sunday night on a wall, he reported indignantly that on that night the magistrates, ("men of understanding"), not only took sides with the mob, but restrained their guard from firing. On the following Wednesday he recorded how, the day before, the mob had already destroyed houses, schools "and many private masses", then cleared the prisoners from Newgate and torched the place. This was the day Blake was apparently among the front runners to Newgate. Twenty-four hours later the government mustered the troops, and Cumberland was writing that the mob, five thousand strong, was, even then, off to deal with the houses of the Duke of Richmond and Lord Shelburne, later young William Pitt's powerful patron. Cumberland had mutiny to report: "The soldiers its said laid down their arms today on being ordered to fire".[6]

The sequence of collusion, confusion and mutiny, in the defence of order and high office, was a cameo of contemporary bungling. Better conducted was the subsequent shooting of a selection of soldiers in the field by Tyburn tree.

In the Gordon Riots of June 1780, Blake witnessed the work of the most spectacular mob of the century. For days on end, London and Southwark were in its fist. The titular motivator was Lord George Gordon, the distraught son of Cosmo George, third duke of Gordon. The nominal cause was the Act of 1778, which entitled Roman Catholic laymen to inherit or dispose of estates, and for priests to work without hindrance, provided allegiance was sworn to the Hanoverian succession. The Act itself was a political bribe from a government incompetent and harrassed, prompted by the dire state of recruitment to the army. The Hessian mercenaries were already over-committed, and now the war with America and her French allies required the enlistment of Catholics in Scotland and Ireland. Lord Gordon, an unstable and virulent anti-Catholic, led a mob some five thousand strong to Parliament on Friday 2 June to demand a repeal of the 1778 Act. The mob had their own antipathies, raised on drink and resentment at the influx of competitive Irish labour. Within a day or two of Lord George Gordon's rally, the mob was attending especially to burning the houses of the Catholic gentry close enough to the King to have negotiated the concession.

Eleven years later, Tom Paine explained the riot in his own way:

The riots of 1780 had no other source than the remains of those prejudices, which the government itself had encouraged. But with respect to England there are also other causes.

Excess and inequality of taxation, however disguised in the means, never fail to appear in their effects. As a great mass of the community are thrown thereby into poverty and discontent, they are constantly on the brink of commotion: and deprived, as they unfortunately are, of the means of information, are easily heated to outrage. Whatever the apparent cause of any riots may be, the real one is always want of happiness. It shows that something is wrong in the system of government, that injures the felicity by which society is to be preserved. [7]

No doubt Blake would have subscribed to this, in the age of "Mental Fight". The tone echoes the debates in the dozens of democratic societies which came later to politicise the gestures of the 'conservative' mob, in radical terms portending revolution. And there is little doubt that in 1780, when Blake was caught in the tumult, his understanding was with the rioters, his regret with the rioting.

Gilchrist gives an account of the involvement:

Blake long remembered an involuntary participation of his own. On the third day, Tuesday, 6th of June, "the Mass-houses" having already been demolished – one, in Blake's near neighbourhood, Warwick Street, Golden Square – and various private houses also; the rioters, flushed with gin and victory, were turning their attention to grander schemes of devastation. That evening, the artist happened to be walking in a route chosen by one of the mobs at large, whose course lay from Justice Hyde's house near Leicester Fields, for the destruction of which less than an hour had sufficed, through Long Acre, past the quiet house of Blake's old Master, engraver Basire, in Great Queen Street, Lincoln's Inn Fields, and down Holborn, bound for Newgate. Suddenly, he encountered the advancing wave of triumphant Blackguardism, and was forced (for from such a great surging mob there is no disentanglement) to go along in the very front rank, and witness the storm and burning of the fortress-like prison, and release of its three hundred inmates. This was a peculiar experience for a spiritual poet; not without peril, had a drunken soldier chanced to have identified him during the after weeks of indiscriminate vengeance: those black weeks when strings of boys under fourteen were hung up in rows to vindicate the offended majesty of the Law. "I never saw boys cry so!" observed Selwyn, connoisseur in hanging, in his Diary. [8]

The "Mass-house" the mob ransacked in Warwick Street was in fact the Portuguese Chapel, run by the Sephardic Jews. In the garden of 23 Golden Square, the mob came across the genuine private "Mass-house" of Count Haslang, the Bavarian envoy and eminent racketeer, and fired it before ransacking the residence. The crowd was on its way past Blake's house into Broad Street, where mob and militia met in carnage, plunder and fire. Four nights later, Blake himself was in front of the mob at the gates of Newgate Prison.

Jails were traditional and easy targets which the mob rarely missed. Among so many across the years, the Clink in Southwark, the sinecure of the Bishop of Winchester, was now opened up. Newgate itself was not

7. Tom Paine, *The Rights of Man*, II, (1792, repr. 1988), p. 166.
8. Gilchrist, *Life of Blake*, pp. 36–37.

much more difficult to deal with than a chapel behind a garden wall. Hardly "fortress-like", gates opened readily, it seems, to pick-axe, sledge-hammer and helping hands holding keys.

After all, the century's way of switching an office into a sinecure had turned jailkeepers into entrepreneurs. Pimps, duns, accomplices, ladies of all talents, drinking pals, dealers, fences, even respectable friends and affectionate relatives, crossed palms with the admission fee, at times extortionate. Access was *gratis* under severe duress.

So considerate assistance from inside was on hand for the mob. And most of the structures would kindle like tinder. Indeed it was this state of things that moved Jeremy Bentham to dream his impossible dream of the impregnable jail in 1791. He reveals in his counter-measures all the defects in Newgate, which confronted the mob surrounding Blake. Jeremy Bentham called it his Panopticon:

The Building circular – an iron cage, glazed – a glass lantern about the size of Ranelagh – the Prisoners in their Cells, occupying the Circumference – The Officers (Governor, Chaplain, Surgeon, &c.) the Centre.

By Blinds, and other contrivances, the Inspectors concealed (except in so far as they think fit to show themselves) from the observation of the Prisoners: hence the sentiment of a sort of invisible omnipresence …

Against Fire (if, under a system of constant and universal inspection, any such accident could be apprehended), a pipe, terminating in a flexible hose, for bringing water down into the central Inspection-Room, from a cistern, of a height sufficient to force it up again by its own pressure, on the mere turning of a cock, and spread it thus over any part within the Building …

The Approach, one only – Gates opening into a walled avenue cut through the area. Hence, no strangers near the building without leave, nor without being surveyed from it as they pass, nor without being known to come on purpose. The gates, of open work, to expose hostile mobs … A mode of fortification like this, if practicable in a city, would have saved the London Prisons.[9]

We know that at times from "a great surging mob there is no disentanglement". But this mob must have declared its approach formidably to Blake where "he happened to be walking", despite the temper of the times, and the recent mayhem outside his home. Then familiar escape lines were countless for him, in the mile and a half between Broad Street and Newgate Jail; and countless and familiar to Blake were the perils of the mob since his childhood.

We may take it that Gilchrist's gloss of "involuntary" is discreet. Blake's reported hustle to Newgate was surely paved with the curiosity which had pulled Samuel Pepys, and cushioned George Cumberland on his wall.

9. Quoted in Jennings, *Pandæmonium*, p. 98.

Though Cumberland had come across soldiers controlled by magistrates favouring the mob days before, the troops were not officially mustered to put down the riots till the day after Blake's Tuesday adventure. It gave some leeway. Most of the spectators of George Cumberland's class had by the Tuesday stayed home, leaving the excitement to artisans, small shopkeepers, journeymen, and Blake. The "spiritual poet" would applaud the troops who refused to fire. The hangings would enrage him. The rioters were opening the prisons; they were against the war, against the king, against the government. It all must have spoken Blake's mind.

It was a few months later, probably in September 1780, that Thomas Stothard shared with Blake a more direct and uncomfortable encounter with the military. Stothard's daughter-in-law, Mrs Bray, recounted the incident some seventy years later. Stothard, with Blake and evidently James Parker, Blake's former fellow apprentice, went on one of their prolonged sailing and sketching trips on the River Medway:

Whilst the trio were one day engaged with the pencil on the shore, they were suddenly surprised by the appearance of some soldiers, who very unceremoniously made them prisoners, under the suspicion of their being spies for the French government; as this country was then at war with France. In vain did they plead that they were only there sketching for their own amusement; it was insisted upon that they could be doing nothing less than surveying for purposes inimical to the safety of Old England. Their provisions were brought on shore, and a tent formed for them of their sails, suspended over the boat-hook and oars, placed as uprights in the ground. There they were detained, with a sentinel placed over them, until intelligence could be received from certain members of the Royal Academy, to whom they appealed, to certify that they were peaceable subjects of his Majesty King George, and not spies for France.

Stothard made a very spirited pen and ink drawing of this scene, whilst under detention. On their liberation, they spent a merry hour with the commanding officer.[10]

With little help from Blake, whose knowledge of seamanship goes unmentioned by anyone, and who seems to have been the cook on board, the crew had negotiated the hazardous traffic down river from Tower Bridge. They passed "the bodies of those unhappy malefactors which were hung up, *in terrorem*, on the margin of the river", and, thirty miles downstream, drew south into the conflux with the Medway. For the Admiralty, the Medway meant, quite simply, Chatham Naval Dockyard. Mrs Bray knew this when she recorded the incident. Blake and the others knew it. They also knew that the French threat of raids on the Medway during the war was real enough. Nevertheless, the sailors hung about.

They had rounded the King's guardship, anchored off Chatham "for the

10. Bentley, *Blake Records*, pp. 19–20. See also *Kent County History*, II, Chatham, pp. 376–78.

purpose of good economy", which passing vessels were required to salute, or feel the range of the dockyard cannon.[11] The expedition clearly did not then sail upstream to make pastoral drawings of the unpatrolled Medway hamlets of Cuxton, Halling and Snodland. It stayed where the action was, as the presence of the military based at Upnor Castle records.

But there were inviting camp-sites along the river-line near Upnor, on the north bank opposite the dockyard. Here the secluded inlet gave Stothard the chance to sketch a nautical adventure, which Blake later engraved. Adventure or not, the guards from the castle, perhaps not with Chatham foremost in mind, clearly felt everyone to be too close to the naval base for comfort. The encounter, usually dismissed as trivial, was not—certainly not for a patrol, with courts martial and the gibbets along the Thames in mind. Of all the waters around London for sketching, the Medway alone was off limits— irresistible.

The defence of the Medway and Chatham Dockyard, serious even in 1940, was crucial two and three hundred years ago. By the time Blake took to the Medway, there were long memories of invasion. In June 1667, the Dutch had occupied Sheerness, raided Gillingham and even hove-to off the Dock-yard. They were then anchored within the jurisdiction of the City of London, a horse ride away. That a threat to the Medway terrified the City was understandable and unforgettable. The presence of the Dutch had troubled Samuel Pepys so much that, as well as fireships, booms (in panic they scuttled newly equipped fireships) and fortifications, he took exceptional measures: "June 12, 1667: By and by, after dinner, my wife out by coach to see her mother; and I in another (being afeared at this busy time to be seen with a woman in a coach, as if I were idle)".

After Samuel Pepys's official and personal initiative, Chatham was developed across another century of incompetence, such as only the Admiralty ashore achieves. By 1774 the dockyard covered sixty-eight acres, all within fortifications, patrolled by thirty-six watchmen, supporting the Marines. After the Compte de Chabrillon casually landed from the river and strolled through the dockyard unchallenged in 1767, it was assumed without question that all foreigners in the Rochester hotels were threatening the security of Chatham, and hence of the realm. Censures, courts marshal and firing squads were frequent, before and after the military were garrisoned at Upnor Castle, over the river from the dockyard.

Authorities everywhere, not only in London, suspected that sketching pencils spelt treachery. It was only two years after Blake found himself arrested that Goethe was jailed at Malcesine for making a totally useless sketch of the Scaliger castle on Lake Garda. It is clear from the reaction of the Upnor Castle patrol that the artists, "engaged with the pencil on the shore", were pushing their luck too far down river.

11. On Friday, August 10, 1787, Reverend Henry Blaine "bade farewell to his dearest friends", left the safety of his parish in Tring, and took ship down the Thames, bound for "the efficacy of sea bathing" at Ramsgate. While the sailors who had "escaped the sea" to hang from gibbets moved him to no more than a moral, "the crowded state of the river" terrified him. But this was nothing to the fraying of his nerves, when the skipper failed, as required "by way of obedience, to lower her topsail", as they passed the King's guardship at the conflux. He saw the flash of the charge, heard the cannon, and waited for the ball, which would make them "feel the effects of disobedience". Even in peacetime, the Medway was as touchy as that. For Henry Blaine, see Edith Sitwell, *English Eccentrics* (London: Faber & Faber, 1933), pp. 195–201.

Figure 2. Blake, wearing his "wide hat", Parker and Stothard, detained by the militia in an inlet of the Medway, as suspected French spies too interested in Chatham Naval Dockyard. (ca 1780). *By permission of The National Gallery of Art, Washington.*

The tone of the contemporary note of the report "received from Mrs Blake" on the affair "during the late war", on a river unnamed, where the three were "taken before some authority as spies", has the ring of truth in its indifference to making an impression.[12] Tatham's reported conclusion, reflecting Catherine Blake, that "they narrowly escaped further trouble perhaps danger", must have come initially from Blake himself, and is close to the mark. The Scaliger castle at Malcesine is now famous for a bronze head of Goethe, in his broad hat, at the entrance. If the Medway incident had gone a step further, we might now have Blake in bronze under his equally distinctive hat at Upnor Castle—or even in Chatham Dockyard.

James Parker's remark, that "he would go out no more on such perilous

12. Bentley, *Blake Records*, p. 621.

expeditions", must have caught Blake's ear. After two indiscreet involvements
he turned to friends too eccentric, or respectable, or ragged for jurisdiction.
And then, as the 1780s moved towards menace, there was immunity from the
Home office in preoccupation with *Innocence*.

CHAPTER THREE

The Future in Draft

In the meantime, Blake was beginning to make his way in the world. In terms evidently derived from Blake himself, writing in *A Father's Memoirs of his Child* in 1806, B. H. Malkin reported how Blake, in his early years "under the eye of Mr Moser", had drawn "nearly all the noble antiquities", until

his peculiar notions began to intercept him in his career . . . On a view of his whole life, he still thinks himself authorised to pronounce, that practice and opportunity very soon teach the language of art: but its spirit and poetry, which are seated in the imagination alone, never can be taught; and these make an artist.

The first recorded engraving by Blake is his 'Joseph of Arimethea' (dated 1773), from a design by Michaelangelo.[1]

There followed a steady run of work for publishers of books varying from *Fencing Familiarized* to the *Universal History of the Holy Bible*. The prints were based both on Blake's own designs and on the work of artists ranging from Stothard and J. Roberts, to Rubens and Raphael, whose paintings the publishers Harrison and Co. used to embellish their *Protestants' Family Bible*.

Alongside the engraving and drawing, Blake developed his painting. Using his time "at the academy and at home", he worked on a series of water-colours covering the familiar antique and medieval subjects. In 1780 the Academy exhibited his 'Death of Earl Godwin'. He seems at this time to have been fairly regularly supplied with commissions, and it was his habit to keep his early efforts beside him for years. In the *Descriptive Catalogue* of 1809, he lists 'The Penance of Jane Shore', which was "done about thirty years ago".[2]

The most impressive figure from 1780 is the well known pencil drawing—"evidently a personification of Morning, or Glad Day", wrote Gilchrist, describing a later engraving of the "nude figure, one foot on earth, just alighted from above, a flood of radiance still encircling his head; his arms outspread, – as exultingly bringing joy and solace to this lower world."[3] If Gilchrist got it wrong, his interpretation, along conventional lines, was fair enough. But Blake rarely expressed the expected, and he 'explained' the drawing another way, with his usual instinctive originality. Taking up the early drawing to engrave in the next century, he added the inscription which interpreted it through his

1. Bentley, *Blake Records*, p. 609.
2. Erdman, ed., *Poetry and Prose*, p. 550.
2. Gilchrist, *Life of Blake*, p. 33.

potent symbol of the Satanic Mill: "Albion rose from where he labourd at the Mill with Slaves:/Giving himself for the Nations he danc'd the dance of Eternal Death."

Another print from these earliest days which presupposes Blake's future thinking is the water-colour 'Pestilence: The Great Plague of London'. The waiting dead are heaved into the cart close by the exit from a tiled outhouse, used as an isolation annex to a larger building. The sick and dying receiving comfort in the foreground include an infant in a young mother's lap. Then in the background, well away from the infection and diminished against the columns of an excluding building, the bellman tolls his warning. Blake's vision settled early. The social divisions touched on here are later deployed in *Experience*.

Engraving work continued to come in for Blake through the next decade from a number of publishers. Stothard was his principal designer down to 1785 but after that year, there was no more from him and Blake more often engraved his own designs.

Blake spent the midsummer of 1781 in the country south of the Thames, upriver four miles from Westminster Bridge, apparently staying with his father's relatives in Battersea. A flirtation came to grief. Polly Wood was a "lively little girl", according to Gilchrist, but lacked the reticence proper to good breeding, since she readily allowed William,

as girls in a humble class will, meaning neither marriage nor harm to "keep company" with her; to pay his court, take mutual walks, and be as love sick as he chose ... When he complained that the favour of her company in a stroll had been extended to another admirer, "Are you a fool?" was the brusque reply—with a scornful glance. "That cured me of jealousy", Blake used naively to relate.[4]

It also landed him on the rebound in the arms of "a bright-eyed, dark-haired brunette", Catherine Sophia Boucher. Catherine took pity, and pity was the beginning of a marriage that lasted till death finished it, forty-five years of housekeeping and labour later.

On Sunday 18 August 1782, the couple was married "according to the Form of the Book of Common-Prayer", in the bright and newly built riverside church of St Mary, Battersea. The previous Tuesday Blake had made out the formal marriage allegation, including the essential oath that he was "of the Parish of Battersea, in the County of Surry", on the slender grounds that he had "been in the said Parish of Battersea for the space of four weeks last past".[5]

Tatham dressed the scene: "with the approbation & consent of his parents", perhaps not so whole-hearted on the paternal side, Blake "married this Interesting beautiful & affectionate Girl":

4. Gilchrist, *Life of Blake*, p. 38.
5. Bentley, *Blake Records*, pp. 21–23.

Nimble with joy & warm with the glow of youth, this bride was presented to her noble bridegroom. The morning of their married life was bright as the noon of their devoted love. The noon as clear as the serene Evening of their mutual Equanimity.[6]

Tatham's fancy might have been nourished by the fact that at the time of writing, 1832, he was busy easing from Blake's widow of five years the bulk of her husband's work. But then, for Catherine Blake, the Tathams were matchless.

Blake had not escaped an ordinary English August during his stay in Battersea. Daily records kept at Sion House across the Thames show that it rained for all but two of the first eighteen days of the month, and the Sunday of the wedding was cool, no better than "mostly clear", with half a gale blowing into the church across the bend in the river. The rain that August prefaced the longest drought on record, which began the year Blake married, 1782, and lasted right through the writing and illustrating of Innocence, to break in 1789.

Catherine signed the marriage register with a cross, a frequent enough practice, apparently not conclusive evidence of illiteracy. A note of Fuzeli's gossip fourteen years later tells us that Blake had "married a maid servant".[7] If the gratuitous recollection rings true in its disparagement, Catherine had put her cross against a lifetime of the unassisted housework she knew so well. We may take it that she was never bought Mr Kendall's "patent Laundress, or Washing Machine", as it came new on the market at three and a half guineas, small size, including a wringer: an "ingenious Invention made wholly of wood", and "highly esteemed by men of science". Alongside Catherine's housekeeping, there was shared labour in the business of earning a living, the common lot of any wife at her level in society, whose husband made or sold anything.

The couple set up lodgings at 23 Green Street, round the corner from Leicester Square. The square was still open, and its old name of Leicester Fields still used. Blake, who had given himself, perhaps intuitively, the title of 'Gentleman' in the record in Battersea Parish Church, was soon moving in gentlewomen's company. He was "honoured by an introduction to the accomplished Mrs Mathew, whose house, No. 27, Rathbone-place, was then frequented by most of the literary and talented people of the day." Rathbone Place is north of Leicester Square, across Oxford Street. Mrs Mathew, "constantly open and ready to cherish persons of genius who stood in need of assistance in their learned and arduous pursuits", sounds laced with the polite condescension Blake found hard to take.[8] She was patron to John Flaxman, to whom Stothard had introduced Blake, and who, it was said, brought Blake to Mrs Mathew's intellectually powdered house parties. Flaxman was at

6. Bentley, *Records*, p. 518.
7. In the diary of Joseph Farington, in Bentley, *Records*, pp. 51–52.
8. Bentley, *Records*, p. 456

this time still making ends meet in nearby Wardour Street. It was most likely Mrs Mathew who persuaded her husband, Reverend Anthony Stephen, to help finance Flaxman's reported initiative in having *Poetical Sketches* by W. B. "printed for private distribution, by the well-known printer and publisher John Nichols".[9]

The anonymous Advertisement patronises "the irregularities and defects to be found in almost every page", by adding that the poet's friends "still believed that they possessed a poetic originality, which merited some respite from oblivion". After all, some of "the productions of untutored youth", were "commenced in his twelfth … year".[10]

W.B.'s reaction must have been mixed, when his eye fell on the reticence of the initials, and the guarded recommendation, as he handled the batch of uncut and unsewn sheets. Depreciatory congratulations never came easy to the "untutored youth". John Flaxman, almost always active in promoting Blake's interests, tried to raise a subscription in April the next year to send him "to finish his studies in Rome". The plan collapsed, and Blake was never to leave England. In the meantime, Flaxman wrote a puff to William Hayley, in which he reminds Hayley of Romney's opinion, that Blake's "historical drawings rank with those of Mr Angelo"; praise indeed, with which went a "Pamphlet of Poems", "the writings of a Mr BLAKE you have heard me mention, his education will plead sufficient excuse to your Liberal mind for the defects of his work".[11] Here again, from his close friend to the man of influence, was proper condescension, polite and not ill-meant in its time; but not easy for Blake to stomach. For all that, *Poetical Sketches* is of unique quality as a collection of early and juvenile verse. Even the derivative verse is not imitative, and there are two poems at least of unprecedented originality in the book, anticipating the *Songs*.

From a commonplace book in the Bodleian Library, we can see just what Blake's juvenile verse should have been like to meet with classroom approval.[12] The manuscript began as a school book of exercises in versification in 1710. Decades later, in the ink and with the pen that wrote the second half of the book, the owner added marginal comments confirming that the poems were exercises from schooldays. At the time they were made, the poetical exercises were unremarkable. Only in later life did the writer feel it worthwhile to record his recollections of years of schoolboy rhyming.

All the school verses appear at the beginning of the book, and none is copied from other authors. As were all pupils, the writer was required to follow the classics. The implications of the precision of the first title are intimidating: 'A Dialogue Between Phillis & Damon in Imitation of The 9th Ode in the 3rd Book of Horace'. Then over the page is a poem 'On the Death of his Royal Highness Prince George of Denmark Who departed

9. See Michael Phillips in *Bulletin of The New York Public Library*, LXXX (1976), on 'The Printing of Poetical Sketches'. A connection with Basire is established. The article is reprinted by D. V. Erdman in *Blake: Prophet Against Empire*, where it is suggested that "one is tempted to throw aside the whole 'Mathew legend' " (p. 93, n. 12).

10. Bentley, *Blake Records*, p. 27.

11. Ibid., p. 27.

12. Ms. Rawl. Poet. 197, in the Bodleian Library.

this life the Day before my Ld Mayors day in the year 1708 this was made on my Ld Mayors day Being the first I euer made'. In the margin is written the word "Exercise". The 'educated' punctuation matches Blake's own. Next comes a heart-cry beginning "O Rest what is it that thou canst not do", an 'Exercise at a breaking up', followed by another with the decisive opening line: "Be gone I say; fly thou from my calm breast". The pupil poet then turned to religion, and "verses on the Cross, made at the request of Mr A. B.", and a piece in quite lively measure on 'The Dissenter's Liberty of Conscience', which tells us a little of the school's background. All the education in versifying was conducted, from the previous century, in a mildly puritan spirit.

The poem in *Poetical Sketches* to come nearest to all these is the worst in the collection, 'A War Song to Englishmen', the least like Blake, and the most likely for magazine publication. For the rest, alongside Shakespeare, Milton, Spenser and other "fond old authors", together with the Bible, it is clear Blake kept his reading up to date, "until the eighteenth century exerted the most extensive influence both in the number of poems affected and in the number of authors who were Blake's sources". So we find no difficulty in listing the 'sources' of the Sketches among the poets of the lifetime of Blake and his father: Akenside, Isaac Watts, Percy's *Reliques*, Chatterton, Thomson, Henry Carey—the list goes on. All are turned to Blake's own advantage, however, in a way a classroom would not have encouraged—all are contaminated with originality. So Blake's stanzas forming 'An Imitation of Spencer' are not "all different and all wrong" from incompetence. Blake follows the "ample precedent during the eighteenth century for writing an irregular stanza", with "a variety of attempts to modulate the form in new ways", which brings to mind "in the perversity of variation Blake's evident disquiet within the convention".[13]

Even more remarkable than the apprentice's "perversity" in the face of poetic convention is the control and originality of the verse he wrote (as Reverend Malkin put it, kindly enough for the headmaster he was), "before the age of fourteen, in the heat of youthful fancy, unchastened by judgment":[14]

'Song'

How sweet I roam'd from field to field,
And tasted all the summer's pride,
Till I the prince of love beheld,
Who in the sunny beams did glide!

He shew'd me lilies for my hair,
And blushing roses for my brow;

13. M. R. Lowery, in *Windows of the Morning* (Yale: Yale University Press, 1940), established the precedence of eighteenth-century sources, especially in relation to James Thomson, *The Seasons*. See also Michael Phillips, 'Blake's Early Poetry', in Paley & Phillips, eds., *Essays . . . Keynes*, p. 3.

14. Bentley, *Blake Records*, p. 428. Malkin's report is generally accepted.

He led me through his gardens fair,
Where all his golden pleasures grow.

With sweet May dews my wings were wet,
And Phoebus fir'd my vocal rage;
He caught me in his silken net,
And shut me in his golden cage.

He loves to sit and hear me sing,
Then, laughing, sports and plays with me;
Then stretches out my golden wing,
And mocks my loss of liberty.

As early as this, it seems, Blake leads us into areas of surmise not pre-
viously explored. Apparently while the boy was finishing with Mr Henry
Pars's place in the Strand, he wrote these lines which engage speculation,
and intimate the poetic challenge to come. And the poem delivers a clear
caveat against reading autobiography into Blake's writing. Without the
contemporary testimony on the juvenile nature of the poem, an argument for a later date associated with Blake's marriage would appear
unanswerable. The "golden cage" would be seen, quite obviously, as "Matrimony's Golden cage" of ten years later.[15] The roaming from field to field
would fit snugly into Blake's pre-nuptial summer among the meadows
between St John's and Wimbledon, and the 'gardens fair' of the up-river,
southern loop of the Thames, especially if we lacked the knowledge that
the 1782 summer was wet, and the carrot crop failed disastrously.

Instead we have a remarkable hint of Blake's distinctive symbolic rec-
onciliations, which totally outweigh the familiar personifications in the
contemporary verse he had read. Then there is the loaded use of the
insignificant word, which becomes almost Blake's monogram. At the
outset, even here, we feel uneasy, as the sense of betrayal develops from
the little word "till" (not 'when') in the third line, which introduces the
prince of love. Actions and identities develop in a symbolic sequence, as
if it were signed by Blake. Our unease shifts into suspicion in the second
verse; then the transition, from the speaker (a child, if we believe
Malkin) to the bird in a cage, is made without explanation, relying on
our instinctive acceptance of the conceptual parallel between the
speaker's state, and the bird's.

It is the nature of Blake's poetry, even this early, that there are so few
lines of transition. Yet there is no sense of abruptness. The reader is held
by the symbolism of transfused actions (child's or bird's), and not dis-
concerted by a visual presence of the speaker (child or bird); and the

15. Michael Phillips, ed., *An Island
in the Moon* (Cambridge: Cambridge University Press, 1986),
chapter 9.

solicitude of the first two verses drifts uncomfortably into the atten-
tiveness of the last two. A link exists at the intellectual, non-visual, core
of the poem, such as we find time and again in Blake's writing, particularly in *Songs of Innocence and of Experience*.

We come across the hints again in another of the *Sketches*, which moves
eighteenth-century verse even further away from the shallow mainstream:

'*Song*'

Love and harmony combine,
And around our souls entwine,
While thy branches mix with mine,
And our roots together join.

Joys upon our branches sit,
Chirping loud, and singing sweet;
Like gentle streams beneath our feet
Innocence and virtue meet.

Thou the golden fruit dost bear,
I am clad in flowers fair;
Thy sweet boughs perfume the air,
And the turtle buildeth there.

There she sits and feeds her young,
Sweet I hear her mournful song;
And thy lovely leaves among,
There is love: I hear his tongue.

There his charming nest doth lay,
There he sleeps the night away;
There he sports along the day,
And doth among our branches play.

Then there is the spectacular maturity of the complex satire in 'Mad
Song', and the less disturbing, but conclusive dismissal of contemporary
fashioned verse, where each prescribed phrase is so often comfortingly
anticipated. In 'To the Muses' Blake sets up fourteen lines of unexception-
able diction, for the Muses of an exercise book, and, having shown how
polite versification should be conducted, dismisses it in its own terms.

'*To the Muses*'

Whether on Ida's shady brow,
Or in the chambers of the East,
The chambers of the sun, that now

From antient melody have ceas'd;

Whether in Heav'n ye wander fair,
Or the green corners of the earth,
Or the blue regions of the air,
Where the melodious winds have birth;

Whether on chrystal rocks ye rove,
Beneath the bosom of the sea
Wand'ring in many a coral grove,
Fair Nine, forsaking Poetry!

How have you left the antient love
That bards of old enjoy'd in you!
The languid strings do scarcely move!
The sound is forc'd, the notes are few!

We shall find Blake turning to contemporary diction again, in unique and masterly fashion, in 'The School Boy'.

Blake's early preoccupation with the devastation wrought by tyranny and war comes clearly through many of the *Sketches*. Though said to have been "a radical all his life", in his youth he did not express support for the American revolt, as he may have done with impunity. That came later, in retrospect, and without impunity. On 20 November 1777, William Pitt, Earl of Chatham, hardly a democrat or a republican, gave the House of Lords his views on the revolt of the American colonies:

This ruinous and ignominious situation, where we cannot act with success, nor suffer with honour, calls upon us to remonstrate in the strongest and loudest language of truth, to rescue the ear of Majesty from the delusions which surround it . . . I know the conquest of English America is an impossibility. You cannot conquer America. If I were an American, as I am an Englishman, while a foreign troop was landed in my country, I would never lay down my arms. Never, never, never.

Quite unremarkably, Blake could have shared the Earl's view, so respectably then held. Expressed in his son's premiership, the Earl's opinion might have made a sermon for Tyburn tree. It was only then, after the Bastille fell and a Gallic 'democracy' threatened to infest England, that the exemplary American revolution demanded Blake's symbolic approval. There is, however, striking evidence in *Poetical Sketches* of his reaction this early to the social and political exploitation, so smoothly, poetically and historically justified by his contemporaries. And it is this

exploitation that dominates Blake's imagination, in the 1780s, and periodically thereafter.

The academic opinions of the Society of Antiquaries, for whom Blake
had done so much youthful copying among the effigies, had no currency
at all for the fashionable poets. For them and their customers, medieval
victories could be too readily and profitably re-shaped as propaganda for
contemporary trade and empire. Medieval kings and bishops were not
to be presented as tyrants, when the conflicts and commerce of their
Georgian successors could be favoured with such glorious historic analogues. The metrical promotion of the empire of commerce, that staple
of eighteenth-century poets, was always associated with the fostering of
notional freedom—what Blake ironically has King Edward call "Liberty,
the *chartered* right of Englishmen"(my italics).

So, typically, James Thomson in his revered sequence, *The Seasons*,
apostrophises "happy Britannia", a land that "teems with wealth", the
"dread of tyrants", and goes on to update the Edwards, kings "dear to
fame", as "The first who deep-impressed/On haughty Gaul the terror of
thy arms". He glances at English naval power and the "crowded ports",
and puts a smile on drudgery:

> *Full are thy cities with the sons of art;*
> *And trade and joy in every busy street*
> *Mingling are heard. Even Drudgery himself*
> *As at the car he sweats, or dusty hews*
> *The palace stone, looks gay.*[16]

For James Thomson, drudgery finds exclusive gaiety in the service of
the powerful.

In the dramatic piece 'King Edward the Third', Blake updates Edward
and his court into his own century. The virtue of regal, martial 'toil' in
the diurnal conduct of war is justified in easy Georgian assumptions.
Clarence tells how the king

> *Toils in his wars, and turns his eyes on this*
> *His native shore, and sees commerce fly round*
> *With his white wings, and sees his golden London,*
> *And her silver Thames throng'd with shining spires*
> *And corded ships; her merchants buzzing round*
> *Like summer bees, and all the golden cities*
> *In his land, overflowing with honey,*
> *Glory may not be dimm'd with clouds of care.*
> *Say, Lords, should not our thoughts be first to commerce?*

16. James Thomson, *The Seasons*
(1730). 'Summer', ll. 1140–85.

My Lord Bishop, would you recommend us agriculture?

Indeed the Lord Bishop would, in terms endearing to his time. And he would go further, in words of "true wisdom", as Clarence observes, that drops "like honey" from his tongue, "as from a worship'd oak!":

> *When I sit at my home, a private man,*
> *My thoughts are on my gardens, and my fields,*
> *How to employ the hand that lacketh bread.*
> *If Industry is in my diocese*
> *Religion will flourish; each man's heart*
> *Is cultivated, and will bring forth fruit:*
> *This is my private duty and my pleasure.*
> *But as I sit in council with my prince,*
> *My thoughts take in the gen'ral good of the whole,*
> *And England is the land favour'd by Commerce;*
> *For Commerce, tho' the child of Agriculture,*
> *Fosters his parent, who else must sweat and toil,*
> *And gain but scanty fare. Then, my dear Lord,*
> *Be England's trade our care; and we, as tradesmen,*
> *Looking to the gain of this our native land.*

The edge to the verse is unmistakable, with the Bishop *elevated* into trade. Clarence points out how the French, the perennial enemy, "like ravening wolves" are "spoiling our naval flocks", till "the merchants do complain". The Bishop divinely confirms the "right that heaven gave" to the English, as "sovereigns / Of the sea". In the meantime, steps must be taken to get the merchants who are "rich enough" to "bestir themselves" in the royal cause. And for the common man's reassurance, Chandos has Whitehall's timeless illusion: "Teach man to think he's a free agent", and he will "build himself a hut and hedge / A spot of ground", and "move onward to plan conveniences, / Till glory fires his breast to enlarge his castle".

For Blake, the spirit motivating this chartered "freedom" is aggressive self-aggrandisement. The King catches the lead, and launches into the battle cry of the sacred cause: "O Liberty, how glorious art thou!"

The satirical leading edge of *Experience* can hardly be missed, as the apprentice revolutionary reacts to his 'sources'—decade after decade of time-serving verse, giving "audience to the world": "What bales, what wealth, what industry, what fleets!"[17]

So, from the beginning, Blake was profoundly aware of the pragmatic deception which bolstered the social structure. His indignation never wavered, and was never qualified.

17. John Dyer, *The Fleece* (1757), III, pp. 626–30.

Ten years later, Tom Paine, in *The Rights of Man*, was to begin a remarkable four or five pages as "an advocate of commerce", by making his point that, "if commerce were permitted to act to the universal extent it is capable, it would extirpate the system of war, and produce a revolution in the uncivilised state of government".[18] It was an advocacy for disaster which Blake would deplore.

Close as he was to Tom Paine's thinking, Blake was no political theorist. To the end of his life, he looked around him, and recorded the effects of the "holy" alliance of commerce, church and state. There was no rationalising for him, no compromise.

No concessions, and no doubt this became the difficulty among the blue-stockings at 27 Rathbone Place, where Gilchrist's embroidery brightens the "legend" of "the agreeable, fascinating, *spirituelle* Mrs Mathew". At her "reunions", he confides, Blake was consorting with literary lionesses, fashionable novelists, improving socialites, guardians of morality:

There would assemble those esteemed ornaments of their sex: unreadable Chapone, of well improved mind; sensible Barbauld; versatile, agreeable Mrs Brooke, novelist and dramatist; learned and awful Mrs Carter, a female Grand Cham of literature.

Among these, and the rest, Mrs Mathew was "by far the most pleasant to think of, because she did not commit herself to a book".[19]

It was in this company that the young J. T. Smith "often heard" Blake "read and sing several of his poems". Once the novelty wore off, appreciation must have been uncertain. It is easy to see how his "unbending deportment" made it tiresome for Blake, of all people, to come to terms either with the company, or with its sophisticated aspirations. However, J. T. Smith reports that Blake

continued to benefit from Mrs Mathew's liberality, and was enabled to continue in partn ership, as a Printseller, with his fellow-pupil, Parker, in a shop, No. 27, next door to his father's, in Broad Street; and being extremely partial to Robert, his youngest brother, considered him as his pupil.

Bob Blake had been one of John Smith's 'playfellows', and his testimony is based on familiar information. His mention of Blake's continuing, rather than starting, in partnership with Parker is intriguing. If the 'liberality' was aimed at preventing a split in the partnership, it failed.[20]

By the end of 1784, Blake had moved away from Green Street, and away from singing his verses to ladies of self-acknowledging genius. From now on, the change in his life, his preoccupations, and above all in the company he kept, was dramatic. He was writing the poems of Innocence.

18. Paine, *Rights of Man*, p. 212 et sq.
19. Gilchrist, *Life of Blake*, pp. 46–8.
20. Bentley, *Blake Records*, p. 457.

From the Common to King Street

When Blake set up in the printing business with Parker at the end of 1784, a particular pleasure was the closeness of his favourite brother, Robert, doubtless still living in the family home next door. Moreover, he now had his brother, ten years his junior, as his pupil.

There was now a small clutch of Blake family shops in Broad Street, on the corners with Marshall Street. Blake's father had died, and was buried in Bunhill Fields on 2 July 1784. The event seems to have changed the fortunes of his family. His son, John, three years William's junior, at once set himself up in business across the street from the family home, at 29 Broad Street. He called himself a baker, and gave his address as Marshall Street, a cut above Broad Street if you were located away from the Carnaby Market end. Tatham defined him more closely as a "Gingerbread Baker", adding "literally" as if quoting Catherine, and that he "became abandoned & miserable & literally, contrary to his parents presage, sought bread at the Door of William. He lived a few reckless days, Enlisted as a Soldier & died". In fact John lasted more than nine years before his fortune hit the contemporary norm and the shop failed. Like so many brought down and out, he "ran away" in 1793, and turned soldier. Blake reported him dead to brother James in November 1802.[1]

William and Catherine moved into 27 Broad Street within months of the father's funeral. With his mother's lifetime experience for support, James Blake, Jr, carried on the haberdashery business. Things drifted, and the next spring he was obliged to make formal application to retain the contract with the only two customers of the business we can name with certainty, since the accounts survive—the Governors to supply haberdashery to St James's Workhouse, and to their King Street school.

For Blake and Catherine certainly, and surely for Robert as well, given the bond between the brothers, these years were graced with long walks in the country, habitually south of the river. There is little evidence that Blake walked for pleasure north of the city. He gives a reason in a letter he wrote on 1 February 1826 to John Linnell, excusing himself from a visit to Hampstead, which he so much enjoyed, especially for the Linnell children's boisterous welcome. He complained that he was "again laid up with a cold in the stomach", such as "the Hampstead Air" invariably brought on, "Except it be the Morning Air", and went on to explain in recollection:

1. Bentley, *Blake Records*, p. 509

*When I was young Hampstead Highgate Hornsea Muswell Hill & even Islington &
all places North of London always laid me up the day after & sometimes two or
three days with precisely the same Complaint & the same torment of the Stomach.
Easily removed but excruciating while it lasts & enfeebling for some time after.*[2]

A physical aversion to "all places North of London" was credible. Jonas
Hanway wrote that the fields there in the 1760s were "displeasing both
to sight and smell. The chain of brick-kilns that surrounds us, like the
scars of the smallpox, makes us lament the ravages of beauty and the
diminution of infant ailments". In the next decade Charles Jenner
expanded the same theme in his *London Eclogues*:

> *Where'er around I cast my wand'ring eyes,*
> *Long burning rows of fetid bricks arise,*
> *And nauseous dunghills swell in mould'ring heaps,*
> *While the fat sow beneath their covert sleeps.*
> *I spy no verdant glade, no gushing rill,*
> *No fountain gushing from the rocky hill,*
> *But stagnant pools adorn our dusty plains,*
> *Where half-starv'd cows wash down their meal of grains.*

Physicians down the decades warned repeatedly of the danger of the
"sickness occasioned" by strolling "in the fields adjoining the town".[3]
The threat of assault by footpads or vagrants was ever present. An
"expedition" anywhere north of London was a foray into country
mauled by hogs, cattle, brick makers, night-soil men, and scavengers
sorting the waste for stuff to take back into town and hawk. Across
Love Lane behind the Jew's Harp House, just past the fashionable security of Marybone Gardens, was sickening enough. East, at Tottenham
Court, past the Farthing Pye House in Green Lane, the cinder sifters
and hogs by the hundred took over exclusively.

Londoners were recommended to walk south for fresh air. It was a
practice Blake followed energetically from childhood. Frederick
Tatham, who gave Catherine house-room when she was widowed,
mentions Blake's day-long country walks. For all its flourishes, much in
Tatham's essay carries an echo of Catherine's conversation. So we seem
to hear her voice setting her widowhood against pleasant, even ambitious, recollections, in Tatham's account of how her husband's

*excessive labour, without the exercise he used formerly to take, (having relinquished
his habit of taking very long Walks) brought on the complaint which afterwards
consumed him. In his youth he and his Wife would start in the Morning early, &*

2. Erdman, ed. , *Poetry and Prose*,
p. 775.

3. George, *London Life*, p. 106.

Figure 3. THE COUNTRY TWENTY FIVE MILES ROUND LONDON ... BY W. F[ADEN] (1790) [section].
Reprinted with permission of The British Library.

This section of the plan of *The Country twenty five miles round London* (1790) covers the area round London most familiar to Blake.

By the time Blake was working on *Songs of Innocence and of Experience*, the city had already spread north to the verge of the the New Road (now partly Euston Road), which ran from Tottenham Court west, past the Farthing Pie House at the top of Green Lane. In his later years, Blake recorded the pleasure he found here at the Green Man Inn. Given this recollection, it is a fair guess that he also knew the renowned ale served up in the Yorkshire Stingo, at the west end of the road, near the turnpike. This was on the track to Hampstead, past "mournful ever-weeping Paddington" and through St John's Wood.

walk out 20 miles & dine at some pretty & sequestered Inn & would return the same day home having travelled 40 miles. Mrs Blake would do this without excessive fatigue. Blake has been known to walk 50 Miles in the day, but being told by some Physician that such long walks were injurious, he discontinued them.[4]

It is clear why Blake's parents always seem advisedly to have walked him south across the river, and why his preference persisted. From his early days he was wandering in the cornfields of Peckham Rye. Dulwich, Sydenham Hill, Norwood, the "lovely hills of Camberwell", and the rolling Commons west to Wimbledon, and on to Malden, Esher and Walton-on-Thames, were all happily within Catherine's recollected distance. From Golden Square, Westminster Bridge led into the country. This was the recommended way out of London. It was the habit of Londoners to loiter on the bridge for some air, a relaxation encouraged with seats along the wall. Then, by the time Blake was married, there was "the bridge at Black-friars . . . a noble monument of taste and public spirit", as an alternative way over the river.

Besides the river crossing, there were civilised, as well as rural attractions, for Blake, his wife and his brother in Surrey. Through Lambeth, in St George's Fields "such ladies as are fond of rural elegance" could even take a rest for "milk and syllabubs" in the Lactarium. There was a room "kept warm with a good fire", and protected with "a conductor to make it a safe place in case of lightning and a garde-robe for ladies". Wholesome milk alone was itself worth a long walk, when milk in town was notoriously and indiscriminately diluted. It was 1791 before the speculators started to exploit St George's Fields, and 1793 before the New Bond Estate populated the road south-west of the river towards Battersea and Wimbledon. Even in 1830, Battersea Field was still

an entirely open space, a good deal of it given up to corn, and the rest grazing fields, which were inhabited by an enormous herd of cows, [an afternoon's walk] from Wimbledon Common, with its wild and lovely scenery . . . the undulating surface of

4. Bentley, *Blake Records*, p. 527.

A few hundred yards north of the New Road, the Jew's Harp House was still rural, and as the decades passed and the fields were cleared, Blake could sit in the tea garden and hear the boys' voices as they bathed in the pond across Love Lane. But he always found south of the river more congenial. It had been commonplace in his earlier lifetime for physicians to spell out the health risks of taking the air among the night fires of the destitute in fields north of the town.

His, and his family's, habitual and recommended escape from "the terrible desart of London" was across Westminster Bridge, marked on the plan between the words RIVER and THAMES. From there, a mile or so to "the fields of corn at Peckham Rye", less to "the lovely hills of Camberwell".

It was west along the south bank of the Thames, that Blake met and married Catherine Boucher in the riverside village of Battersea. It was an easy walk from here to Wimbledon, where children from the Poland Street workhouse incredibly drew the intervention of the first Countess Spencer.

the ground, together with several thick plantations and the fine views over the surrounding country. [5]

However, Blake made it plain that, for all the recreation to be found among the vales and hills, "Where man is not nature is barren",[6] and a walk to Wimbledon in the years of his early marriage brought him among the cottagers, with whom workhouse children found shelter, rescued from the burial ground behind his home in Broad Street. More than this, he knew they would now never be sent back to Pawlett's Garden. Wimbledon Common rejoiced for him with the voices of children he knew. If the concept of Innocence took substance from reality, the matrix was here.

We may get a measure of the rescue Blake watched from the decades leading up to it round the country. At the start of the century, the Freemen of Colchester, Essex, were complaining that it was not only the "idleness and disorders amongst the meaner sort of people here for the want of *Workhouses* to employ them", but also the fearsome mortality rate of parish children put out to nurses, that motivated the extended provision of these institutions. There had been "hospitals for the maintenance of impotent men and women", and the "refreshment of poor people" as long ago as the reign of Henry V. And the "Poore-house and Hospital in Colchester" itself had housed the poor and infirm since 1612.

In was in the 1650s, however, that the word 'workhouse', long established for any place of indigent industry, took on the sense Blake knew. It announced the arrival of "an institution, administered by the Guardians of the Poor, in which paupers are lodged and the able-bodied set to work."

More than this, from the start the workhouse was also "a house of correction for the disorderly", exemplifying the received wisdom which fired Blake's anger: that crime and poverty are analogous. The workhouse came to terrify the disabled and poor, as a place to die. Well into the present century it was still the "foundation of all indoor relief". It took the Second World War to finish it off.[7]

By 1700 the advantageous economics of a 'working house' had been recognised long enough for every busy ratepayer and clergyman to commend it. At the same time, the death rate among infants put out to nurse was intolerably fearsome, and a weight on many a "feeling mind". So the foundlings were gathered into the workhouses, after a Parliamentary report of 1716 noted:

[many] children are inhumanely suffered to die by the barbarity of nurses, who are

5. *Surrey County History*, II, 8, p. 120. For the Lactarium, see George, *London Life*, pp. 93 and 341.
6. *The Marriage of Heaven and Hell*, plate 10.
7. Thomas Kitson Cromwell, *History and Description of the Ancient Town and Borough of Colchester* (London: Robert Jennings, 1825, 2 vols.), II, p. 331, and *Oxford English Dictionary* (ed. 1991), 'workhouse'. On hospitals, Blake wrote in *The Song of Los*:

These were the Churches:
    Hospitals: Castles: Palaces:
Like nets & gins & traps to catch the
    joys of Eternity.

'Hospitals' here are at times misunderstood to be schools, misdirecting once more Blake's aim towards education. A hospital, the ancient name for an alms–house, was essentially a refuge for the indigent, sick or infirm. It came often to be associated with the workhouse: 'the poor house and hospital'. Analogously the workhouse could be referred to as the infirmary, often on maps. A school (Christ's Hospital, Grey Coat Hospital) was not a hospital unless it was a hospice. Even then it was normally shown on a map as a school. It was not schools, but the places where the unwanted were locked away, that Blake lined up with the churches, castles and palaces. The US sense for workhouse (1888): 'a prison, or house of correction for petty offenders', is unknown in UK.

a sort of people void of commiseration or religion, hir'd by the churchwardens to take off a burthen from the parish at the cheapest and easiest rates they can.

Often, it was later said, by the generous spoon-feeding of infants on gin.

The parish of St James was among the first to respond to the consequent Act of 1722. It was proposed that "all the poor children now kept at parish nurses, instead of being starv'd or misus'd by them, as is so much complained of, will be duly taken care of, and be bred up to Labour and Industry, Virtue and Religion," in their workhouse built in Pawlett's Garden.[8]

But in Blake's century, an undertaking, however well intentioned, was rarely effective. Self-interest, profit (that is, 'the benefit of society'), invariably intervened. By 1742, in Colchester (again an ordinary yardstick), "[the] Workhouse Corporation became indeed too much the property of a few, who perhaps made too great an advantage of it; it also became a powerful tool in the hands of those odious things, parties".[9] By the year Blake was born, a report circulated his neighbourhood, saying "that the officers of one parish in Westminster received money for more than five hundred bastards, and reared but one out of all that number." Exaggeration maybe, but not necessarily—the temptation facing parish officers was to reckon the unlikely life expectation of the foundling, against the lump-sum received to maintain the child. The result was often, as Jonas Hanway wrote as late as 1766, "saddling the spit": a parish feast, which was based on

an opinion that a parish child's life is worth no more than eight or ten months' purchase, and that there is a chance of its being but so many days, and consequently occasioning a speedy release from all expense, and the money may go on good cheer.

It was a century when old sinecures, however crude, were tenaciously protected at all levels, while as always the familiar spiral of history disabled reform. In time the cure-all of the workhouse became the death of its inmates. The only solution was a reversion to an old alternative, that the children must be sent to nurses in the country.

By 1762, Jonas Hanway had forced through an Act of Parliament requiring all the parishes within the walls to keep registers of their "infant poor". These showed that of a hundred children registered under one year old, only seven survived to the age of three. Hanway remorselessly pursued reform, "going from one workhouse to another in the morning, and from one Member of Parliament to another in the afternoon, for day after day, year after year", hearing simply from some workhouse officers that "all our children have died", and being

8. George, *London Life*, pp. 215–16.
9. Cromwell, *History of Colchester*, II, p. 333.

dismissed by members of Parliament, until his persistence led to the Act of 1767. People called it "the act for keeping children alive". It required all parish children to be sent out of London to nurses in the country, infants under two years old at least five miles, children under six, at least three miles.[10]

For the parish of St James, the nurses were across the river at Wimbledon, which just met the requirements of distance. Indeed the Governors of the Poor in St James's were named as an example to follow. Some years before Hanway's Act required it, they had already arranged that

several cottagers on Wimbledon Common, fit and proper to be entrusted with care of children, were paid three shillings a week for each child they rescued from mouldering away in the Workhouse ... Five or six being placed in one house brought in the nurse a good income.[11]

Despite the effect of the Hanway's Act, in 1770 children still alive in London workhouses were sleeping and dying ten and more to a bed, as they were brought back from the country. It was the next move that broke with history. The year after the American War ended, Blake watched it happen, as he spent most of the summer in the rolling country south of the Thames. It was the year the meticulous book-keeper to the Governors of St James's Workhouse began his record of a series of unprecedented undertakings in child care.

From Green Street or Broad Street, it was six miles to "the purple heights of Wimbledon",[12] perhaps five if the walkers took the new footbridge from Chelsea, and called in to see Catherine's parents in Battersea. On Wimbledon Common, among the rescued children he knew and their nurses, Blake saw the care go beyond mere relief. Those who could walk "were sent to school, and threepence a week paid their respective mistresses for instructing them to read and sew".

The Governors of the Poor in Blake's parish were now bringing a unique initiative to the problem of infant destitution. At times luck, such as Thomas Stothard himself had enjoyed as a boy, helped them along. The children at Wimbledon were visited by people of quality. On 30 August 1782, "Mr Harper of Knightsbridge" applied to the Committee to take "James Squires now at Nurse in Wimbledon to live with him". But the Governors knew that bringing back the friends of Jimmy Squires to finish their late childhood in the workhouse "was a dreadful period to the children, and the feeling Mind"

little schools were established at the Workhouse, and every care taken of them that the nature of the case would admit of. But ... it became necessary to separate healthy chil-

10. See Jonas Hanway, *An earnest Appeal for Mercy for the Children of the Poor* (1766), p. 29 et sq., and George, *London Life*, pp. 58–60, pp. 214–18.

11. See *English Historical Documents* vol. 10, pp. 555–58; vol. 11, p. 439 et seq.

12. Gilchrist, *Life of Blake*, p. 40.

dren from the diseases and infirmities incident to old age; and from pernicious vice and immorality that sometimes are visible in the best-regulated Charities.[13]

The "little schools established at the Workhouse" were invariably "staffed" by one or more of the inmates, nominated as nurses and teachers. This being so, nothing is recorded in the minutes of the St James's Workhouse relating to a teacher, whether helpful, incompetent or sadistic. Education was minimal, lasting perhaps half an hour a day. Having taken bread and prayed, the children were at work with the flax and the wool six days a week, by seven o'clock at the latest, finishing at six in the evening. Sickness were endemic. As the Committee acknowledged, the parish children were a minority among the discardings of penury, accident and senility. To change their lives, on 2 April 1782, the Governors of the Poor completed the purchase of "the House, Stables and Riding House, late Mr Durrell's, in King Street . . . for Two Thousand Two Hundred Pounds".

King Street is now Kingly Street, a few minutes walk south of Oxford Circus. Earlier in the eighteenth century, "Mr Durrell's place" had been a riding academy run by M. Foubert, whose name survived in M. Foubert's Passage, now Foubert Place, off Regent Street. Having bought the buildings, the Governors rented the ride and stables fronting on M. Foubert's Passage to a livery stableman, and spent in all a further £7,415 on converting the rest of the premises into a school and living accommodation.

"Mr Durrell's place", just across Carnaby Market from Broad Street, now became known variously as the King Street school, the house in King Street and the Parish School of Industry. The last title belies the enlightenment of the men whose initiative established and administered the King Street school. It was not to become a traditional school of industry for some years, and the avoidance of this happening is minuted in the details of the school's teaching. And the Governors initially never advertised it, as one might expect, as a School of Industry.

At a meeting in the Vestry of St James on 24 October 1783, the Governors were able to draft a notice for apprenticeships for their poor children, for whom they could claim a preference:

[since] in September 1782 the Governors and Directors of the Poor . . . caused all the Poor Children belonging to the Parish between the Age of Seven and thirteen years to be removed from the St James's Workhouse in Poland St & placed in a House purchased for their reception late Mr Durrell's in King St Golden Square. There are about a Hundred Boys and a Hundred Girls . . . who have the advantage of a good example and daily instruction.

13. For the children and nurses at Wimbledon, the St James's workhouse and the King Street school, see my *Blake's Innocence and Experience Retraced* (London: Athlone, 1986), *passim*, especially the first chapter. All references are given there, the main source being the minutes and accounts of the Governors of the workhouse and the school, mss, D. 1869–72 and 1856, in the Victoria Library, Buckingham Palace Road, Westminster.

The Governors acted with remarkable efficiency. Within five months of the transfer of the deeds of the house in King Street, they had moved there all the children from the workhouse.

Further to this, on 11 October 1782, the book-keeper recorded that, having retained the younger children a year longer than normal with the nurses, they had "caused 20 boys and 46 girls who were above 7 years of age and at Nurse in the Country to be brought to the house [in King Street] who are now maintained therein". This sustained and objective rescue of the children from the proximity of death in the workhouse was familiar to Blake both as a neighbour and, closer than that, because his family had trading links with both the school and the workhouse. He and Catherine (and Blake's brother, Robert, come to that) knew so well the people in the coach-hire caravans that were trundling the children across Westminster Bridge, that they could have got a lift back to Green Street, if they were out walking that day.

Perhaps earlier, but at the latest from 9 August 1782, "Mr Blake Haberdasher" was being paid to supply the workhouse. By November 29 that year, "the Schoolhouse" also appears in the Blake accounts. The Governors of the Poor simply extended James Blake's workhouse contract to the school, soon after the first children were enrolled. The payments, for supplies both to the workhouse and the school, continue regularly.

However when various tradesmen submitted samples and letters in response to an advertisement for contracts in April 1784, the senior James Blake's name was missing. We may speculate that he was terminally ill and the business temporarily neglected. The last of at least forty-nine fortnightly payments from the Governors of the Poor to the Blake haberdashery business, £1. 13s. 6d., was made on 11 June. James Blake, Sr, was buried three weeks later, on 4 July.

It was a considerable income to recover. Some four months after Blake moved from Green Street to 27 Broad Street, his elder brother next door, surely having discussed the matter, applied formally to rescue the contract from the incursions of Messrs Jones & Co, Haberdashers, who had received the huge payment of £7. 17s. 7d. on 14 October 1784. So it was at 4 p.m. on 1 April 1785, that the Governors of the Poor, meeting in the workhouse, heard their book-keeper read "a letter from Mr Blake", which he had copied in his minutes, preserving the family's scant punctuation:

A Letter from Mr. Blake was delivd to the Board & read Copy thof is as follows

   Gentn

   As at this Season of the year you appoint your several Trades persons permit me to offer myself to serve you with the Articles of Haberdashery for I flatter myself I am able to supply the Infirmary & School of Industry with every Article upon as low terms as any house in London & being an Inhabitant of this Psh & my family for many years hope a preference may be given me for which should I succeed shall make it my study to deliver for the use of the same such Articles as will bear the strictest examination sho.d any be found not agreable or otherwise not suiting shall be happy to provide such as will every way answer the use intended or exchange the Articles if not approved – I remain Gent.n for Mother & Self

Your very hble Serv.t

Ja.s Blake

Broad S.t Golden Sqr:
Resolved that Consideration be referred to the next Board [14]

James Blake's use of "school of industry" and "infirmary" is interesting. He gave the school no airs, and was politely euphemistic about the workhouse. The application succeeded. Though the Committee named no supplier, they continued to pay James for haberdashery "For the Schoolhouse". It seems the large deliveries from Messrs Jones & Co. to the workhouse were not yet exhausted. It is a totally safe assumption that Blake, of all people, together with Robert, took the opportunity to deliver the goods to both school and workhouse, and to take a look around, especially at the children.

If nothing else, the precisely minuted inspections of improvement in the children's progress measure the enlightenment Blake witnessed in the King Street school. While eighteen months was about the time "common" children normally spent in school, the destitute pupils in the King Street school could be there for five years; and longer if a "comfortable" apprenticeship could not be found for them.

For the next five or six years, coinciding precisely with the writing of the poems of Innocence, the Governors ensured that the children in their school of industry learnt everything usually taught in the London day Charity Schools, where places were coveted since they held forth "advantages for the *first degree* among the lower orders".

The important qualification is, with emphasis, "the *first degree*". It was mistaken, as Mrs Sarah Trimmer later made plain, to spread charity school education downwards through the lower orders,

to train them all in a way which will most probably raise their ideas above those servile offices which must be filled by some members of the community and in which they may be equally happy with the highest, if they will do their duty. [15]

The Governors and Directors of the Poor in Blake's parish were soon

14. The original is copied in Gardner, *Retraced*, p. 12.

15. Sarah Trimmer, *Reflections upon the Education of Children in Charity Schools* (1792), pp. 7, 13, and 23–24. See Gardner, *Retraced*, pp. 83–85.

breaking the code outrageously. On 3 December 1782, no more than a
few months after they had emptied the workhouse of the children,
they examined their progress in the house in King Street,

*as to their several qualifications and found several very backward in their learning
particularly those who came from the Workhouse and they desired Mr Whitaker the
Master to take the utmost pains in his power to bring them forwards.*

Mr Whitaker was very probably as little qualified as Robert Atchison,
his contemporary at the Foundling Hospital, "a Mechanic" who turned
teacher, he said, when his eyes failed him.

It was an age when clergymen were ready to fight elections with
unscrupulous, unchristian tenacity for Masterships of the Free Grammar Schools. With their connections to Oxford and Cambridge, here
was a privileged step to preferment, even to a bishopstool. But the work
of Mr Whitaker or Robert Atchison was beneath their contemplation.
Nonetheless, though it took them best part of a year, by 12 September
1783, the Governors had replaced Mr Whitaker with a clergyman
schoolmaster, a nomination unthinkable even for "children of the first
degree among the lower orders" in the best Charity Schools, and incredible for these workhouse children, if it were not documented—and this
some seventy years before Lord Macaulay recognised teachers still as
"the refuse of all other callings, discarded footmen and ruined pedlars".

However, as the meticulous book-keeper records, the foundlings in
their King Street school now had Reverend John Mossop to teach them.
Eight months later "the Committee examined the Boys writing &
ciphering books and found them much improved." However the Governors refused John Mossop's request for an extra room, since they
expected to admit more children. He threatened to leave. They allowed
him the room. Miss Elizabeth Pinnard had been appointed with him, as
his assistant schoolmistress, each initially on three months probation.
John Mossop must have been a remarkable man, and Blake doubtless
knew them both well. We may find Miss Pinnard introduced to us in *An
Island in the Moon*. John Mossop could well be there too.

The Governors of the Poor went regularly to Wimbledon to review
the nursing provision. In September 1784, they instructed the surgeon,
James Swift, that "the children at Nurse at Wimbledon who have not
had the smallpox be inoculated, and that they should be housed at
Holloways, Lord Spencer's farm for the time being". Inoculation was
common enough by this time. But the success of the socially organised
Wimbledon programme is to be matched against the failure of the
scheme set up two years earlier in Clapham, to inoculate children

either in a dispensary there, or in their homes.[16] It seems the close interest of the surgeon, and someone even more influential, were factors.

More important than the inoculation to the children was doubtless the fact that "good milk can be had at a farmhouse near the spot". The surgeon understandably considered this "an advantage", since milk delivered in London was thin and soiled. Fetched by the milk-sellers from the cowmen in St George's Fields, the parks or Battersea Field, it was diluted first from a tap in their cellars, then, for ill-luck, a second time from the horse trough before the roundsman scored it up on the customer's door.

James Swift also took care of the nurses. On 10 January 1783, the Governors "ordered that Ann Finch Nurse of No 8 be allowed a pint of Beer a day for a week by the recommendation of the Surgeon". At the same meeting, under the weather or not, she was sent three more children. More remarkably still, the book-keeper recorded, "if two children die with a nurse in a year, she is discontinued, as it seems to imply want of skill or attention or both".

The extent of the care comes impressively through the records of the workhouse and the King Street school. Not only this, the open handed tone the book-keeper reports at this time is something we so rarely meet. So it comes as a pleasure, and no surprise, to read that the Governors rode to Wimbledon frequently. The annual accounts through the 1780s give details of convivial expenditure "for coach hire caravans and expences in going to visit the Poor children at Nurse in the country; and also for a Dinner for the Nurses and said children as usual at Christmas". Beyond this, the medical arrangements suggest that the Governors and the foundlings even enjoyed the intervention of the first Countess Spencer. The first Earl Spencer became lord of the manor of Wimbledon in 1755. Soon after, he built a handsome town house in the parish of St James, opposite Green Park. It seems the move brought the Governors of the workhouse an invaluable patron. The Countess took a charitable interest in poor children, helping to found in 1758 (and re-found fifteen years later) the charity school in Wimbledon. Known as the Round School, it still exists. The Countess outlived her husband by some thirty years, until 1814, and gave so much help to Mrs Sarah Trimmer in her work of severe social concern, that she raised the indignation of her family.

From what comes later, it seems more than coincidence that, as the Countess moved into luxury in the parish of St James, the foundlings moved from the workhouse to Wimbledon. We know that she looked with practical concern in the 1780s on the destitute children put out to nurse on the Common.

16. A. S. Turbeville, ed., *Johnson's England* (Oxford: Clarendon Press, 1933), vol. 2, p. 282.

She favoured James Swift for her family, though he lived away from Wimbledon, by the Thames in Putney. When her grandson, John, fell off his horse in January 1794, and "got a deep cut on his chin", as the ground was "hard with frost", the boy was promptly taken to Putney. James Swift "closed the chin up, dressed it carefully, and Jack has felt no pain since". At the time, the apothecary-surgeon in Wimbledon was John Sandford, the illegitimate son of Somerset aristocracy, who landed in the village in 1784, and worked his way into the job. That the local man was thought unfit to treat young John Charles Spencer is unremarkable; that the Governors of the Poor at the time shared the view of the Countess for their foundlings was something we may now come to expect. After James Swift inoculated them, the children convalesced away from Wimbledon itself, at a farm on the Spencer estates. There is a sheen of Countess Spencer on the reality of rescue, postulating an uncommonly rare sense of community.[17]

It is difficult to imagine circumstances more compelling for Blake than this provision for children of no consequence, brought close to him through the family haberdashery business: the workhouse, where "the living go to bed with the dead", against Wimbledon Common and King Street. For some five or six between-war years of peace after Blake was married, his neighbours directed this enlightened undertaking in community care, with an impetus that was genuinely charitable and sustained. It occupied precisely the years Blake spent with Robert close by as his pupil, spanning the most influential and intense relationship of his life.

By 1787, as Blake nursed and guided his brother towards death, the Governors of the Poor along the street were coming grievously, perhaps inevitably, to the conclusion that Mrs Sarah Trimmer's disciplinary reforms for the regulation of the poor were the best they could expect, and that the Countess Spencer's expostulating relatives were right all along.

Mostly already written, within months *Songs of Innocence* was ready for engraving. We may see the book as a timeless record of a rescue tragically abandoned to the rising tide of Experience.[18] It engulfed the King Street school, the bricks of which still underpin Regent Street.

The forlorn generosity towards those destitute children William Blake knew so well was simply not worth a footnote in history.

17. The information on the first Countess Spencer, and her relation with Sarah Trimmer and James Swift, was kindly passed to me by Richard Milward, from his comprehensive knowledge of Wimbledon's history, when he came across the reference in my own *Retraced*. This enabled the link to be followed up. Incidentally, it was Jack, who fell on his chin and was patched up by James Swift, who was chiefly res-ponsible for carrying the great Reform Bill of 1832. While most institutions for the poor were otherwise ill-served, the physi-cians and surgeons associated with them were generally good.

18. My *Retraced* covers the evidence in detail.

"Good News for Morning Tea"

Though it was said at the time that "very few of the Engravers keep Copper-plate presses in their houses", it is reasonably certain that Blake installed one when he moved to 27 Broad Street, most likely with money from his father's legacy, and maybe from Mrs Mathew. There was certainly room in the house (three floors, attic and basement) to accommodate the Parkers, the Blakes and the press with no discomfort by contemporary expectations, and to leave room for the shop.

It is evident that Blake had the press with him in Lambeth in 1795, and during the three years he spent on the south coast from September in 1800. It was here that Hayley, watching the progress of his Ballads, was impressed with the way Blake and "his excellent Wife (a true Helpmate!) pass the plates thro' a rolling press in their own cottage together".

Such wifely cooperation was less voluntary than Hayley's gallant parenthesis colours it for Lady Hesketh's eye. Catherine had already fulfilled the invariable expectation of the times twenty years earlier, as printer's assistant and by helping alongside Parker's wife in the shop, from first light to late night lock-up and after. The chance of friction, especially with Blake around, must have been high.

For the short time the Blake and Parker partnership survived, most profitably promising were high quality engravings of demure subjects, then much in vogue. The prices were high, and it is said that Blake earned no less than £80 for one such "decorative" print, 'The Fall of Rosamond'.[1]

Alongside the knowledge that money might be made in the business, there was some sweet taste of recognition, the more pleasant for being shared with his brother Robert.

In May 1784, Blake had exhibited two water-colours at the Royal Academy, with titles that sound to have a commercial ring to them: 'A Breach in a City the Morning after the Battle', and 'War Unchained by an Angel – Fire, Pestilence and Famine Following'. The next year, four more water-colours went to the Academy Exhibition: three based on the story of Joseph, and one from Gray's *The Bard*. A gathering of Blake's friends, Fuseli, Flaxman, J. T. Smith (Nollekens, that is) and Stothard, also exhibited, together with the dandified and patronised Richard Cosway, whom we soon hear of in *An Island in the Moon*. Gilchrist admired these 1785 water-colours by Blake, the last to go to the Academy for many years:

1. See Bentley, *Blake Records*, pp. 29 and 75, and Robert Essick, *William Blake: Printmaker* (Princeton: Princeton University Press, 1980), chapter 7.

The latter series I have seen. The drawings are interesting for their imaginative merit, and as specimens, full of soft tranquil beauty, of Blake's earlier style: a very different one from that of his later and better-known works. Conceived in a dramatic spirit, they are executed in a subdued key, of which extravagance is the last defect to suggest itself. The design is correct and blameless, not to say tame (for Blake), the colour full, harmonious and sober.[2]

Reflecting Stothard's later assured reputation, Gilchrist suggests that Blake "was at this period of his life influenced to his advantage as a designer by contact with Stothard's graceful mind", an influence Blake himself would have furiously denied.

Far more profound than any other was the influence on Blake of his younger brother, Robert, who had already been admitted to the Academy on 2 April 1782, to study as an engraver. The brothers' relationship developed into a spiritual understanding, which for Blake was not dissolved by Robert's early death. It will turn out to be crucial, too, that Robert must have shared with his brother a delivery man's knowledge of the neighbourly rescue of destitute children, while the Rector of St James's ministered to the supremely rich in the parish, half a mile and light years away in his church opposite Albany.

It was during these optimistic months while he was financially, if temporarily, comfortable, that Blake put together his account of oddball islanders, living "near by a mighty continent" on the moon, "which small island seems to have some affinity to England. & what is more extraordinary the people are so much alike & their language so much the same that you would think you was among your friends."[3]

While he was among friends, some young and rough cut, some with intellectual and fashionable pretensions, Blake's mind was turning to the project of an illustrated book of verse for children. No doubt the initial motivation was profit for the print shop. But writing to commercial order (even his own) was only Blake's line under necessity. Inevitably, circumstances, relationships, the way his neighbours lived— all this was the day-long stimulus to his imagination, and radically determined what he wrote. So it is, that even the reactions of the self-regarding eccentrics he lodges on "an island in the moon" are tempered in his creative solicitude for children in distress; and he was not alone in this preoccupation in the 1780s. At a less committed level, it was shared by friends who matured into "radicals". While Blake had his eye on his Islanders, Joseph Priestley, of all people, was opening Sunday schools for deprived children in Clapham.[4]

With an unexpected persistence among the bombast and flasks of dephlogisticated air, the inhabitants of *An Island in the Moon* condone the

2. Gilchrist, *Life of Blake*, p. 58.
3. The opening words to *An Island in the Moon*.
4. 'Sunday school' entered the language in 1783, for an unsullied endeavour. 'Radicals' did not have that name for another two decades.

interventions and pastimes of children. Perhaps unexpectedly in the context, the topics recur in all but two of the manuscript's eleven chapters; stranger still, is the unembarrassing presence, in the febrile academic circle, of a collection of urchins clearly close to Blake, presented in the character of Quid the Cynic. With an unselfconscious ease reminiscent of Chaucer, he brings his neighbours' impoverished offspring into social intimacy with the pretensions of the "the better sort" of eccentric; and the poor are not mocked. Apparently, even more surely with them, "you would think you was among friends".

The satire that runs through the piece in no way sets out to diminish education or educational charity. Its first target is the prissiness and irrelevance of educators, and it reflects for us, as through a distorting mirror, Blake's empathy with vulnerable children in the mid-1780s. From the forlorn envy of Miss Gittipin's exegesis on fashion and unattainable style in chapter 8 to the end, Blake's common companionship is expressed in lines which are better than anything earlier in the piece. Then, collected at the end of the satire, are the poems he later adapted for *Songs of Innocence*.[5]

This transfer of texts from a satire to Innocence has led to endless speculation. At the centre of the problem has always been 'Holy Thursday', the poem on the charity schools' annual service in St Paul's, and its contrary in *Experience*. Reading back from our times to the occasion in St Paul's, we have rarely seen the children as other than flogged, scrubbed and marched through London into their seats; as if, in a century of ingrained dirt, with his lovely phrase "their innocent faces clean", Blake jeered. It is a response which his illustration, showing them out of step and gossiping, enjoying what was always a day out for Londoners, has oddly done little to disturb. We forget the eternal schoolchild's preference for an escape, anywhere, from a desk; and, as a critical guide, we paste beneath Blake's lines the stock report of *The Times* on the day, invariably commending its readers on having opened their philanthropic purses "to sympathy and to brotherly love".

As always, a newspaper was selling itself, and brought "good news for morning tea". In its columns the hymn-singing children all became "orphaned innocents": so many "adopted children of public benevolence", "under the humane direction of the worthy Patrons". In fact, very few charity school children were orphaned, except in some of the schools turned hospitals. Leaning towards these, *The Times* reports were simply an early slant on the feel-good factor for the readers. What the press reports do for us is to identify our first difficulty: to reconcile the thousands of children gathered in St Paul's Cathedral with Blake's Innocence, rather than with the 'innocence' of a newspaper editor.

5. See Phillips, ed., *Island*, chap. 9, p. 11; Gardner, *Retraced*, pp. 26, 29 and 49. The subject is covered in chapter 7 below.

We are mistaken to lump all charity schools with hospital schools, or with schools of industry, which did take in destitute orphans. Blake knew that some charity schools, but far from all, had been moved into workhouses; and he knew the ambivalent reaction, at once congratulatory and resentful, of parents whose children had been "pushed aside" by the admission of children of lower class into the successful, locally controlled day charity schools of London. In 'Holy Thursday' in *Songs of Innocence*, Blake etched his approval, not simply of a privilege accorded the poor, but of a right. It would never sell *The Times*—not then, not now.

To counter our twentieth century assumptions, let us go back to the invention of the two kinds of school, charitable and industrial.

In the time of Blake's grandfather, alongside the solution of settling parish children in the workhouses, two parallel initiatives in child care served to place common children profitably in society. They were the school of industry and the charity school. Each survived well beyond the years when Blake wrote of "the better sort" of child in *Experience*, and each was approved by the establishment, as an essential support of degree.

The history of confusion among these institutions, bred from ancestral economic and social wheeler-dealing in children's lives, has always shadowed our reading of the *Songs*. In 1690 John Locke had seen "the mind at birth as a blank sheet to be written on, the child as virgin soil to be exploited". Nine years later, in a *Report to the Board of Trade*, he came to the conclusion which characterised the coming century, in its concept of service, its charitable economy and the recipe of physical and spiritual "welfare". In his old age, in baleful detail, Locke authorised the exploitation of deprived children for the next hundred years or more. The hierarchs of the Board of Trade were assiduous in taking heed:

The children of labouring people are an ordinary burthen to the parish, and are usually maintained in idleness . . . The most effectual remedy for this that we are able to . . . propose, is, that working schools be set up in each parish, to which the children . . . above three and under fourteen years . . . not otherwise employed for their livelihood . . . shall be obliged to come . . . and from their infancy be inured to work, which is of no small consequence for the making of them sober and industrious all their lives after . . . If care can be taken, that they have each of them a bellyful of bread daily at school, they will be in no danger of famishing . . . And to this may be added also, without any trouble, in cold weather, if it be thought needful, a little warm water gruel, for the same fire that warms the room, may be made use to boil a pot of it.

Another advantage also of bringing poor children thus to a working school, is, that ... they may be obliged to come constantly to church ... whereby they may be brought into some sense of religion, whereas ordinarily now, in their loose and idle way of bringing up, they are as utter strangers both to religion and morality as they are to industry.

Here John Locke drew the plan for the parish schools of industry, which proliferated across the country, until the reforms at the beginning of the nineteenth century changed things; it was the plan which Blake's neighbours redrafted unrecognisably into the King Street school; and it was the plan, "of respectable antiquity", which was dusted over and updated by educationists as Blake was writing *Songs of Experience*, even before Pitt proposed "the extension of schools of industry" as a way to stifle unrest.

Alongside John Locke's institutions, we may watch "the middle sort" set about safeguarding their status. On the initiative of people like the six tradesmen who set up the Grey Coat school in Westminster (a soap and candles dealer, cheesemonger, draper, bookseller, broomseller and a tanner) the charity schools began their ambivalent progress through the century. The beginning was self-interest serving charity. [6]

We may see charity schools typified as a trust to serve this class of child in the record of the schools in Colchester. Ten years after John Locke was writing to the Board of Trade, the town set up "Charity-schools belonging to the Church of England", and later "to the Protestant Dissenters". Supplementing the income from rents, bequests and stock, the annual "subscriptions of the inhabitants of the town" were "one pound four shillings, collected quarterly; for which every subscriber is allowed the privilege of nominating, in rotation, a boy or girl".

So the control of the school lay crucially with the subscribers, parents and friends, twelve of whom were appointed alongside the minister, treasurer and secretary, as trustees. "The subscribers at large" met every quarter-day, "observing the state of the schools, and satisfying themselves as to the proficiency of the children."

The children's day was the familiar routine of catechism, prayers, the Bible, reading, writing, cyphering and house craft. They were provided with, and enjoyed, their Blue Coat dress, seen by us, but not by them, as a "uniform". Their status in humble respectability was guaranteed in the oversight of the trustees and benefactors, who nominated them, and in the fact that they were directed "to join in the public service, which they attend morning and evening ... with decency and advantage".

Such a "decent" reception by the clergy sealed the superiority of the charity school children. It was out of the question for John Locke's children "above three and under fourteen years", and "from their infancy

6. See Gardner, *Retraced*, chapter 4. The standard work is Mary G. Jones, *The Charity School Movement: a Study of Eighteenth-Century Puritanism in Action* (Cambridge: Cambridge University Press, 1938).

LEFT *Figure 4*. The Grey Coat Hospital, Grey-coat Place, Westminster, one of the former Charity Schools transformed, and now a girls' school. *Photograph by Mary R. Gardner.*

OPPOSITE *Figure 5*. The eighteenth-century Charity School children, in the dress they so cherished, still stand in the wall of the Grey Coat Hospital, St Margaret's, Westminster. *Photograph by Mary R. Gardner.*

inured to work", drafted into a separate service. They also lacked the powerful benefit of intervention by trustees and subscribing parents. Parents such as these were particularly influential in the day charity schools in London, when Blake came to be interested in them.

Most charity schools retained their initial identity, until in 1812 the trustees agreed that "the children of these schools, and those of the intended National Schools should be educated together, by the same master and mistress".[7] This straight amalgamation in itself exemplifies the quality of teaching in the charity schools which survived down-grading to "industrial" status. It is the quality which Blake had recognised in the London charity schools, as "sweet instruction" for working class children, and which he found incredibly emulated for destitute children in the King Street school.

The general identity of charity school children comes through an appeal in *The Spectator*, as early as 6 February 1712, for funds for fifty boys "who would be clothed, and take their seats (at the charge of some generous benefactors) in St Bride's church on Sunday next". The appeal is prefixed with the commendation of the charity schools, since "it is rather from the good management of those institutions, than from the number and value of the benefactions to them, that they make so great a figure". After a promise to "compound with any lady in a hooped petti-coat, if she give the price of one half-yard of silk towards clothing, feed-

7. Cromwell, *History of Colchester*, II, pp. 381–89.

ing, and instructing an innocent helpless creature of her own sex in one of these schools", the writer appeals to the reader for assistance, and in making his bid outlines for us, in their classic state, the background and expectations of the charity school pupils whom Blake was to hear chattering and singing in St Paul's on Holy Thursday. *The Spectator* approaches the "generous mind" of man: make a gift to a charity school, and

do it for public good; do it for one who will become an honest artificer. Would you do it for the sake of heaven; give it to one who shall be instructed in the worship of him for whose sake you gave it. It is, methinks, a most laudable institution this, if it were of no other expectation than that of producing a race of good and useful servants, who will have more than a liberal [that is, gentrifying], a religious education.

It is the common vice of children, to run too much among the servants; from such as are educated in these places they would see nothing but lowliness in a servant, which would not be disingenuous in the child. All the ill offices and defamatory whispers, which take their birth from domestics, would be prevented, if this charity could be made universal.

It is no surprise to read the list of personal advantages that accrue for charitable deeds. It is surprising, at first, to read the recommendation that the charity school child may be rescued from the influence of domestic servants; strange, that an offspring of a family apparently comfortable enough to be waited upon should even approach a charity school for a servile education. A 'liberal' private academy with gentrifying pretensions would seem more likely.

The crux is the nature and universal availability of domestic service in the eighteenth century. The workhouse governors were repeatedly driven to off-load a girl into service for a pound or two. Worse, the overseer was required as a priority in practice, to discount the law safeguarding the interests of the apprentice, and "to bind out poor children apprentice, no matter to whom or to what trade, but to take especial care that the master live in another parish", so passing the charge of a settlement. Though *The Spectator* aims a little higher, we are close to the social level from which the 'classic' charity school child came, and for whom William Blake clearly saw the London schools offering such a socially reshaping opportunity.

The "especial care" laid on the overseer meant that even a smart labourer, who sported a gold watch, could always get his hands on a maid-servant as unpaid drudge. Indeed, at times, the most dire poverty hardly meant lack of an "apprentice". A widow existing in a garret or cellar, running a street stall, or a faggot-hawking outfit, shifting night soil or watering milk, could always pick up a child, if not from the workhouse, then off the streets.

Against this, a child from "the underclass" could have the luck to be taken as a servant at a level well above this, even in a haberdashery or print shop in Broad Street, where the family might, if times were hard, consider a charity school suitable for its own offspring. It seems to be the domestic "defamatory whispers" among the children of these households that *The Spectator* deplores. It is these children who would be shielded in charity schools from insidious ideas, since it is they who may eventually seek service at a genteel level, some of them with improper ambition, among "well regulated families, that set apart an hour in every morning for tea and bread and butter"; and, of course, for *The Spectator* "punctually served up".[8]

Here is the original charity school child personified, a cut well above the industrial drilling outlined by John Locke, for derelict infants from the age of three, a cut below the child to whom Blake later gave such a glorious "liberal" voice in 'The School Boy'. The schools of industry were uniformly unremitting as John Locke defined them, while some of the charity schools failed to survive the suppressive exploitation of the century in their designated form. As was so often confirmed,

8. *The Spectator*, no. 10 (12 March 1710).

the Creator of the universe has appointed every thing to a certain purpose ... In like manner, it is in the dispositions of society, the civil economy is formed in a chain, as well as the natural: and in either case the breach but of one link puts the whole in disorder.[9]

To assist divine dispensation, it was the way of "people of condition" to subvert any institution that tended to release the underclass, and too many charity schools were diverted to supporting the sheer weight of poverty. Directed by the newspapers of the day, looking back we tend only to notice these charity schools, lined up with workhouses or reformed into hospital schools. Blake, of course, knew different.

From the start of the century, the simple addition of a house for pauper children had converted the Grey Coat charity school into a hospital. It was by the pound near the Artillery Ground in St Margaret's, Westminster, and Blake knew it notoriously well, as we shall see. A little later, the girls' charity school in St James's was "reformed" into a working school. Such reformation was aided by the fact that the Society for Promoting Christian Knowledge had a special interest, not only in charity schools (with the Society of Patrons it organised the 'Holy Thursday' services in St Paul's), but indirectly in the workhouses. Such concerns tended to come together.

For some twenty years after the Workhouse Act of 1722, relentless efforts were made to "inure the children to labour and industry" in the redesignated charity schools. It meant abandoning much of what was portentously called the "literary" teaching. But it was not easy to find tasks simple enough for frail children, material waste was expensive, and defective work was unsellable, even the girls' needlework. Competent instruction was hard to come by, the trustees were less inclined to supervise degenerate schools, and parental intervention dissolved.

Preaching at the children, parents, trustees and journalists in the annual charity school service in 1766, Dean Tucker of Gloucester confessed that "it clearly appears that the setting up of working schools or the introduction of labour into our present charity schools is not so easy as many people have thought".[10] Many of the governors, and especially the parents, associated with the London day charity schools resisted such denigration. As late as 1792, even Mrs Sarah Trimmer (no silly radical she) was still protesting that no time could be spared from the "literary curriculum" in the charity schools, for the kind of drill in drudgery the children faced in the modern and admirable school of industry she had helped set up in Marylebone. What is more, she went on to record the "superior advantages" of the charity schools, and their "decided pre-eminence over all the subsisting establishments of gratuitous instruction, as the money collected for them is usually sufficient to afford clothing for the children, as well as learning".

9. Ibid., no. 404 (13 June 1712).
10. Jones, *Charity School*, p. 94.

By this time, the schools of industry and workhouse schools were adapting to the provision of juvenile labour for the modern mills and workshops, "essential in the highest degree to the comfort and convenience of the higher orders of society",[11] while the charity schoolboy was required to sit on the stools and cast the accounts for the tradesmen and managers of an age of expanding industry. With a politic stress, the policy still echoes today.

The educationists' dilemma is clear. With unbecoming regularity, the divinely appointed links in society were corroded by luck, ambition and even talent; and broken by disaster. Given parental interest and the rather indeterminate nature of their intake (children "of some condition"), the true charity schools inevitably generated social change. Pre-eminent among these were the London day charity schools. Answerable to distinguished local governors, and monitored directly by parents who were far from intimidated, they put their pupils in the way of "unfair competition with their betters", so that

they crowded out the children of tradesmen in the already overstocked manual trades, and, because they could read and write and cast accounts, they forced their way into the business of shopkeepers and retailers of commodities, and even pushed aside the children of a superior class of domestic service.[12]

It was a grudging gratification at this educational success which brought Mrs Trimmer its own concern. The breeding up of "beggars to what are called scholars" offended the authorised version of divine dispensation. But such excessive "modulation of indispensable subordination, of necessary obedience, and of equitable right" for charity school children, could only fulfil Blake's dearest hopes.[13]

What is more, in their King Street school, the Governors of the Poor in a few short years had even reversed the educational "deconstruction" practised for decades. They had initiated on charity school lines what should have been a John Locke school of industry, and, handy dandy, Blake was walking among life's real beggars who were being bred above their status, not by chance, but by intent. Almost inconceivably, across Carnaby Market he was watching the Governors of the King Street school compound the fracture of Urizen's "civil economy ... formed in a chain". If so, "marked was the improvement of the children in the charity schools that they threatened not only the economic, but also the social, order",[14] what might Blake not expect from this undertaking by his neighbours, for the foundlings from the workhouse and from the nurses at Wimbledon?

Soon after his brother wrote to the Governors of the Poor on 1 April

11. Trimmer, *Reflections*, pp. 23–26. The annual charity school subscription came to something like £1 20s, at a time when an artisan's wage was about 60 pence a week. The subscriber would nominate a child to the school.

12. Jones, *Charity School*, p. 32.

13. See *The Observer*, Sunday 4 December 1791. Jones, *Charity School*, p. 86. Gardner, *Retraced*, pp. 32–37.

14. Jones, *Charity School*, p. 86.

1784, to rescue his haberdashery contract, Blake moved away from the print shop into 28 Poland Street, up the road from the workhouse entrance and opposite the side door to the Pantheon. He soon slipped into *An Island in the Moon* the poems he had written about children living at peace among nurses, while others paraded into St Paul's, dressed "in grey & blue & green". He knew the children's feelings as they filled the cathedral with excited murmurings. He knew that for them, "when many of their contemporaries went in rags, to be neatly and warmly clad helped to suggest the self respect that went with a higher standard of living".[15]

As the chattering stopped and St Paul's overflowed with song on the children's own Holy Thursday in 1784, Blake knew that the workhouse children in the King Street school had been granted a special self-respect, because of "the Hats & Cloaks allowed them" from the previous 13 January; just as if they were charity school children dressed for St Paul's Cathedral.[16]

15. Dorothy Marshall, *English People in the Eighteenth Century* (London: Longman, Green & Co., 1956), p. 162.

16. For Blake's presence at an annual charity school service in St Paul's, see Gardner, *Retraced*, pp. 34–36, and chapter 8 below.

"Goodyness, that's sales"

We cannot say whether it was the failure of the business in the print shop, a change of heart, or sheer discord that motivated Blake's move to Poland Street, while he was toying with alterations to *An Island in the Moon*. The house was up the road across Great Marlborough Street, where Blake's lifelong patron Thomas Butts lived in comfort, no more than a minute or two away. The narrow plot behind the house in Poland Street backed on to a timber yard which opened into Oxford Street, an improvement in this respect on Pawlett's Garden, and the proximity of Carnaby Market.

At the same time Blake was considering the commercial advantage of printing his own illustrated book of poems for children. He had already engraved illustrations for bibles, books of poetry, educational manuals, magazines and pocket books. But it seems that before 1786 no more than two or three of these engravings were of designs by Blake himself. Almost invariably the designer was Stothard.[1] The attraction of writing, designing, engraving and selling a book uniquely his own is clear, quite apart from the chance of profit. What is more likely to sell, or more simple to write, than rhymes for children?

He had many successful examples to follow. The format was cheap, little more than a chapbook. It is not surprising that in *Songs of Innocence* Blake seems to borrow "styles and motifs from children's books and the picturesque vignette illustrations with which he was familiar as a copy engraver".[2]

Books of verse for children at the time were invariably illustrated, commonly with a single woodcut or engraving to go with each poem, as in Christopher Smart's *Hymns for the Amusement of Children* (1770), in penny histories and in metrical admonitions like Francis Quarles's *Emblemes*— a survivor across two centuries of change in taste and fashion.

The commercial viability of Quarles's Jacobean 'fancies' well into the nineteenth century, against the sophistication of children's books and the advance of 'liberal' education, is a solemn warning against easy generalisation. With Francis Quarles still selling, Blake might well have assumed that 'innocent' rhymes would meet the market. However, whatever Blake's 'sources', their influence was always superficial.[3]

Quarles published his *Emblemes*, 'Hieroglyphikes of the Life of Man', as far back as 1635. The poems, in varying metres but uniformly based on scriptural texts, were embellished with quaint engravings, quota-

1. See Bentley, *Records*, appendix 4.

2. Essick, *Printmaker*, p. 138. A number of Blake's 'borrowings' is discussed. See also Zachary Leader, *Reading Blake's Songs* (Boston: Routledge & Kegan Paul, 1981), pp. 1–36.

3. See David Bindman, *Blake as an Artist* (New York: E. P. Dutton, 1977), pp. 60–62.

tions from the Fathers and epigrams. They were rigorously improving, and much in favour among settlers in eighteenth century Boston. Their very nature (a picture and a stretch of verse "free from dross and ribauldry") made them the indestructible template of adult literature precisely suitable for children.

If we may take Francis Quarles's 'Hieroglyphikes', a hundred and fifty years in print, as a 'source' for *Songs of Innocence*, perhaps anything may be contemplated. Indeed the identification of source material seems an indifferent pursuit, and rarely throws light on the *Songs*. If Quarles influenced Blake, more so did Quarles shape from his grave the minatory rhymes published by John Marshall, so alien to Blake, and profitably contemporary with *Innocence*. In the mid-eighties Marshall and others became increasingly aware of an ambivalence in taste, which they hastened to promote. Alongside a more insidious persuasion, there was money in a return to direct severity in books for the "lower classes". On a higher social shelf, late century novelettes, contrived in a more "liberal" tone of improvement, tempted the kind of young gentle-folk Blake introduces to us in *Experience*.

That Blake was little influenced by "sources" may simply suggest discrimination on his part. But then there were the commercial practices, habits of mind, religious and moral foreclosures, which he set aside. Had he treated any of these with consequence, *Innocence* could not have survived as one of "the Two Contrary States of the Human Soul". Clearly the purpose was compelling, which led Blake to discount imperatives of such depth, duration and advantage, as he drafted and relief-etched *Songs of Innocence*.

Experience reports the grafting of a new stock of cultivated indifference on to the reprise of an old alienation, which *Innocence* had reformed: "Two Contrary States". So it is not only *Experience* that is offset sharply against the span of history which preceded its printing.

By the time Quarles's eighteen children had made him a grandfather, the old man was already old fashioned. Men of letters considered him "fit only for schoolboys". But that may have ensured his literary longevity, especially across the years of king's "great bawdy-house at Whitehall".

If the seed of *Songs of Innocence* was the notion of a book of verse for children, Blake had historic justification for assuming their cultivated interest, which some two centuries of instruction had inbred. It was, of course, an instruction Blake himself missed. He also missed the prescriptive support that schoolmasters gave to their pupils' recreational reading, which released him from boyhood, more or less alone to do as he would in the fields of English literature.

The books recommended by schoolmasters assiduously reflected parental preference. This means that in their lists we have the nominees from which the commercial publishers of Blake's day developed their sales, and this is the output against which a new imprint from 27 Broad Street would be matched for popularity.

While books for children changed so much in Blake's lifetime, the carry-over from the previous century was strong. With Francis Quarles nine years in his grave, Clem Barksdale recommended his own methods to parents, and invited custom for his text-book, in an idyll which Frederick Tatham, with his gift for a verbal gesture, would still have admired over a century later:

These following exercises, you may suppose, had their birth by the fire-side, while the Master and his Scholars burnt away the long Winter-nights: the Master proposing the Latin Sentences, as they came to mind, and the ten Scholars in their courses rendring these in the English verse. Certainly there is no hurt.[4]

Clem Barksdale then stresses the need for "no hurt" in books read, not only in, but out of school. Indeed we find little difference between them, when Charles Hoole, Master of the Free School at Rotherham, lists the allowable poets for recreational reading in the puff for his text-book seven years later:

let them procure some pretty delightful and honest English Poems, by perusal whereof they may become acquainted with the Harmony of English Poesie . . . Mr Hardwick's late Translation of Mantuan, Mr Sandys of Ovid, Mr Ogleby's of Virgil, will abundantly supply them with Heroick Verses; which after they can truly and readily make, they can converse with others, that take liberty to sport it on Lyrick verses. Amongst all of which, Mr Herbert's Poems are most worthy to be mentioned in the first place, and next to them I conceive Mr Quarles divine Poems, and his divine Fansies; besides which, you may allow many others full of wit and elegance.

Provided, Hoole cautions, you "admit none which are stuf't with drollary and ribauldry". The normal boy simply had to seek this elsewhere.

By a reversal incomprehensible to us, having mastered the epic, the pupil, progressing in poetic good manners, could rise to fable and the lyric. He then returned to the epic for leisure. Having "become acquainted with variety of meeter", pupils could be set exercises in "a Fable of Aesop into what kind of verse you please to appoint them", or epigrams and emblems, with, of course, Quarles as their model,

4. Clem Barksdale, *Noctes Hibernae* (1653), sign. A2, in the Bodleian Library. The book cost twopence.

or the like Flourishes of wit, which you think will more delight them and help their fancies. And when you see that they begin to exercise their own invention, you may leave them to themselves, to make verses upon any occasion or subject . . . Chapman's English translation of Homer will delight your Scholars to read at leisure.[5]

Charles Hoole's substantial literary diet was aimed pre-eminently at feeding parental aspirations, by nourishing social awareness in their children. So he excluded the commonplace, most familiar book of verse of all at the time, the hundreds of metrical versions of that "Divine Poeme", the Psalms of David; among them, and ubiquitously popular, was 'Thom Sternholds wretched pricksong of the people", which even semi-literate verse makers, who "farther then that dare not pretend to the least sprigg of ye Poetts lawrell", set their reluctant muse to improving.[6]

At the start of the eighteenth century, death in detail was something the young were bred to face with equanimity condensed in platitude. Weaned from the "spiritual milk" of their primers, all children were fed the potted lives of the martyrs (fortified with the delights of Homer for "the better sort"), brought to death through mutilation in crude woodcuts for the "capacity of the young". In this line, more ferocious than Francis Quarles was James Janeway's *A Token for Children, being an Exact Account of the Conversion, Holy and Exemplary Lives, and Joyful Deaths of Several Young Children*, issued in 1671 and cradled into the future as proselytes worked their variations. In 1683 John Keach brought out *War with the Devil*, to an accompaniment of 'Hymns and Spiritual Songs'. Eight years later Nathaniel Crouch hit upon self-righteous sex in his *Youths Divine Pastime*, with its intimacies of coarse shock, illustrated with uninhibited piety: intimacies, however, even "the better sort" of child could not have missed at home, given the closeness of domesticity, particularly before bedrooms led off landings.

These verses, engraved with biblical revelations, still came into the hands of their Georgian grandchildren. And the Bible was still "adopted for young minds". But as the decades passed, "for the better sort", biblical lessons were often more tediously conveyed by the curate. Underpinning all there were Robin Hood and the *Pilgrim's Progress* "from this World to that which is to come", old bestiaries, and, everywhere, for "drollary and ribauldry", chapbooks and street ballads, sensational, topical, crudely pornographic, usually illustrated, stuck up in shops, taverns and houses, and stuffed surreptitiously to fall to bits in countless pockets. The old occupants of the nurseries were still around, but by coarse Queen Anne's time Jack Horner had left his corner to fiddle under the skirts of the cook's maid.

If we find it difficult to comprehend old Francis Quarles's verse as a "flourish of wit", the fault seems to be ours. In his and Charles Hoole's

5. Charles Hoole, *A New Discovery of the Old Art of Teaching Schoole* (1660), in the Bodleian Library (8.° A 6(2) Med.BS), pp. 157–59, 188, 196.

6. See J. Philips, ms. Rawl. Poet. 30. fol. 5, and ms. Rawl. Poet. 110, dedication, in the Bodleian. The efforts were interminably copied in commonplace books. See mss. Rawl. Poet. 37, 67, 74, 95, 97, 100, 201, 204, 208, among so many more, which record the prevalence of versification in all its forms.

time, the hand-me-downs of adult literature allowed to children as light reading served to reinforce the "cultural", and therefore socially correct, rather than severely moral training they also endured in school. As towards Blake's lifetime children's books came to be sold with profit and loss more closely in mind, publishers still made sure that they continued to bolster parental expectations. But time had changed attitudes. A more sophisticated emphasis was required. Always alongside an inviolable sense of social status, it now settled on the *material* advantages for children, that lay in dedication to a code of preferment and duty.

A change in philosophical assumptions on the very nature of child-hood, as "rational theology" improved the start of the new century, has been typified in two apiarian emblems for children. Back in 1686, John Bunyan had warned his readers in *A Book for Boys and Girls*, that when they "ran up and down and played", they "thus from God have strayed". He went on to stress, for customary good measure, that

> *Death's a cold Comforter to Girls and Boys,*
> *Who wedded are unto their Childish Toys,*

and then brought the propriety of terror down to a "Country rhime" in an emblem:

> *This Bee an emblem truly is of Sin*
> *Whose Sweet unto many Death hath been.*

By 1715 Isaac Watts was peddling a less conclusive, more tendentious lesson on the modern virtue of busy-ness in his *Divine Songs*:

> *How doth the little busy bee*
> *Improve each shining hour –*

followed with a qualified approval of morally and materially profitable recreation:

> *In Books, or Work, or healthful Play,*
> *Let my first Years be past,*
> *That I may give for every Day*
> *Some good Account at last.*

It has been said that early in Blake's century, the "old fundamental-ism", the certainty of natural sinfulness as a birthright, was superseded by the rational certainty that "a child began life in a state of innocence. He was, quite literally, a different creature".[7]

Still a long way from Blake's Innocence, we may just make it out on the horizon. But it can hardly be said that "rational theology" reached down to many bedrooms or nurseries. The notion of infant innocence may have been briefly cherished by the intellectually privileged but it never extended to the underclass, and was buried for two centuries under "commercial freedom" and "the practice of education".

The incontrovertible authority for the times on childhood and the raising of children was "Mr Locke's excellent Treatise of *Education*, known to everybody". Educationists applied and rephrased Locke's "letters of gold", all to be marked on the minds of children. Since these minds were "blank Paper, or smooth Wax ... capable of any impression", the inscription of "true religion", was "of the greatest importance".

By the time Blake was born, Locke's theories had been absorbed into the educational commerce of the century. In 1764 Richard Hurd commended again Mr Locke's "Lectures on the good old chapter of *Education*, which many others indeed have discussed but none with such good sense and with as constant an eye to the use and business of the world." John Locke achieved equal status with Newton, when Queen Caroline had their busts set up together in her grounds at Richmond. They were, she said, "the Glory of their Country, and stamp'd a Dignity on Human Nature", and *The Gentleman's Magazine* announced that these grounds had now been transformed into a "rural *Temple* sacred to *Learning and Virtue*".

Newton's influence on the social assumptions of the eighteenth century was immense, not only through his discoveries. Unwittingly he sealed the century's contract between "the Opressors & the Opressed", into which John Locke wrote the conditions. Newton had felt compelled to install a divinity to hold fast his cosmos. As he interlinked his planetary systems in a tracery of gravitation, he concluded:

it is inconceivable, that inanimate brute matter should, without the mediation of something else, which is not material, operate upon and affect other matter without mutual contact ... Gravity must be caused by an agent ... And though the matter were divided at first into several systems, and every system by a divine power constituted like ours; yet would the outer systems descend towards the middlemost; so that the frame of things could not always subsist without a divine power to conserve it.[8]

"A divine power *constituted like ours*": for the eighteenth century, the status quo was both divinely settled and scientifically approved. The redesignated universe was geared to England's social "systems", which

7. See John Rowe Townsend, *Written for Children* (London: Bodley Head, rev. ed. 1990), pp. 6–11, and Samuel F. Pickering, Jr, *John Locke and Children's Books in Eighteenth Century England* (Knoxville: University of Tennessee, 1981), pp. 10–15.

8. Third letter to Bentley, *Opera*, vol. IV.

endured into our own century, as the social cohesion of Blake's Innocence, which challenged it, was applauded into the nursery.

So it is perhaps with little conviction that we have heard a most
respected Newtonian advocate, and populariser of Locke's theories on
childhood, nominated as a "source" for *Songs of Innocence*. This was the
"pious and learned Doctor Watts", whose *Divine Songs* were "little poems
of devotion and systems of instruction ... for the Use of Children" for a
century and a half after their appearance in 1715. Watts's *Songs* were set to
catch all young readers, whether they belonged to the established
church or not, "baptised in Infancy or not", and whether of "high or low
degree".

It was only ten years before Blake married that Dr Johnson wrote of
Watts in his *Life*, deploring the fact that his rhymes were "not always
sufficiently correspondent", but adding that

*his lines are commonly smooth and easy, and his thoughts always religiously pure;
but who is there that, to so much piety and innocence, does not wish for a greater
measure of sprightliness and vigour! He is at least one of the few poets with whom
youth and ignorance may be safely pleased; and happy will be that reader whose
mind is disposed, by his verses or his prose, to imitate him in all but his nonconformity.*

In the year *Songs of Innocence* came out, Sarah Trimmer announced
that "of all the Religious Books that have been written for Children, I
know of none that is committed to memory with so much delight, as
the Divine Songs of Dr Watts". A few years later, Watts rose from his
grave, as it were, to become one of the poets peddled round the country
in penny tracts, with a government seal of approval, for children "of low
degree". Sales were sustained in thousands. Apparently popularity had
little to do with "sprightliness and vigour", and the establishment knew
it. In the years of *Experience* and stifled insurrection, the Home Office
shrewdly brought Isaac Watts to John Bunyan's elected readers: "children that do walk the street".

But all the philosophical revisions on the nature of childhood failed
to discredit the historic, commonplace understanding, that children
were simply little adults, conceived and born in sin. Watts was himself
prepared to remind young Christians of "no repentance in the grave",
followed by "Darkness, Fire and Chains". He had learned well from
Francis Quarles, who not only wrote *Divine Poems*, but, intimately and
gravely, *A Feast for Worms*. And Quarles, Secretary to Archbishop Ussher,
was no black Calvinist. And James Janeway's *Token* of their "joyful
deaths" was reprinted for children to savour, well into Blake's old age,
with John Bunyan, and Francis Quarles for authoritative support. The

background against which Blake relief-etched his *Songs* had no smooth contours.[9]

So we cannot follow the lead into Blake's *Innocence*, which the "rational theology" earlier in the century seemed to invite. What is more, both the parents and their children, whom Blake may have seen as his customers when the scheme for a book first crossed his mind, had been nurtured in an alternative "rational theology", which became, quite simply, a new fundamentalism.

It was set out on 6 February 1712, for readers of *The Spectator*, in the "handsome paragraph of Dr Snape's sermon", which rounds off the piece on charity schools:

The wise Providence has amply compensated the disadvantages of the poor and indigent, in wanting many of the conveniences of this life, by a more abundant provision of their happiness in the next. Had they been higher born, or more richly endowed, they would have wanted this manner of education, of which those only enjoy the benefit, who are low enough to submit to it; where they have such advantages without money, and without price, as the rich cannot purchase with it. The learning which is given, is generally more edifying to them, than that which is sold to others. Thus do they become exalted in goodness, by being depressed in fortune, and their poverty is, in reality, their preferment.

This was the conclusive sweetener across the century, taken with "a dish of bohea and a slice of bread and butter". It solaced the rich from the lips of their Rector in St James's church, Piccadilly, while Blake was writing and colouring both *Innocence* and *Experience*. This was the reassurance under the "the direful Web of religion", the "woven darkness" laid out for mankind by the episcopal deity Blake called Urizen. Serviced with the ferocity of the law, which protected a silk handkerchief with the hangman's noose, it underpinned the wealth of imperial aggrandisement and commerce, the bulk of it mopped up by the grandees and sinecurists who chartered the streets Blake walked, and the Thames he crossed. It was a reassurance threaded so old and taut that its holy irony even consoled Tom Dacre and his pals in *Innocence*, come down through the embers from the coffins of black. The children of the house, who would watch the boy drop from the chimney, knew from their books: they must pity Tom Dacre, but not change his state.

Clerical authority coarsened materially through the century towards Blake's time. Churchmen, who had earlier balked at the Hanoverian modification of the old divine right of kings, became in mid-century

as absolute for the church and state as Dr Johnson himself. George III, unlike his

9. See J. H. P. Pafford, ed., *Isaac Watts: Divine Songs Attempted in Easy Language for the Use of Children* (London: Oxford University Press, 1971), for two facsimiles of Watts's verses, and Pickering, *Locke*, pp. 144–45.

great-grandfather, had few subjects more loyal than his clergy or gentry. After all life was good for them … It is not surprising that they discovered spiritual values of the highest order in the hierarchic nature of society … The slow growth of society was the work of time and history, imperfections as well as perfections were but a part of the mysterious Providential process.[10]

Toward the last decades of the century, parents who carried silk handkerchiefs pursued gentility for their children, as an aspect of virtue as well as status. By then, children's books were on the shelves with admonitions candied in good breeding and "learning". They had developed from the initiative of John Newbery, whose financial opportunism in mid-century matched that of the higher clergy. His trick was to refashion children's books more to their liking, and to point both story-line and moral towards the promotion of his patent medicines.

John Newbery's initial step up from apprenticeship was into the bedroom of his master's widow, when he was twenty-four. The widow had come into possession of a printing house in Reading. Six years later, in 1743, Newbery moved to London, brought a new tone to writing for children, and never missed a chance to sell a powder. Interminably and assiduously, he bound the promotion of infallible nostrums into the pages of his books for the young. Among dozens of remedies, from St Paul's Churchyard he made a fortune through Greenough's Tinctures for Teeth alone. Though more of his readers still died of rotten teeth than of smallpox, his profits never faltered, but then he had readily to hand more than one remedy for smallpox. Ahead of all else he recommended Dr James's Fever Powder, which featured as the supreme cure-all through his tales. Among supplementary powders and pills, it set up endless opportunities for dramatic shifts of fortune. However death from neglecting any recommended remedy was just as final for John Newbery as death from divine retribution—but (avoidable with a purchase) a great relief to the readers. His successors in the two Newbery shops kept up the service into the nineties with Pectoral Lozenges of Blois, which covered, at a rough count of the press columns, a dozen "Asthmatic, Phthisicky and Consumptive Complaints", at the same time as they were "contributing to sweeten the breath".

A remedy came consistently from Newbery with one of two commendations, both still on file today. A cure-all may be the latest triumph of science. So "the King had been pleased to grant to the inventor a Patent" for the violet soap promoted by Newbery and sold by haberdashers ("one square will last a person, washing once a day, for three months"), indispensable "for ladies, Boarding Schools and infants". On the other hand, it may be of ancient efficacy. The Pectoral Lozenges

10. J. H. Plumb, *The First Four Georges* (London: Batsford, 1956), pp. 26—27.

had everything implied for them. "Prepared in England for upwards of 150 years", they were now "made and sold by ... the Grandson to the Inventor, who was an eminent Apothecary to King William and Queen Anne".

Parents were gratified. Children picked up the right priorities. New science was grafted on to good old stock. Basing them on preferment and oligarchy, Newbery fed his promotions into the Juvenile Library he had opened at 259 Oxford Street. Both through selling and lending, Newbery brought not only sweet breath and white skin to daughters and mothers, but also some release from Joyful Death in hardback. He paid strict lip-service to the pre-eminence of Locke and Newton, but let neither obstruct his eighteenth-century business sense. John Bunyan had noted of *The Pilgrim's Progress* that it had appealed to "young ladies and young Gentlewomen", readers whom Newbery courted with flare. On the other hand, "the very children that do walk the street", whom John Bunyan was concerned to reach and please, were for Newbery beyond the pale of commerce.

Locke had laid it down that instruction should be tempered with delight. Playthings should make learning a pastime, and books were best written "fit to *engage* the liking of children". At the same time, it was "*ill-chosen*" to flatter a child with rewards, since "he that will give his son *Apples*, or *Sugar-plumbs*, to make him learn Book does but authorise his Love of Pleasure, and cocker up that dangerous Propensity, which he aught by all Means to subdue and stifle in him".[11]

At the same time, the setting of good and bad examples was better than any discourse. Newbery's writers set them in an endless trail, beginning with his first book of verse and pastimes, *A Little Pretty Pocket-Book* in 1744. Beginning as he went on, he had it generously illustrated for "Instruction and Amusement". If, as did so many parents, Blake's mother bought her children a later edition for sixpence, for an extra twopence she could have a ball (for boys) and a pincushion (for girls), coloured red one side, black the other. Ten pins came with each. William could then do as Tommy in the rhymes—stick pins in red for his good deeds, black for his bad, and count his virtues against his vices— ten pins in the red, and Tommy in the tale hit the jackpot for a penny. Parents approved. Ten in the black, and the rod came out. The use of a game was authorised by Locke, the bribe and the beating were Newbery's diversion, in line with his middle class customers' instincts, into which the theory of education never has percolated far. If Blake initially modelled *Innocence* on Newbery's books for children, he missed it all, from philosophy down to pincushion.

With philosophy in reserve, it was Newbery the sales director who most influenced generations of children, from a level at times beneath

11. See Pickering, *Locke*, pp. 70, 172, 222–30.

perception, so that an awareness of the essential relationship, between pleasure and profit, between virtue and affluence, survived as an unquestioned precept into old age.

From his early days, Newbery diverted magnanimity into the Special Offer. In 1749, *Nurse Truelove's Christmas-Box* was "GIVEN GRATIS, By J. NEWBERY, at the Bible and Sun in St Paul's Church-yard, over against the North Door of the Church", the customer "only paying One Penny for the Binding". Soon the binding for Nurse Trulove's Special Offer inevitably rose to two-pence. Parents learnt that "children who were good" could come to the North Door for the books and the naughty were to "have none".

As, in book after book, readers met characters who overcame afflictions (mental, physical and spiritual) with the aid of infallible remedies, so the virtuous child, judicious in the choice of a nostrum, was parent of the successful adult. Beyond that, customers were assured that a child in dire poverty who reacted with fortitude to adversity was destined to finish life in comfort and even the Manor House. Little Goody Two-Shoes was the memorable case, and, like all Newbery's undertakings, extensively imitated. But with humility and rectitude dressing penury in silks, the corollary was inevitable: the destitute who grew up incurably destitute were "lacking in moral virtue", and in consequence "undeserving".

It was a corollary that became axiomatic. It was an axiom few others than Blake discounted—none so conclusively. It was an axiom the Little Vagabond in *Experience* dismissed so cockily, that years after Blake died his first editor still could not take it. In 1839, J. G. Wilkinson was content if his edition of *Songs of Innocence and of Experience* might give "one impulse to the New Spiritualism which is now dawning on the world", to counter Alan Cunningham's "Mercantile ethics". At the same time, the New Spiritualism was not expected to stomach the impudent assumptions of the Little Vagabond, and Wilkinson, even from the safety of anonymity, on second thought expediently excluded the poem.[12]

Newbery was never diffident about a self-complimentary title page. When Blake was a child of four, decades before the grand ideas of an extensively 'liberal' education permeated children's 'literature', Newbery brought out *The Newtonian System of Philosophy Adopted to the Capacities of young Gentlemen and Ladies*. The 'Philosophy' was "made entertaining by Objects with which they are intimately acquainted." Then the customers were advertised that, with the condescension of learning, "their old Friend Mr. Newbery" had generously included "a variety of Copper-plate Cuts to illustrate and confirm the Doctrines advanced".

Hop scotch, hoops, tops, cricket—all figure in the illustrative games, here and elsewhere, in line with Newbery's practice, making child's play

12. J. J. G. Wilkinson, ed., *Songs of Innocence and of Experience* (London: Pickering, 1839), p. xx.

of morality, Newton and nostrums. We may see these, without the moral injunctions and sales talk, as the styles which Blake borrowed as "graphic accompaniments" to the poems of Innocence. Again, however, our recollection of mere borrowing is incidental, as it does nothing to clarify Blake's transforming achievement.

In *Innocence*, the illustrated games are not in Newbery's sense "illustrative". As Blake coloured them while his mind faced Experience, he pictured a social bond, an inclusive nurture which most children, both poor and (as it turns out) rich, simply lacked. The meaning which his readers would familiarly expect was not there. Since the pictures in *Innocence* conveyed neither moral nor manners nor information, for most customers they would seem to say nothing.

'Innocent', with minds of impressionable wax, Newbery's readers may have been. To this end, and in line with more refined expectations, he polished the coarseness of the witches, giants and ogres of the previous century. He was competing for the custom of children who could still be faced with the "Joyful Deaths" of James Janeway, if they had an aunt appreciative of his turn of mind. The booksellers covered themselves all ways. They became careful to address their "innocent" readers with the deference their pennies merited: "little Gentlemen and Ladies". Innocence was not absolute, but relative to status, in line with all other value judgements. So Newbery's Juvenile Library leads our minds inexorably away from the children of Blake's *Innocence*. In the Library we meet the sophisticated insouciance of the children who emerge from the nurseries of Experience.

The community of care in *Innocence* is a self-contained statement: nurture is simply every child's birthright. The claim is staked, then the 'contrary' sharpens its validity, in the paradox that the breeding of betterment is itself a spiritual deprivation. In *Experience* we are the closer to Blake's 'sources' in their gainsaying.

After all, from boyhood, he shaped his reading in literature alongside the unchallenged acceptability of myths in the Goody Two-Shoes vein, where application, virtue and submission took Goody from watergruel to a coronet, and the sureness of 'Heaven hereafter'. By 1780 a follow-up, *The Entertaining History of Little Goody Goosecap*, brought the orphan Francis a fortune of ten thousand pounds from a repentant wicked uncle, and married her, charity school educated and unsullied, into the family of Lady Bountiful.

It was a theme to encourage the ambitious classes, a kind of fairy tale with a profitable twist. Yet Blake ignored the hint of the market for the children he characterised among the nurses, though 1785 was the year *The Renowned History of Primrose Prettyface* related how innocence and upbringing combined to raise Primrose "from being the Daughter of a poor Cottager, to great Riches, and the Dignity of the Lady of the Manor".

Such topics as these led Mrs Sarah Trimmer to a good deal of tut-tutting a few years later. She applauded the new choice of an orphan, Francis, as the escalating heroine, in preference to Goody Two-Shoes, whose ill-treatment by Grips and Graspall she considered to have been misconceived by the author. Care must be taken not "to prejudice the poor against the higher orders, and to set them against parish officers" and she felt it politic and proper "to have a veil thrown over the faults of oppressive "squires and hard-hearted overseers".

Another anxiety for Mrs Trimmer was the story-line that made education promote a change in status. The basic schooling of the "lowest classes" was essentially an instrument of social stability, not an incentive. It was "very wrong", she understandably wrote, to encourage

girls of the lower order to aspire to marriage with persons in stations far superior to their own, or to put into the heads of young gentlemen, at an early age, an idea, that when they grow up they may, without impropriety, marry servant-maids.[13]

13. Quoted in Pickering, *Locke*, pp. 51 and 239. Sarah Trimmer does not warn against the reverse arrangement—the lady marrying the serving man.

Mrs Trimmer could have approved Tom Dacre as a candidate for fictional preferment—but perhaps not the chimney boy who tells us about Tom Dacre. Odd. And how she would have fitted in "lovely Lyca" is anyone's guess.

"I am glad you are come, said Quid"

During the 1780s, "a growing array of commercial manuals, historical miscellanies and conduct books for children, young adults and the poor, also sternly warned of the dangers of fashion, trading manners, upstart riches and the vulgarity of under-breeding."[1]

The publisher in the 1780s who most successfully exploited the need to discipline "the natural temper" was John Marshall.[2] Contrary to the practice of Newbery, it was not his way to sweeten instruction with too many dainties. The approach had changed, and children who took up his books were expected to read them "with a sincere desire of being instructed in their duty, both towards God and man". Had Blake thought to offer the book he was contemplating in 1785 to Marshall for printing, instead of doing it himself, rejection would have been certain.

Almost every book Marshall advertised in his list of that year was one of a course in propriety, moral and religious. While Newbery in his day had cared little about the tone of his authors, provided the lessons embraced a treat and the sale of a packet of pills, Marshall and his associated writers exercised what amounted to a customer-oriented censorship. Newbery's books were often syndicated, but with none of the cohesion the word implies. John Marshall used a small and conveniently supervised group of writers, each responsible for her own book: *her* book. All but two of the titles in the 1785 list were written by ladies, who now and for the future more or less orchestrated the market.

Newbery's books continued to sell, their lessons and warnings still larded with sweetmeats and nostrums. Janeway and his lieutenants were on the shelves, to be bought by aunts who disliked children. But it was through the 1780s, while Blake was recording the spiritual liberation and nurture of Innocence, that Marshall and his team worked one line for "the better sort", and another "for the labouring classes" which so appealed to the Home Office in the years of Experience, and set the groundbase for its chapbook propaganda.

For Marshall's ladies, Ellenor Fenn (Mrs Teachwell), Dorothy and Mary Ann Kilner, Sarah Trimmer and the rest, no approach was too basic and direct. Dorothy Kilner addressed the "Young Readers" straight in 1784:

Whoever you are, that have now taken this little book into your hand, I hope you

1. James R. Raven, *English Popular Literature, and the Image of Business 1760–1790.* Unpublished thesis (Cambridge, 1985), vol. 1, p. 12.
2. See Pickering, *Locke*, chapter 6.

intend to read it with a sincere desire of being instructed in your duty both towards God and man; and a fixed determination to endeavour to practise what shall therein be taught you.[3]

The tone is typical, though profit remained a priority. The message always plugged the diminutive readers into other publications by Marshall, in a technique adapted from Newbery's. It is difficult to imagine the book Blake gives the nurse to hold for the children on his title-page of *Innocence* to be a topical John Marshall publication. On the other hand, we can readily characterise the sophisticated reading that absorbs the "experienced" girl in 'Nurses Song'.

While John Marshall's lady authors were consolidating morality after the American War, Mrs Anna Laetitia Barbauld refreshed the children's book fair, and so earned reflected immortality as a plausible "source" of *Innocence*. It is not that she changed the taste in reading; but she added a course of unprecedented hymns: in prose! While the *Divine Songs* of Dr Watts both flourished in hardback and, towards the end of the century, came to be hawked abroad among the improving penny tracts "for the under classes", in 1781 Mrs Barbauld refined the tone and untied the scansion for their betters.

So, shortly before Blake thought about a book of verse for the young, Mrs Barbauld was dangerously but successfully courting heresy. She justified herself by confessing misgivings on the propriety of poetry being "lowered to the capacities of children". It was a view not only unexpressed earlier, but beyond contemplation. "Little poems of devotion" for children, "from the dawn of reason through its gradations of advance in the morning of life" carried even Dr Johnson's seal of authority. Against this, and against two centuries of compulsory scansion drummed out on desks, Mrs Barbauld published her *Hymns in Prose for Children* in cadences "nearly as agreeable to the ear as a more regular rhythmus". *Hymns*, in *prose?*

The remarkable initiative was not only instantly popular, but imitated and distinctively approved for generations. Mrs Trimmer, Mary Wollstonecraft, Crabb Robinson, Hazlitt and Coleridge all paid "debts of gratitude" to Mrs Anna Barbauld. But she was never considered to have the moral staunchness required "for the under classes". *Hymns in Prose* never got on to Marshall's Cheap Tract circuit.

If prose for hymns was an innovation, the aim of these prose hymns was not. It remained, with a more genteel emphasis, "to fill the heart with religious sentiments and affections", by making the Deity "obvious to the senses",[4] and in this way to achieve "large advances towards that habitual piety, without which religion can scarcely regulate conduct".

3. *Letters from a Mother to her Children*, quoted in Pickering, *Locke*, pp. 186–87.
4. Mary Wollstonecraft, *Thoughts on the Education of Daughters* (1787), p. 16.

The technique was to picture an idyllic flora, and populate it with fauna endowed with "responsive" senses:

The hedges are bordered with tufts of primroses, and yellow cowslips that hang down their heads ... The young animals of every kind are sporting about, they feel themselves happy, they are glad to be alive. They may thank him in their hearts, but we can thank him with our tongues; we are better than they, and can praise him better.[5]

Echoes of Mrs Barbauld have often been heard in Blake's lines, and it has been suggested that *Songs of Innocence* is generally "free from obtrusive allusions, particularly if one excludes from consideration the models, like Barbauld and Watts", which Blake was "consciously superseding".[6]

It is hard to imagine Blake press-ganged into the "cursed Barbauld crew", or even being faced with "consciously" refusing to sign on.[7] Events, circumstance, his brother, his neighbours and their children shaped Blake's thinking in *Songs of Innocence*, where the motivation was simply neither "literary" nor moral. Rather the spiritual and social illumination of the *Songs* is highlighted against the contemporary "literature" of manipulation. With a change worrying in its simplicity, in *Innocence* it is the Shepherd, not the child, whose "tongue shall be filled with praise".

The transfer reshapes relationships and the assumptions on which they are based. "Hallelujah" from the lips of a parent or guardian would be rare enough; but here the voice giving praise predicates the pastoral Saviour himself. Blake discounts the prescriptive duty of children to give thanks. Beyond that, he draws children, nurses and the Saviour, into an affinity of grace, which dissolves distinctions of status and age; and beyond that, the Shepherd/Saviour rejoices with voice and hand in the transforming concept.

Innocence discounts two centuries of injunctions and formalities, on which social order and even national survival were supposedly founded. "Familiarity in Superiors", Sir Richard Steele had remarked half a century earlier, is "Condescension". That was the kindliest way of putting it. "To stoop, so far as a particular action is concerned, from one's position of dignity or pride"—this was considered good breeding. Such condescension to one's inferiors was praiseworthy, not patronising.

Here again Blake disregards the inhibiting manners and minute distinctions of his age, as if he were unaware of them. While even Tom Paine, defending the poor against their exposure to "vice and legal barbarity", declared them disadvantageously "bred up without morals", Blake never looked for such "breeding" in them, and was apparently unaware of their "morality". For him the utterly poor were simply neighbours.[8]

5. Anna Barbauld, *Hymns in Prose for Children* (1781), III et sq., p. 12.
6. Michael J. Tolley, 'Blake's Songs of Spring' in Paley & Phillips, eds., *Essays ... Keynes*, p. 106.
7. Charles Lamb's phrase. He was one of the few writers who disapproved.
8. Paine, *Rights of Man*, p. 218.

Perhaps it was Blake's too ready entertainment of common children and their teachers at 27 Broad Street that helped to break up the partnership with James Parker. When Blake moved out to 27 Poland Street, he had been working on *An Island in the Moon* for some time, and we meet there the unshod urchins as easy company for Quid (as we may take it Blake names himself), alongside the eccentric philosophers, surgeons and lawyers. This social cohesion, soon transformed into Innocence, is extended into intellectually affluent salons and demonstration rooms on the Island. It seems it was also extended to Catherine Blake's sitting room.

As Blake was making up his mind about who was to sing what in *An Island*, and watching life improve for the workhouse children, London altogether was becoming more congenial, at least for citizens not condemned to sleep in the shambles. England was enjoying the middle years of a decade of unaccustomed peace. As politicians applied their minds to the advantages of another war, minds applied to science brought housewives the washing machine. It is a tribute to the tenacity of the speculators, that against the wrath of the washerwomen, and with labour as cheap as faggots, "Mr Rogerson's specification" not only survived, but was developed. By the end of the eighties, Mr Kendall at 7 Charing Cross was selling his improved, more "ingenious Invention made wholly of wood, and highly esteemed by men of science". The large machine, to take thirty shirts, cost six guineas.

Carriages and coaches now had the advantage of anti-attrition axletrees from the manufactory in Chamber Street, Goodman's Fields, where the patentees advertised their status by offering attendance on "the Nobility, Gentry, &c." only "from Ten to Four" in the day. Meanwhile Luke Ideson, the efficient vestry clerk of St James's parish, had been working against graft and neglect to ensure that, as the streets were paved, the new stones were not simply dropped over uncleared sewers. He wanted holes fenced, carriers, casks, carriages and cattle kept off the pavements; and, incidentally, an end to the practice of simply dropping tiles and bricks and debris from housetops. Night soil and refuse was to be dumped at least half a mile from the city, a vast amelioration, except to the fields north of Oxford Street.

In this one street alone there were more lamps, of two or four branches, "enclosed in crystal globes", than there were in "all the city of Paris. Even the great roads for seven or eight miles round are crowded with them which makes the effect exceedingly grand".[9]

The Victorian age of gaslight looked back with distaste on the cotton rags soaked in fish blubber which smoked in these crystals through the 1780s. But then their magic was such that the Prince of

9. *The Observer*, 4 December 1791, and George, *London Life*, pp. 110–11.

Monaco, visiting George III, thought the street lighting was illumination set up in his honour. And the crystals of blubber brought work to
the lamp-lighters lodged east in the city, where their bunks commonly
rode in the debris of bilge water half-bailed out of cellars. The point
was made frequently, that children in the workhouses, even before the
opening of the King Street school, were better accommodated than
this. The upgrading of the city, in a brightness extraordinary to the
Prince of Monaco, still floated on seemingly changeless foundations of
distress.

Soon after Blake moved to Poland Street the Governors paid "the
patentee for three reverbrators fixed" over the entrance to the workhouse, opposite and just down the road. The new lamps flickered and
reflected, summer and winter, over men, mothers and infants hanging
about on the pavement waiting for the lock to turn. Almost alongside,
there was illumination more to the liking of Miss Elizabeth Pinnard,
the schoolmistress Blake doubtless met in the King Street school.

The Pantheon, opened when Blake was a boy, with its entrance in
Oxford Street and a side entrance opposite Blake's Poland Street house,
was the most startling building in London. A vast building, with a
glazed dome fashioned on the Pantheon in Rome, Ionic and Corinthian
columns, ceilings and panels "painted like Raphael's *loggias* in the Vati-
can", "stuccos in the best taste of the grotesque", galleries, halls, assembly rooms, statues framed in tabernacles, it "engrossed the conversation
of the polite world". In its early years, the recommendation of a peeress
was required for admission, but by Miss Pinnard's time this had been
set aside, "on account of the rigour with which ladies of easy virtue
were exempted from admission".[10]

So far was the fall, that now bills for concerts in the Pantheon had
spread to the walls of tenements in Milk Street, off Cheapside, where
on May Day the maids were mocked in their dance by the chimney
boys, the soot in their hair covered for the occasion in cast-off wigs.

Albeit on the soundest commercial principles, the come-down
across the decade from ambassadors and the Lord Chancellor, to "a very
numerous assembly of fashionable people" at best, was sad but inevitable. Peace, however demeaning, had its priorities, and by 1783 was celebrated in the elegant structure in the Great Room of the Pantheon,
"chiefly composed of warlike implements", with a hint of regret, it was
said, "now rendered useless".

The excitement of 15 September 1784, was the flight of Vincenzo
Lunardi, "the first aerial traveller in the English atmosphere". When,
with Mr Biggin's attention "allotted to the philosophical experiments
and observations", and his own to "the use of the vertical cars, in

10. See Stanley Gardner, *Blake*
(London: Evans Bros., 1962), pp.
61–66.

depressing the Balloon at pleasure", Lunardi contemplated the sky, he decided that "the impatience of the multitude made it inadvisable to proceed in filling the Balloon so as to give it the force it was intended to have", and the process was halted. So, despite the presence of the Prince of Wales, the courtiers of King Mob misdirected this demonstration of "the pretended art of sailing in a vessel thro' the air or atmosphere".[11]

In the upset, Mr Biggin and his instruments were left forgotten on the grass. The last gun was fired at five past two. The balloon was elevated with hydrogen, "inflammable air or gas", supplied by Dr George Fordyce, chemist and physician at St Thomas's Hospital, who lived on one stupendous meal a day, and often walked the wards all morning after indulging all night.

As hydrogen lifted Lunardi from the Artillery Ground in Moor-fields, King Mob was gratified, and "almost at one instant, passed from incredulity and menace, into the most extravagant expressions of approbation and joy". After drifting over the heads of Londoners "about the size of a tennis ball", Lunardi landed "between four and five o'clock", in a meadow called Long Mead, in the parish of Standon in Hertfordshire, outside the brewhouse of Mr Thomas Read, where Elizabeth Brett, spinster, was working the mash rudder. She was first to see the "strange large body in the air ... with a man in it". While she and the farmer anchored the balloon, two labourers, "being likewise requested to assist in holding the rope, both made their excuses, one of them, George Philips, saying he was too short, and John Mills saying that he did not like it".

Elizabeth Brett was required to make her mark under a "voluntary declaration and deposition on oath" of the incident. Inflammable gas had been earth-bound in illiteracy. Lunardi's balloon was celebrated commercially in high fashion, soon after it was installed in the roof of the Pantheon.

"Like other beauties" it was suggested, the Pantheon was "best seen by candle-light". With twenty thousand lights "reflected from an immense number of looking-glasses" (and that not in the largest room),

the first object which presented itself was Lunardi's balloon, suspended from the centre of the dome, like a vast umbrella from Brobdignagg ... Eleven beautiful ladies also, sat in a circle, repairing it with their needles, like the nymphs in Romance, fitting out their airy knight.[12]

11. Aeronautics, defined in these words in Chambers's *Cyclopædia* (1753 edn.).
12. Vincent Lunardi, *An Account of the First Aërial Voyage in England,* (1784), quoted in Jennings, *Pandæmonium,* pp. 80–82.

Ladies more cushioned in life than Elizabeth Pinnard, the schoolmistress from King Street, looked up at Lunardi's balloon and imagined it on their heads. Other needles, in cellars and stalls, decorated the balloon hats and

Lunardi hats for haberdashers like Blake's brother to sell. Some of them were frilled, no doubt, with extras sewn by Ann Davies. She was a foundling who came from the nurses at Wimbledon, to be taught by Miss Pinnard, and then to be apprenticed by the school Governors to Thomas Singer, the trimming maker in Blake's Poland Street.

The ladies of the town, with leisure to sport the bombasted hats, were celebrating Lunardi almost before he had picked himself up from the formidable arms of Mistress Brett. After 1787 it seems Mr Singer had to set Ann Davies to work on modified trimmings, as novelty required. But the fashion remained aeronautic. By 1787 parachute hats had arrived.[13]

The seasons through which the fashion of the balloon version lasted help us with the date for Blake's work on *An Island in the Moon*. The first three philosophers we meet on the Island, to make us feel we are "among friends", are Suction the Epicurean, Quid the Cynic and Sipsop the Pythagorean. Blake gives us the reason for the names: "I call them by the names of those sects tho the sects are not ever mentioned there as being quite out of date however the things still remain, and the vanities are the same."

If we imagine these three philosophers landed from Lunardi's balloon in Poland Street, Suction the Epicurean, lavish with his drink, looks like Robert Blake; Quid the Cynic, chewing his "Quid of bitterness"[14] is Blake himself; and Sipsop the Pythagorean, who believes souls transmigrate, and so eats "neither fish, nor flesh nor fowl", but exists on sips and sops, resembles Robert's friend, Mrs Mathew's son, William Henry, an apprentice to a surgeon. Since it turns his stomach, he is thinking to quit turning the knife in human flesh as well.

We join them, "sat together thinking of nothing" in Blake's parlour, engrossed in their own private jokes at the expense of the visitors. We share this family location for much of the action that follows. Into the room comes Etruscan Column, the Antiquarian. His fancy is taken with Etruscans, the imitation antique pots enamelled by artists with "encaustic fire" and marketed at about a guinea each by Josiah Wedgwood and others at the time. So much for antiquarianism on "an island in the moon", or around Broad Street.

"After an abundance of Enquiries to no purpose", Etruscan Column "sat himself down & described something that nobody listend to so they were employd when Mrs Gimblett came in tipsy"[15] and, while lost in self-contemplation, "seemed to listen with great attention while the Antiquarian seemd to be talking of virtuous cats"; which I guess was an intended mishearing of "encaustic casts".

Mrs Gimblett is "thinking of the shape of her eyes & mouth", and the

13. C. W. & P. Cunnington, *A Dictionary of English Costume* (London: A. & C. Black, 1965), p. 9. The parachute, a device for keeping a balloon grounded, came to England in 1785.

14. For the identities of characters already reasonably established, see references in Phillips, *Island*.

Suction: This was contemporary slang for 'imbibing strong drink' (*OED*). If Suction refers us to Blake's brother, Robert, the conviviality is in line with what little we know of him.

Quid: Acceptably identified as Blake himself. The bitterness of a quid of tobacco was associated with cynicism. *The Gentleman's Magazine* (1727) had: 'Spitting about the church . . . as if he had a quid in his mouth.' Then in 1805: 'I chewed my quid of bitterness' (*OED*).

Sipsop, the Pythagorean: The Pythagoreans accepted the transmigration of souls, and so ate no meat, fish or foul. Flesh and blood turned Sipsop's stomach; perhaps he sipped on sops.

15. Underlining indicates Blake's working erasures throughout. The only surviving manuscript, which is in the Fitzwilliam Museum, has many gaps and was never finally drafted by Blake. The erasures are restored and marked in Phillips, ed., *Island*.

Antiquarian "of his eternal fame", while the others contain their laughter, when "in a great hurry, Inflammable Gass the Wind finder" enters. The Windfinder was a scientist of explosive indifference to his onlookers, and representative of any number of gaseous experimenters living around the Pantheon in the 1780s.

It is the same with Jack Tearguts, the surgeon whose ferocity, when he plunged "the knife in up to the hilt in a single drive and thrust his fist in. and all in a Quarter of an hour", so intimidated Sipsop his apprentice.

We know Blake had John Hunter in mind when he wrote of Jack Tearguts, as he failed to scrawl out the originating name effectively. "Jack" to the resurrection men, Hunter lived in Golden Square when Blake was young. Golden Square was fashionable, and handy for corpses smuggled through Tylers Court from the graveyard behind Broad Street. Hunter ran private classes in anatomy and surgery at home, and had the refusal of all animals dying in the Tower and other menageries. By 1783 he had moved himself and his demonstration room, which furnished his 'museum', to nearby Leicester Fields.

Jack's elder brother, William, was in the same line. He had his anatomical theatre with its adjacent burial ground in Great Windmill Street. Even closer to Poland Street was the anatomist Joshua Brookes, who lectured across the cadavers of criminals in Blenheim Street, and kept his own animals caged in his garden at the back of the Pantheon. Blake's fiction derives its strength from precise identities, substantiated in local circumstance.

It is these characters in *An Island in the Moon* comprising the roll-call of capricious authority, who have imposed themselves on the attention of readers; among them, Jacko, off stage but familiar, and, by every assumption, one of a very much "better sort". They are the targets for Blake's satire. But they are measured on their Island by more humble yet spirited souls, whose actions and reactions are unlettered. They are the unsophisticated neighbours, alert and unimpressed, by whom the satire is steadied. And they are clearly closest, most congenial, to Blake.

It is as a matter of course, without even allowing the scholars and philosophers the contemporary politeness of condescension, that Blake includes in their rare company, not only adults of uncertain class, but children of unrestrained ebullience. The Islanders, of whatever status, share an unembarrassed relationship which anticipates the social cohesion unique in *Songs of Innocence*. Nothing more implicitly speaks Blake's mind.

Across the garrulous pedantry and exploding flasks of academics, the main theme of the satire develops from the intimate location of Quid's house, through the activities and attitudes of a circle of less self-important friends; and after the initial quick-fire, this main theme gets under way when, joining Quid and company in the first chapter, "Obtuse Angle entering the room having made a gentle bow, proceeded to empty his pockets of a vast number of papers".

Obtuse Angle fancies himself as a mathematician. "A man is a fool ifaith not to understand the Mathematics", he lectures the more eminent academics. He is a schoolmaster. I suppose the "vast number of papers" are those which every teacher carries round: stuff for marking. His pretensions are not confined to mathematics. And he has some unrepentant and cocky pupils who inflate his omniscience. He is obtuse in all senses. He claims that he "always understood better when he shut his eyes". He does so while he scratches his head, perilous in front of pupils like his.

In the second chapter, one of only six lines, we meet his assistant and their charges. Of Obtuse Angle's pupils, or recent pupils, Tilly Lally is a Siptipidist, which is still Blake's secret; but his name takes him near to being labelled "fiddle sticks", and he has a laugh as loud as a cherry clapper. Another is "Arodobo, the dean of Morocco", which, I take it, makes him the Dean of the Guild of Morocco-men. They hawked the back streets and alleys, and hung around the parlours of public houses with illegal lottery insurance. Arodobo is young, but the true professionals all started young. Then there is Little Scopprell, diminutive and unpredictable as a little top, and reminiscent of Blake's childhood in the haberdashery shop. With them is Miss Gittipin, who can only be their familiar schoolmistress, from the way they set her up throughout the piece. Present as well, before the names were crossed out, were Quid himself, Sipsop and Suction. So here at home, with Gibble Gabble (that is Mrs Inflammable Gass) a typically intrusive acquaintance, is the circle of Blake's closest friends. Quite properly, among them it seems we now meet Catherine Blake, as Mrs Nannicantipot.[16]

Come the next chapter, and Tilly Lally, Little Scopprell and Aradobo at once wind up Obtuse Angle with a co-ordinated sequence of red herring questions. It is classic classroom tactics. Obtusely, he takes the bait; and, interestingly, Miss Gittipin only just misses getting into the dialogue. As we know, 'Miss' and 'Sir' has always been the way to address teacher, with extra polish during the team work of serving up red herrings:

Ah said Tilly Lally I did not hear it. what was it Obtuse Angle. pooh said he Nonsense. Mhm said Tilly Lally—it was Phoebus said the Epicurean <u>Miss</u> Ah that was the Gentleman said Aradobo. Pray Sir said Tilly Lally who was Phoebus. Obtuse Angle answered the heathens in old ages usd to have Gods that they

16. *Tilly Lally*: Seems to be a variation of Tilly Fally—'fiddlesticks'. Interestingly Lallygag turns up in US in the mid-nineteenth century meaning 'fooling around', origin unknown (*OED*).

Scopprell: A scopperil was a little top (*OED*). Small enough to be spun by finger and thumb, it was made by fixing a pointed peg through a disc, usually a button mould or flat button. We are back with Blake as a child among the ribbons and lace. The word was applied to a restless child: 'Little Scopprell'.

worshipd & they usd to sacrifice to them you have read about that in the bible, Ah said Arodobo I thought I had read of Phebus in the Bible.—Arodobo you should always think of what you read before you speak said Obtuse Angle—Ha Ha Ha he means Pharaoh said Tilly Lally.

In the next but one chapter, "Obtuse Angle Scopprell Aradobo & Tilly Lally are all met in Obtuse Angles study". And the baiting of teacher continues,[17] accelerating from an initial question whether Chatterton was "a Mathematicum", till Obtuse Angle is manipulated into the classic mistake of appealing to another pupil; and gets, of course, the classic response of impertinent support:

Oh no Sir I thought that he was not but I askd to know whether he was.—How can that be said Obtuse Angle How could you ask & think that he was not—why said he. It came into my head that he was not—why said Obtuse Angle you said that he was. Did I say so Law I did not think I said that—Did not he said Obtuse Angle Yes said Scopprell. But I meant said Arodobo I I I cant think Law Sir I wish youd tell me. how it is—Then Obtuse Angle put his chin in his hand & said when ever you think you must always think for yourself—How Sir said Arodobo. whenever I think I must think myself—I think I do—In the first place said he with a grin—Poo Poo said Obtuse Angle dont be a fool—

Then Tilly Lally took up a Quadrant & askd what is this gimcrank for. Is not this a sundial. yes said Scopprell. but its broke—at this moment the three Philosophers enterd and lowring darkness hoverd oer th assembly.

To suit them for the rarified atmosphere of the Island, both pupils and master are cerebrally involved in matters more or less remote from the schoolroom. But the pace of this dialogue matches Blake's intimate interest at first hand in the schooling of boys like Tilly Lally, Arodobo and Scopprell, whose lack of seemliness disqualifies any recognition of Obtuse Angle as a tutor of "the better sort". Beyond that, implicit throughout is Blake's unspoken rejection of prescriptive and tendentious education, long standing in custom and usage. It is a rejection the more absolute and compelling for being presented as it is. Here, among rough schoolboys, is the burlesque prelude to the reshaping in *Innocence* of the patterns for living laid down through the century by the great and the good.

We may now guess at the identity of the school-teachers Blake allows on the Island. Miss Elizabeth Pinnard, we recollect, would have taught young Ann Davies, as assistant mistress to Revd John Mossop in the King Street school. Perhaps we may take the hint, that a Miss Pinnard would have to tell boys to "get a pin" no more than once for the

17. Chapter 5. 'In a burlesque of the Cogito of Descartes', Phillips, ed., *Island*, pp. 74–75, with lengthy quotation.

nick-name Gittipin to stick. We may be sure that Blake knew her better than many other characters he names. Miss Gittipin in *An Island* has all the sense of regret and inferiority he must have met in Miss Pinnard, when he handed her haberdashery in King Street. In one line, he sketches her with tenderness. While Obtuse Angle and Steelyard are in conversation, she enters with Scopprell, and breaks in: "Now here said Miss Gittipin I never saw such company in my life. you are always talking of your books I like to be where we talk". But she lets go the highflown stuff of the philosophers, and gets down to fashion and envy. She is sure she can

never see any pleasure. thers Miss Filligreework she goes out in her coaches & her footman & her maids & Stormonts & Balloon hats & a pair of Gloves every day . . . I might as well be in a nunnery There they go in Post chaises & Stages to Vauxhall & Ranelagh And I hardly know what a coach is. except when I go to Mr Jacko's he knows what riding is <u>& he will ride</u> & his wife is the most agreeable woman you hardly know she has a tongue in her head and he is the funniest fellow. & I do believe he'll go in partnership with his master. & they have black servants lodge at their house I never saw such a place in my life he says he has Six & twenty rooms in his house. and I believe it & he is not such a liar as Quid thinks he is. <u>but he is always envying</u>.

Blake took out Miss Gittipin's aside about Quid's envy, one assumes since it was too close to himself as Quid. We know how Blake noticed that others less gifted than he so often prospered, among them Richard Cosway. This was Jacko to Miss Gittipin, because of his grinning likeness to the monkey of that name, which performed famously, mounted on a horse, in Astley's Amphitheatre over in Lambeth, at Sadler's Wells and in the Royal Circus.[18]

Seventeen years older than Blake, Cosway had worked his way through Henry Pars's Drawing School to become a full Academician by 1771. Ten years later he married Maria Hadfield, the half Italian daughter of an Irish innkeeper in Leghorn. Always socially alert, Cosway kept her in seclusion till she could behave and speak something like the English, which accounts for Miss Gittipin's remark on her agreeable reticence. She was created baroness by Francis l. By 1784 the Cosways resided in part of Schomberg House, Pall Mall, which was jammed with carriages for Maria's Sunday evening concerts. It is no wonder that Miss Gittipin had "never seen such a place". Cosway had taken over the house from James Graham, an impressive quack physician, who had decorated the apartments the year before "in celestial soul transporting" style as a "Temple of Health and Hymen".

18. Chapter 8. For Jacko as Richard Cosway, see R. J. Shroyer, 'Mr Jacko knows what riding is', in *Blake: An Illustrated Quarterly* (Spring 1979), pp. 250–56. General Jacko is illustrated grinning and riding a mastiff, one of his acts. See also Erdman, *Prophet*, pp. 95–97.

Cosway's tastefully erotic miniatures were "not only fashionable, but fashion itself", after Mrs Fitzherbert sat for him. His income was said to be £10,000 a year. The Prince of Wales made him painter in ordinary. Translated to Cosway in real life, it is the Prince, no less, who is the "master" Miss Gittipin believes Jacko will "go in partnership with".

The assured nature of Jacko's identity with Richard Cosway breeds tantalising speculations. One fascinating question is how Miss Gittipin, the insecure schoolmistress, burdened with Little Scoprell, familiarly found his wife "the most agreeable woman", when she went "to Mr Jacko's". More tantalising still is it, to speculate on Blake's own knowledge, so brilliantly passed on to Miss Gittipin. Knowledge could have come, of course, from talk among the artists, engravers and magazine editors of Blake's acquaintance. But then, there is the aside given to Miss Gittipin that Jacko is not "the liar Quid thinks he is", and the meaningful deletion about Quid's "always envying".

Almost everything related to the Islanders sounds first-hand. If this passage is no different, it could make Blake a visitor to Schomberg House in the mid-1780s, so close to the throne that Cosway could walk along its private passage to Carlton Palace Gardens.[19] However fleetingly close Blake may have come to social distinction, by contrast to his life, genius did not trammel the sustained elevation of Richard Cosway.

When Steelyard the Lawgiver tells Miss Gittipin to hold her tongue, she proceeds "to use every Provoking speech". Little Scopprell's knee-jerk retort comes surely from a schoolboy commending his teacher, with the loyalty of polite insolence: "I think the Ladies discources Mr Steelyard are some of them more improving than any book, that is the way I have got some of my knowledge".

She is addressed by Little Scopprell as 'Miss': "no Miss . . . indeed miss", school fashion. She suffers his cheek in silence when she sings, and he commends her: "Charming, truly elegant", and again, "Miss Gittipin, you sing like a harpsichord".

It is plain that Quid, Miss Gittipin and Little Scopprell are close. When Quid sings his song of Matrimony, "the universal Poultice this", Scopprell checks him impertinently for having "the face to make game of Matrimony", and both Quid's and Miss Gittipin's initial responses are deleted: "What you skipping flea how dare ye? Ill dash you through your chair says the cynic This Quid (cries out Miss Gittipin) always spoils good company in this manner & its a shame."

Apart from simple adjustments, the allocation of songs and the needs of versification, these deletions occur, it seems, when the dialogue comes too close to home. The familiarity, in the main, includes Little Scopprell, Tilly Lally, Miss Gittipin, Obtuse Angle and Quid himself; not

19. See references in *The Survey of London*'s volumes on St James's and Westminster.

often the more illustrious Islanders. It seems this is the intimacy most spontaneous to Blake, and so subject to second thoughts.

Not appearing in the satire, but named as a pal of Tilly Lally's is Joe Bradley, at whose initiative in stealing molasses Scopprell rejoices, before he turns to cheek Miss Gittipin again:

O ay said Tilly Lally. Joe Bradley & I was going along one day in the Sugar house Joe Bradley saw for he had but one eye   —saw a treacle Jar Sohe goes of his blind side & dips his hand up to the shoulder in treacle. here Il lick lick lick said he Ha Ha Ha Ha Ha For he had but one eye Ha Ha Ha Ho then sung Scopprell
                    And I ask the Gods no more
                        no more no more
                        no more no more

Miss Gittipin said he you sing like a harpsichord . let your bounty descend to our fair ears and favour us with a fine song [20]

There was a chandler named Joseph Bradley selling pots from his house in Tyler's Court, the alley which led into St James's burial ground from the north-west corner of Carnaby Market. As the only access, Tyler's Court saw much sad and surreptitious traffic, the dead tolled in, and cadavers smuggled out. On 4 May 1787, Joseph Bradley applied to the Governors of the workhouse and school "to serve the poor with earthenware". As one would expect for a tradesman so handy, he was as successful as James Blake, and the Governors approved him on 18 May. If Bradley also served the sugar house with earthenware, his son of the same name would know his way around without a second eye; and, coming from Tyler's Court, he would very likely be a pupil of Miss Pinnard's at the nearby King Street school.

The tone Blake gives the incident rings with reality. It is matched in the book-keeper's minute on 13 December 1785, of an escapade in the King Street school. Matron Frith caught Andrew Davelin and Thomas Willcott late one Sunday night making a paste with butter and flour, "the paste wet on the drawer and the Sauce Pan ready to boil it". Andrew Davelin knew what was coming, and "for fear of punishment made his escape". Thomas Willcott was "sent to the workhouse".

Blake takes his fiction so close to the living. In the Easter game of cricket with Bill, who was so poor he "ran without shoes to save his pumps", it was Joe Bradley who bowled the ball "in a tansey", and saved Miss Gittipin's blushes.[21] Then he cleaned the mess with Tilly Lally's handkerchief.

It is this handkerchief which earlier understandably "smeard the

20. Chapter 9. *Sugar house*: 'House' could refer to a large building. The King Street school was normally minuted as 'the house in King Street'.

21. The tansy pudding, not the plant. The custom was tansy pudding at Easter, like mince pies at Christmas. Samuel Pepys took Betty Martin over to the King's Head in Lambeth on the Friday after Easter in 1666, where he 'spent an hour or two with pleasure with her, and ate a tansy'. Blake first had Joe wrap the ball in a turd. His crossing-out made Joe Bradley less indelicately disreputable, and incidentally gave us the time of year he had in mind. But back to Blake's actuality: would Joe Bradley of Tyler's Court on the day so waste a tansy pudding, some other missile being to hand?

glass worse than ever", before Tilly Lally and Scopprell, "pumping at the air pump", burst the "bottle of wind" Inflammable Gass had "took up in the bog house". The domestic familiarity of the "scientific" set-up was commonplace. Anywhere could be a laboratory. Dr Johnson was "observed" by Boswell "all his life very fond" of "an apparatus for chymical experiments" in his garret in Gough Square. Christopher Smart brought the air-pump and suction into bedlam and *Rejoice in the Lamb*. Shelley's room at Oxford was cluttered with "an electrical machine, an air pump, the galvanic trough, a solar microscope, and large glass jars and receivers". As Blake wrote at the outset, his *Island in the Moon* was recognisable in its "affinity to England", explosions being frequent in both places. Without the help of the likes of Tilly Lally and Scopprell, in England Robert Boyle himself often over-exerted his air-pump.

The unique and telling touch is the scruffy handkerchief and the enthusiastic intervention. We know where Blake's mind is centred. The Island has an "affinity" to Golden Square, as in climactic chaos the observers all finish in a heap at the foot of the stairs to avoid their lungs being "destroyed with the Flogiston". It is a kind of full stop before the company enjoys a series of verses, including the three poems taken later into *Songs of Innocence*. And then there is the cricketing song of Tilly Lally, not transferred to *Innocence*, but reflected in the illustration to 'The Ecchoing Green'.

Apart from characters we can readily link to real life, speculation on the friends Blake ballooned to the Island is irresistible and elusive. So there is no direct evidence that Obtuse Angle leads us to Rev'd John Mossop; at the same time, Obtuse Angle is harrassed by boys identifiable with those returning from Wimbledon Common, to worry John Mossop in the King Street school. We know Blake knew John Mossop well, through the haberdashery contract. Then, tantalisingly, Obtuse Angle had a study in Quid's house. John Mossop had no study in the school, asked the Governors for one on 21 May 1784, and was refused; threatening to resign, he got his room the following September. During this time, Blake was in 27 Broad Street, next to the haberdashery business, most likely with *An Island in the Moon* on the table in front of him.

Identities aside, the talk still takes us vividly into the company of the likes of the Wimbledon/King Street crew: adult, pestered, opinionated, burdened with regret; young and cocky Cockney. All of them—Obtuse Angle, Miss Gittipin, Sipsop, Arodobo, Young Scopprell, Tilly Lally, Joe Bradley—all of them drift across the Island in the Moon as clouds of recollection: the neighbours Blake knew. Through them he implicitly speaks his preoccupation in the 1780s.

For the final gathering of verse, we are moved to the house of Steelyard the Lawgiver. Steelyard we recognise. This is a caricature of John Flaxman, Blake's close friend, whose fame was yet to come. From 1782 to 1787 he was working from his house in Wardour Street, "weighing up" (as if with a steelyard) and collecting the watch rate from door to door, where he had to "stand & bear every fools insult", "with an ink-bottle in his button-hole". Though hopeful he would "live to see Filligree work", his chief worry at the time was that he would lose "the parish business", or suffer the shame of being put on "constable duty".[22] Steelyard is one with Obtuse Angle, Miss Gittipin and the rest in his social insecurity, as was Blake's friend Flaxman at the time.

It is in his house that, trying "every method to get good humour", Miss Gittipin prays Obtuse Angle to sing his song 'Upon a holy thursday'. The day in June may have been Holy Thursday for Joe Bradley; it was not for the Rector of St James's church, Piccadilly, even when Blake took it into *Songs of Innocence*.

22. Chapter 8, p. 11. *Steelyard*: this was a balance with a long arm and slide for the object to be weighed, against a weighted short arm, commonly used in all trades. For Steelyard/Flaxman, see Erdman, *Prophet*, pp. 109–13.

From the Ruins of Time

Perhaps the most striking absentee from *An Island in the Moon* is the character who should have taken the moral conduct of Tilly Lally, Young Scopprell and the rest in hand. It is odd that Blake missed mining such a rich satirical vein. Some clergyman, bred at third or fourth hand on the theories of Mr Locke, could have brought discipline and propriety to the pupils on the Island; someone like Reverend Mr Barlow, the epitome of all tutors, who dominated the generations in three volumes, while he instructed Harry Sandford and Tommy Merton in interminable virtue.[1]

One of Mr Barlow's associates occupied the moral ground in most children's books, and books on how to teach school. It seems that Blake mined a more intimate reality of local schooling in his satire, than either Mr Barlow intoned, or Mrs Sarah Trimmer prescribed.

No doubt Reverend John Mossop got through the right lessons on duty and humility. But the Governors' minutes in the early 1780s make little or no mention of the moral initiative they expected, either from Mr Mossop, Miss Pinnard or from the teachers at Wimbledon. The Governors simply directed that the children attend daily the chapel in Berwick Street, boys and girls separately, when the place was not needed for the charity school children; the old chapel, that was, opposite Fryingpan Alley, in the other direction from St James's, Piccadilly. They went, no doubt, clad in their "Hats & Cloaks", these children of "the meanest sort", incredibly fingering their pocket money. It was a share-out of £1. 14s. 5d., "being encouragement", the book-keeper had recorded, "for their good behaviour".

The emphasis in the minutes relating to the King Street school was firmly on matters of practical care. Sick children were to be moved to Wimbledon, writing and ciphering books were inspected. "A well of excellent spring water . . . without any communication on either side with sewer or drain" was found under the cellar of the school, and piped to the kitchen. The children were required to bathe in the summer; with old fashioned propriety, boys and girls apart.

In 1783 the Governors rejected an application by a Mr Becknel to install forty-five spinning-wheels in the school. He can only have been incredulous that in the 1780s the Governors of the Poor "did not think spinning of Jersey the best employment" for these children in "the lowest order of poverty". The same consideration extended to the

1. Thomas Day, *The History of Sandford and Merton* (3 vols., 1783–7), *passim.*

apprenticing of the children. When boys from other workhouse schools were packed off to sea or chimney sweeping, and girls indiscriminately put out to service and milk selling, tradesmen were visited and approved before a King Street child was apprenticed. Moreover the Governors looked separately at each case, and were prepared to hold a child in school till they were assured of "a proper place" being found.[2] Yet, in an age when charitable works were accountable and their reward an acceptable self-esteem, the scrupulous book-keeper minuted no mention of the expense of the rescue, and no self-gratification.

We can readily understand the impact of this neighbourly initiative on Blake's mind while he tutored his brother, Robert. In these "years of toleration"[3] the initiative went far beyond the expectations of so many putative radicals he respected, such as Richard Price, Thomas Paine, Jonas Hanway, William Godwin and Joseph Priestley. For them all, education was "the chief instrument of human advance"; but the best they could do was to organise the fashionably new Sunday-schools.

In 1783, three years after Robert Raikes, the editor of the *Gloucester Journal* hit on the idea, the city's clergy had taken up the scheme of "rendering the Lord's Day subservient to the ends of instruction, which has hitherto been prostituted to bad purposes". With hindsight, we may read the seeds of the subsequent disgrace of the movement in that initial phrase about "bad purposes". But when Joseph Priestley set up in unlikely coalition with Hannah More in 1785, a year after the First Circular Letter of the Sunday School Society had gone out, he did so in the trust that "persons of all denominations of the protestant faith will be induced to unite" in the "laborious undertaking" of providing the poorest children with "safe books".

The initial aim, later so subverted, was to break illiteracy. When he joined with the evangelical Anglicans of Clapham to approve the Society's "most liberal and catholic principles ... with all the energy and zeal which characterised his powerful mind",[4] Priestley epitomised, in its best sense, the cautious betterment, against which the King Street undertaking may be matched. The Sunday School Society's pitch was "two hundred and forty children, taught every Sunday by several masters",[5] against Reverend Mossop and Miss Pinnard as many as need be, all week, and pocket money.

The 1790s changed the Sunday-schools, and changed "the house in King Street", to "induce patience and submission to poverty" in the young. They changed Priestley, they changed Blake and they hardened Hannah More. But it is no surprise that, while the impoverished children of Clapham were being garnered into the first Sunday-schools for some basic instruction, Blake should show his interest in the more

2. For references see my *Retraced*, especially chapter 1. In October 1785 the Governors declined to allow Mary Blake to be apprenticed to 'Mr Dawson', because it was 'not a proper place'. They kept the girl at school till June the next year, when she went to 'Mr Southern of St James Street'.

3. For the 'years of toleration' in the 1780s, see Albert A. Goodwin, *The Friends of Liberty* (London: Hutchinson, 1979), chapter 3.

4. Jones, *Charity School*, p. 148, p. 152.

5. *Gloucester Journal*, 3 November 1783, and John Wesley, 1784, quoted in *OED*, 'Sunday-school'.

effective education offered to children of the labouring poor in the charity schools. That interest is demonstrated by his presence at one of the annual charity school services in St Paul's when the demand for seats was so heavy, that no casual places were allocated.

From the beginning of the century Londoners had filled the streets and applauded the procession of charity school children to their annual service. It was turned into a festival, and no church could take the crowds of parents and subscribers. As early as 1712 Wren was blocking proposals to move the service to St Paul's, on the grounds that "accommodations for the children and spectators" would damage the cathedral. It was Thursday 2 May 1782, before some four thousand five hundred 'little boys & girls', in a congregation said to number eight thousand, took over Wren's cathedral and hauled themselves up the wooden galleries to wave to their parents, teachers and friends.[6]

Small wonder that Blake made sure he joined them, and then celebrated the occasion, especially as the children's invasion of St Paul's coincided precisely with the passing of Gilbert's Act of social reform. The Act optimistically reinvented the moribund office of Guardian of the Poor, which Blake rescued from the oblivion that soon swallowed the Act, when he relief-etched it immortally in the last line of 'Holy Thursday' in *Innocence*.

These Guardians of the Poor, "to be chosen out of the honestest, discreetest, and charitable inhabitants", reoccupied an ancient and honoured dignity.[7] The title was first used at the start of the century. But across the decades it had become impossible to find men of standing willing to take on a responsibility that was upsetting, thankless and burdensome: the management of care for the legions of indigence. So both office and title had long fallen into disuse, when they were conveniently revived and frequently named in relation to their duties in Gilbert's Act.[8]

Of direct interest to Blake, in abolishing the workhouse test the Act required parishes to make accommodation and provision for parish children. Crucially admissions and allocations were the responsibility of the newly designated Guardians of the Poor. The Act did not require anything like the separate "house in King Street", which Blake's neighbours had organised even as the ink on the Act was drying, or the extent of education and care he knew there so familiarly. On the other hand, the 1782 Act provides a gloss of immediacy on his memorable valediction to the Guardians, with, literally, the onus of a child's life or death laid upon them by Parliament: "Then cherish pity lest you drive an angel from your door".

Gilbert's Act had directed that:

6. See Gardner, *Retraced*, pp. 34–35, p. 129.

7. Guardian of the Poor. *OED* gives the first occurrence of the word as 1782, in Gilbert's Act, and the second as Blake's 'Holy Thursday'. But the title appears in 1698. For this, and the decay of the office, see Gardner, *Retraced*, pp. 39–41.

8. Act 22 Geo. III (1782). It turned out to be a dead letter. For the duties of the Guardians of the Poor, see Gardner, *Retraced*, pp. 39–42, and n. 5.

all infant children of tender years . . . chargeable to the parish . . . be sent to the poor House as aforesaid, or be placed by the guardian or guardians of the poor, with the approbation of the visitor, with some reputable person or persons in or near the parish . . . until such child or children shall be of sufficient age to be put into service or bound apprentice.

In the way of legislators forever, while the Guardians' commitments were extensively specified, the provision was neither directed nor funded. Blake's typical challenge to these revived and repeatedly recorded officers is too recollective of a topical reform to be coincidental. The unerring injunction, "cherish pity", is not only incisive in its place as the full stop of a poem on more privileged children, but sharpened against the euphoria of revived enlightenment. The hierarchs' valediction to the legislators trails through *Experience*.

Not only the 1782 date is interesting. Gilbert's Act stipulated that the Guardians of the Poor should take responsibility "from and after the twenty-fifth day of *March*, which shall be in the years of our Lord one thousand seven hundred and eighty three". Given the intense demand for seats at the anniversary service, it is unlikely that the guardians, newly appointed for 31 March, were accommodated in St Paul's by Thursday 12 June 1783, without some special provision.

We are into time scale of *An Island in the Moon*, and the drafting of the lines that became 'Holy Thursday'. The radiance of the poem and explicitly his deleted reference to "the chief chanters commands" declare Blake's presence in St Paul's. If not in 1783, it seems that he got himself a ticket for Thursday 10 June 1784. By then he could look back on a year's endeavour by the newly harrassed guardians, no doubt by then well in need of his conclusive after-thought: "cherish pity".

Since tickets for this highlight of the London year were always in great demand, and strictly allocated by the Patrons and by the Society for Promoting Christian Knowledge, the fact that Blake acquired one confirms his support for the charity school movement. It is easy to see his motive, since "so marked was the improvement of the children in the charity schools that they threatened not only the economic, but also the social order".[9] Surrounded by thousands of brightly dressed and excitable children, Blake's mind must have turned to the foundlings who were nurtured at Wimbledon and in the King Street school, to something near the state of the children glorifying the cathedral: "multitudes of lambs . . . cherish pity".

Then it seems we hear the voices of the children even in the secular title of 'Holy Thursday', which Blake adopted for this ecclesiastically unscheduled day. He must have been listening to the pals of Joe Bradley.

9. Jones, *Charity School*, p. 86.

For the charity school service, the Patrons always avoided Ascension Day and Maundy Thursday, the Holy Thursdays of the church calendar. In exceptional circumstances, Thursday was even abandoned for an unpopular Wednesday. It happened in 1780, and back in 1766, the year Dean Josiah Tucker lectured the children on the problem of getting them to do work of any retail value. The Holy Thursdays of the Church itself were never turned over to the children.

So Blake's and the children's Holy Thursday was nothing to do with the cloth. However it sounds to be just the cocky abbreviation Joe Bradley would use, for an occasion as portentous as "the Annual Service for the Charity School Children, under the Direction of the Society for Propagating Christian Knowledge"—a day out of the desks, a jaunt through the streets, and a climb into the roof of St Paul's: a proper Holy Thursday for Tilly Lally and the King Street pupils, if only they had qualified to mix.

If, when he sings of the happenings "upon a holy thursday", Obtuse Angle echoes his pupils' irreverence, it suits Blake's characterised irony to the letter. The Islanders had "playd at forfeits & tryd every method to get good humour", before Miss Gittipin (who else?) prayed the schoolmaster to "sing us a song", which reduced the company to fifteen minutes expressive silence. Beyond this, a schoolboy's colloquial nickname, familiar as such to all his readers, fits precisely the angle of Blake's vision in *Innocence*, where the designation is established as a title; it becomes the children's signature. The same signature is carried over to their dead and dying contemporaries in the contrary state of *Experience*.

While Blake allocated the 'holy thursday' lines unhesitatingly to the schoolmaster among the Islanders, he took much longer to make up his mind about the singer of the next song. 'When the tongues of children were heard on the green' was moved from Mrs Sigtagatist's grandmother or mother, to Mrs Nannicantipot's elder relative. But it seems they all had the lines at second hand from a nurse, who does not appear among them.

The way towards *Songs of Innocence* is traced further when Quid himself takes over from Miss Gittipin and Tilly Lally the ominous verses on the father deliberately striding away from his son, who is later rescued in *Innocence*:

> *O father father where are you going*
> *O do not walk so fast*
> *O speak father speak to your little boy*
> *Or else I shall be lost*
>
> *The night it was dark & no father was there*

And the child was wet with dew
The mire was deep & the child did weep
And away the vapour flew.

Here nobody could sing any longer, till Tilly Lally pluckd up a spirit & he sung . . .

his ditty about Joe Bradley taking his own initiative at a cricket match. Again this game, and Miss Gittipin's ghostly walk in the forest which follows, are deliberately recollected in the illustrations Blake set to the poems of *Innocence*.[10] There is an essential link between the relief-etchings of *Innocence*, and the relationships intimated so surely in *An Island in the Moon*. It seems that in *Innocence* the reality behind the Islanders is underscored.

The reality became tragic. In February 1787 Robert died. The loss profoundly affected Blake's recording of both *Innocence* and *Experience*, and his brother remained with him as a presence all his life. Many years later on 6 May 1800, Blake wrote a letter of condolence to William Hayley on the death of his illegitimate son, Tom. Tom was twenty years old, and had been apprenticed as a sculptor to John Flaxman. At this distance of time, the youth's occupation and early death still drew from Blake recollections of his brother, who died at much the same age:

Thirteen years ago. I lost a brother & with his spirit I converse daily & hourly in the Spirit. & See him in my remembrance in the regions of my Imagination. I hear his advice & even now write from his Dictate—Forgive me for expressing to you my Enthusiasm which I wish all to partake of Since it is to me a Source of Immortal Joy even in this world by it I am the companion of Angels. May you continue to be so more & more & to be more and more persuaded. that every Mortal loss is an Immortal Gain. The Ruins of Time builds Mansions in Eternity.

Blake told John Linnell, and Catherine confirmed, that those thirteen years earlier, "he sat up for a whole fortnight with his brother Robert during his last illness & upon his going to bed which he did as soon as Robert died he slept for three days and nights". "Blake's peace of mind was much broken", was J.T. Smith's quiet way of putting it.[11]

It is fair to say that for us the "Mansions in Eternity" built from those "Ruins of Time" was *Songs of Innocence and of Experience*. Within a twelve-month or so of his brother's death, Blake etched the tiny plates, measuring about two by two and a half inches, making up the sequences *All Religions are One* and *There is No Natural Religion*. They appear as a kind of prelude to *Innocence*, angels aloft, pipers, gestures of acclaim, flourishing trees, girls and boys absorbed in reading in the open air; and "all

10. Phillips, ed., *Island*, chapter 11, and 'The Little Boy Lost', 'The Little Boy Found', and 'The Ecchoing Green', in *Innocence*.
11. Bentley, *Blake Records*, p. 459.

through these pictures, we see the vine of Education and the birds of song and flight outreaching the rational statements".[12]

At the same period, Blake provided an engraving as the frontispiece of one of the many editions of Lavater's *Aphorisms*, so widely advertised and profitable. Henry Fuseli, who designed the engraving, suggested that Blake, "if he meant to know himself", should mark a copy of the book with those aphorisms which were agreeable to him, or "left a sense of uneasiness". In playing this game, Blake passed over without comment these two sentences, which epitomise so much of his later thinking:

280 He who seeks to imbitter innocent pleasure, has a cancer in his heart.
495 The cruelty of the effeminate is more dreadful than that of the hardy.

At the same time, he marked as "heavenly" the aphorism:

343 Who are the saints of humanity? those whom perpetual habits of goodness and of grandeur have made nearly unconscious that what they do is good or grand.

"Heroes with infantine simplicity", Blake stressed. Then he had already underlined aphorism number

328 Keep him at least three paces distant who hates bread, music, and the laugh of a child.

Blake marked this "the best in the book." *Bread* is the interesting word.[13]

The priorities are clear, in times that were changing for the worse as he marked the book. By 29 May 1787, the recollection of Robert's death-bed still raw, Blake knew that the Governors of the "House in Poland Street" had turned their minds from the provision of care, to the cost of bread; and taking into their most serious consideration the great number of Idle poor harbored in the Workhouse and who appear to be capable of providing for themselves, were unanimously of the opinion that difference should be made in the manner of their lodging from the deserving sick and infirm poor, and also in the quantity and quality of the Provisions.

Two weeks later, on 14 June, they put out an advertisement from the King Street school for "a Sober Man Capable of Instructing a number of Boys in picking Cotton in an expeditious and workmanlike manner".[14]

Then, on 19 October, the Governors corrected the creative accounting of five or six years, and reckoned the profit they had missed. The book-keeper recorded that, since July, 1,640 shirts had been made by

12. David V. Erdman, ed., *The Illuminated Blake* (London: Oxford University Press, 1975), p. 29.

13. See Erdman, ed., *Poetry and Prose*, p. 583.

14. See Gardner, *Retraced*, p. 86ff, p. 193 and n.9.

fifty-four of the girls, besides 1,135 table cloths and 206 shifts—income, £86 7s 8d, making a profit of £31 against the outlay for the girls' upkeep, now subject to strict monitoring. Moreover, "about 8 boys are employed making shoes for all the Poor of the Parish others of them in making their own Cloths and some in Picking Cotton. The other Boys are kept constantly at School." The educational afterthought confirms the new priorities. Reverend John Mossop had gone, together with "Hats & Cloaks" and pocket money. Though instruction had been appropriately side-lined, the King Street school was not yet totally industrialised. Despite the boys' cobbling, unsurprisingly the Governors still had to buy shoes in bulk even for the inmates. Though not yet fully restored among the children brought back from Wimbledon, the application of atavistic principles was already working away as Blake turned his mind to illustrating *Songs of Innocence*.

When, soon after his brother died, he turned to the poems he had written about children in the country, he must have seen that he had not written a book "designed for the perusal of young Ladies and Gentlemen". If nothing else, the initial inclusion of 'The Little Girl Lost' and 'Found' in *Innocence* puts an enigmatic question against the prospective age of its readership. Then, motivated, as ever, irresistibly by common truth, he had left out so many features essential to "the generality of works published for the amusement and moral instruction of youth". He had written of the wrong children, in the wrong language for the market. The precious cadences of acceptable heroines ("Oh no father, one can never be tired of doing good; the doing of one kind act always makes one wish to do another")—these would not slide from his pen. He could now hardly miss recognising his "failing": no message, no genuflexion, no family (except Lyca's, originally and significantly), no fortitude, no parson, no class, no niceness, no obedience, no gratitude, no high tone, no breeding—nothing that would sell at 159 Oxford Street; but instead something that would stand tangibly as a "State of the Human Soul", while it could puzzle even his most receptive contemporaries beyond credulity.

It is fair to say that Blake's most enduring and accessible poetry was generated from the relationships—humane, indifferent, or evil—among the people living around him. In *Songs of Experience* this is self-evident; but it is true no less for *Innocence*. In the children redeemed and nurtured at Wimbledon and taken from their workhouse beds into the King Street school, we come upon the groundwork of a vision. In his century, Blake could hardly make poetry and art of King Street within breathing distance of a slaughterhouse; but a related community of children in the village of Wimbledon fitted the rural framework of art.

By discounting a fashion for children's books, and transforming a threadbare pastoral tradition, he immortalised the triumph of untarnished charity. He called it Innocence. He had watched it flourish with tragic brevity on a familiar Common south of the Thames.

With his mind focused by his brother's death, he turned deliberately to illustrating the poems on this state of "organised *Innocence*": the sustaining, interdependent community, centred upon children and graced by the Saviour. We may acknowledge it as an ideal. But Blake and his brother had watched it come to some reality, imperfectly, locally and briefly, through the intransigent history of indifference. For a few years, the children of the streets were no longer excommunicated by the self-interest of privilege, and the lamb of God seemed no longer abandoned.

By the time he turned to illustrating his record of Innocence, Blake had long been familiar with developments in printing. In *An Island in the Moon*, he had already parodied his friend, George Cumberland's, "proposals for a new method of engraving or etching a text on copper for printing, instead of from letterpress".

The parody takes edge, doubtless because the method was not new, but common knowledge among professionals. Word and illustration could be brought together by the poet and artist, who would then "have all the writing Engraved instead of Printed". As early as this too, we have the first brief evidence, at the back of *An Island in the Moon*, of Blake practising the mirror writing essential to the technique.[15]

Against this prosaic background, there is the tradition of Robert's spiritual intervention with some final detail. Any such intervention is most credible as the induced end to prolonged thought by Blake himself:

After intently thinking by day and dreaming by night, during long weeks and months, of his cherished object, the image of his vanished pupil and brother at last blended with it. In a vision of the night, the form of Robert stood before him, and revealed the wished-for secret, directing him to the technical mode by which could be produced a fac-simile of song and design.[16]

One way or another, Blake had the solution; by 1788 he was master of this new technique of printing from relief-etched copperplate.

The conventional method of intaglio etching was to cover the whole copper plate with etching-ground. This prevented the acid from biting into the metal, except where the surface of the ground was subsequently cut through with a metal needle or tool to form the design. The plate was then inked and the surface wiped clean, leaving the area bitten by the acid charged with ink.

15. See Phillips, ed., *Island*, chapters 10–12 and f16v, and the findings of Geoffrey Keynes and G. E. Bentley acknowledged there.

16. Gilchrist, *Life of Blake*, p. 71.

Blake's method reversed this process. He initially wrote his text in reverse on the copper plate and added the illustration. To do this he used a fine brush and, essentially, his specially formulated acid-resistant liquid. A wax wall was then formed round the edge of the plate. The acid was then added, biting into the surface, other than the text and design protected by Blake's brush-strokes. The plate was cleaned, and only the relief surfaces meticulously inked, with the shallows bitten by the acid kept free of ink. The printed impression was touched up and finished off in water colour.[17]

Blake now made another inspired commercial mistake. In the redirection and range of the illustrations, which make them unique, he abandoned (if he ever considered) the book-artist's first principle, especially for the young: that the illustration should be "a simple statement matching the verse", and should not "out-do the text".[18]) From the early plates in *Innocence*, and then time and again, Blake's illustrations "out-do the text" with a visual statement which qualifies, amplifies or enriches the verse, but never belittles it in the way of a matching illustration.

Within months of perfecting his printing technique, Blake began to sketch a series of emblems in the Notebook which he had recently taken over from his dead brother. His first entry in the precious book was the title, which he centred on a whole page:

Ideas
of
Good & Evil[19]

So apposite is this to "the Two Contrary States of the Human Soul", that it seems Blake's imagination was seeded with the idea of setting *Innocence* against a 'Contrary State' soon after Robert died. What is more, some months later, he scribbled a definition on to the fly-leaf of a copy of Swedenborg's *Divine Love and Divine Wisdom*: "Suffering & Distress i.e. Experience" by means of which mankind acquired "understanding". And since he had already noted that "If God is any thing he is Understanding",[20] we sense the divinity Blake identified in the victims of adversity, and the "contrary" spiritual deprivation in their exploiters.

The tragic paradox that is *Songs of Innocence and of Experience* had taken hold of Blake's mind in the months after his brother died, and it seems he had the word he wanted for the "Contrary State". He was soon committing to his new mode of printing the lines he transferred to *Innocence* from *An Island in the Moon*. As he did so, he made one or two crucial changes in the texts.

But even before Obtuse Angle was given his "holy thursday" song on the island, Blake had erased the impossible presence of the chanter,

17. This account is based on Michael Phillips, 'From Manuscript Draft to Illuminated Book', *The Book Collector* (Spring, 1979), and his 'Printing Blake's Songs' 1789–94, in *The Library* (September, 1991). Robert Essick's *William Blake: Printmaker* is authoritative. I have no first-hand knowledge of Blake's working methods. For the various copies of the *Songs* Blake made, see G. E. Bentley, *Blake Books: Annotated Catalogues of William Blake's Writings* ... (Oxford: Clarendon Press, 1977), pp. 364–432.

18. "An illustration for a child, as they [John Newbery and his successors] were well aware, need not be large, nor should it attempt to out-do the text; in fact it is an advantage if it is a simple statement matching the verse ... For the more mature child ... what seemed to be called for were evocative headpieces." Iona and Peter Opie, eds., *The Oxford Nursery Rhyme Book* (Oxford: Clarendon Press, 1955), pp. ix–x.

19. Erdman, ed., *Notebook*, N. 14. The superb editing and presentation of the Notebook that Blake cherished all his life throws a unique and intimate light on his work.

20. See Erdman, ed., *Poetry and Prose*, p. 602.

with the children in attentive expectation: "multitudes of lambs/And all in order sit waiting the chief chanters commands". Had the line been less of a disaster, the idea of the "lambs" sitting "in order" might indeed have suited the mock reverence of the Islanders. Instead, by forestalling the choirmaster and taking the timing back five minutes, as "thousands of little boys & girls" wave to their friends, Blake handed over the cathedral to the irrepressible children. The effect is transforming. He then recollected that the Guardians of the Poor were not usually reverend or Reverends. In *Innocence* he made them "aged".

In *An Island in the Moon*, among the London children climbing around St Paul's, Obtuse Angle was apparently recognising boys and girls from nearby schools, whose colours Blake familiarly knew. The schools were all clustered just south of Petty France, on the way across Tothill Fields, to the footbridge for Battersea and Wimbledon.

The Blue Coat school was almost opposite the Lady Dacre's Almshouses, eponymously Tom Dacre's home. Since 1709, a Blue Coat boy still stands above the door of this elegant school-house, today reviewing the activity in Caxton Street. The Green Coat school is recollected in Greencoat Place. From 1701, the Grey Coat school, behind its two painted statues of charity children, happily still flourishes in Greycoat Place.

The children in red coats seem to have been lost in unrecorded time, unless Mr Emery Hill dressed his children in red. Hill's School stood alongside his almshouses, in Rochester Row opposite the Green Coat school and its adjacent Bridewell, and backing on to Tothill Fields. The school is gone, but the bust of Mr Hill still looks out from his rebuilt almshouses across Rochester Row, now a road, no longer an avenue of trees.

When he scanned the "flowers of London town" in the galleries in St Paul's, initially it seems Blake's eye caught the colours of his local schools: "*grey* & blue & green". But by 1788 "those children wearing grey uniforms" had hit the headlines. They had been so mistreated for so long by an infamous matron, that they fired the Grey Coat hospital. They were brought to court. But, against all the odds, the law came down on the side, not of authority, but of the oppressed. The matron was dismissed.

The severity and outcome of this Grey Coat fire was unique among the injustices that too often disgraced schools—hospital schools in particular. While none of these troubles, though common knowledge, spoilt Holy Thursday for the children or for their parents, notoriously interested only in their own offsprings, it is a pity that the story did not break a few years earlier. It could have been juicily chewed by Quid on the island in the moon. But it was 1788, scandal was intense and Blake was illustrating 'Holy Thursday' for *Innocence*. Grey coats were out.[21]

21. See Gardner, *Retraced*, pp. 31–42. The Blue Coat building is now in the keeping of the National Trust, open to visitors. No Red Coat school appears on Rocque's map of London, 1747. One wonders what colour the Governors uniquely chose for the workhouse children in the King Street school.

Blake made a virtue of necessity. He both dissociated *Innocence* from the topical affair of juvenile fire-raising and the malpractice of office, and he brightened the dome of St Paul's with children picked out in "red & blue & green". It helped both text and illustration to recollect the day for the festival of organised spontaneity that it was.

All London turned out to watch these privileged children, "neatly and warmly clad", talking and waving as they walked "two by two", friend out of step among school friends. This is no march, but simply the timeless and only safe way to crocodile children through streets. The girls are led by one teacher, so relaxed she perhaps carries a book: to read in her seat? Clockwise they follow the boys, who are led into the cathedral by the "wand bearers": "honorary lay officials of St Paul's", with a "tall slender staff of white wood . . . borne as a sign of office."[22] Blake takes us there.

These vestry beadles had, of course, no status as Guardians of the Poor, and their "wands as white as snow" have nothing to do with chastity—theirs or others. Inside the cathedral the gossiping goes on, and the excitement of recognition is irresistible. Again Blake brings to this holiday Thursday his common touch. His imagination rejoices with the children and their working parents, who might for once next day even have bought *The Times*. And it was here, in a church service, that he first brought together in his poetry the link between children and lambs. It was no pastoral format that moved him, but the cared-for rejoicing of children. Even set among the explosive Islanders, the holy thursday lines are already as true to Innocence as that.

So it was children and lambs, not child and lamb, that first fired Blake's imagination: a communal togetherness. As the identity of individual lamb and child develops singularly from here, in both text and illustration, the essential exclusion from *Innocence* is of those ingratiating nursery endearments so extensively printed: "sweet lamb, pretty lamb, poor lamb".

Then the shepherd, who pipes in the 'Introduction' to *Innocence*, does so with a difference. The eighteenth was a century when many "a tuneful shepherd charm'd the list'ning glade", and was recognised as playing to the poet's music. But the shepherd in *Innocence* neither pipes for the poet, nor charms the air. From the start, he pipes of that essential element of Innocence, which the Little Vagabond insufferably in *Experience* demands as God-given: "pleasant glee"; and at once the lamb is tuned in at the behest of a child. A unique visionary order is established, which Blake, the illustrator, bracketed in working references when he populated the interwoven side panels of the plate: sower, printer, teacher, nurse—the structure of *Innocence*. The child's tears of

22. *OED*, 'wand', 7a and 15. The girls are not led by a matron, as is often suggested. Most of the children walking (those in day schools) knew no matron; and no matron would readily take on the teacher's job of walking children through the streets—then or now.

joy at the piper's song are a moving response, more profound as we read the book which it introduces.

There is no hint of the biblical tradition in this initial pastoral regard for the claims of childhood. But even when the identity of Christ the Shepherd comes into *Innocence*, the Shepherd still fulfils the child's need. The charity of rescue and nurture becomes a Christian imperative as absolute as that.

Blake established the precedence of care in more practical terms when he designed the title-page, taking over "a stock motif" of "instruction with delight" from the genre of children's books, while avoiding "the heavy handed moralising". In particular, "a similar arrangement of woman, book, and two children comprises the Frontispiece in John Newbery's *A Little Pretty Pocket-Book, Intended for the Instruction and Amusement of Little Master Tommy, and Pretty Miss Polly*" published in 1767.[23]

However the objective detail Blake illustrates is more telling than either the "similar arrangement", or his dismissal of moral uplift. The mentor in the *Pocket-Book* wears a decolletage and is coiffured into the right status. This is in effect more restrictive than the simple cap of Blake's nurse, who takes the attention of two children, more or less of an age, and respects their childhood. Against Blake's open countryside, Newbery's "little lady" and her junior brother, already bewigged into premature propriety, are caught in a lesson that is a private, family affair. The lad's left leg is mincingly outstretched. Here is the beginning of some early pointe-work, directed by the raised arm of a lady who has trodden the salons. It is a straight illustration of eighteenth-century 'liberal education': pure Newbery, for "the better sort", plainly, if paradoxically, closer to Experience than to Innocence, as the boy is taught to dance his way through the "cords of twisted self conceit". Against this, in its selfless cohesion, Blake's title-page exemplifies the "care & sweet instruction", which was for him a precious benediction.[24]

Back on the island in the moon, the charity children, still "in grey & blue & green" as they took over St Paul's, put Mrs Nannicantipot 'in Mind' of another occasion, when a rural benediction came to children of far less account. She had another quid of philanthropy for the Islanders to chew. She gave them her 'mothers song' beginning,

> *When the tongues of children are heard on the green*
> *And laughing is heard on the hill*
> *My heart is at rest within my breast*
> *And everything else is still.*

23. Essick, *Printmaker*, p. 138. Newbery's frontispiece is there reproduced as figure 134.

24. *The Four Zoas*, plates 6 and 21.

Mrs Nannicantipot's mother was plainly an uncultured woman to find composure in the spontaneous laughter of children, unrelated to conduct. Such a reassuringly naive response would surely qualify her as a foster mother to move in with her song, when Blake illustrated it for *Innocence*.

So, if it originally and genuinely belonged to her, 'Mother's Song' would have suited as a title. Instead it became a 'Nurse's Song'. It seems the poem is back with its primary voice. The lines then fit the illustration Blake gives it for *Innocence*, where the nurse calmly reads her book while supervising seven children at play, all more or less the same age, and manifestly not siblings.

The title, the immediacy of the lines, and the illustration all presuppose Blake's personal knowledge of the nurse in charge of children in the countryside. This generates the poem, which is then lent to Mrs Nannicantipot, as it suits her mood, before Blake retrieves it for *Innocence*, with an illustration that conclusively recollects its source: the contentment he knew familiarly well among the foundlings with the nurses at Wimbledon.

In illustrating the texts of *Innocence*, Blake's mind returned repeatedly to the ideal of nurture, either in pastoral analogues or by direct intervention. The clearest and most general statement of such intervention is again curiously related to the activities of Tilly Lally, Joe Bradley and the rest. Again, in illustrating 'The Ecchoing Green' at the end of the decade, he records the actuality of care familiar to him in earlier years.

On the first plate, the batsman has let fly so hard at the ball, that his bat has swung out of his right hand. The ball flies over the hedge, past the outstretched arms of the fielder on the boundary. The youths off the field of play to the right enjoy the excitement with all the indifference typical of spectators round a village green. Alongside the text, a player stands with proper nonchalance, resting on his bat.

Provided bare-foot Joe Bradley was not around, this was a very civilised, social and therapeutic game, already so recognised by educationists. The Marine Society had introduced it to boys in their ship-school, and Blake is here recording, among the children "organised" in Innocence, an essential ingredient in their upbringing: God is "pleasant".

While the text of 'The Ecchoing Green' has Old John "Sitting under the oak/Among the old folk", Blake uses the illustration to bring the community together there. Old John sits with a companion of his own age, a child at their knees looking up at them. The rest of the seating round the tree is taken up by nurses and young children even less interested in cricket than are the spectators. The children on the green have found, not only nurture, but a place in the community; the "contrary" will be the alienation of *Experience*, whether polite or necessitous.

As early as 'The Ecchoing Green', Blake uses his technique of transposing text and illustration, to achieve a visual and literary interrelated continuity. The first illustration visually sets the nursing of the "little ones weary" alongside the sport and recollected rejoicing of the opening two verses; but the first mention of this nurture, where "Round the laps of their mothers / Many sisters and brothers" seem already "weary", is withheld till the second plate, alongside the visual departure from the sport on the green.

If there is any doubt about the nursing identity of the mothers who care for the children under the oak, it is dispelled in the second plate, where it is impossible to see the single young female as the natural mother of all her charges. Here the mother (the title easily used by anyone, and unfailingly by her children, for 'nurse'), carries an infant, with a weary child at her skirt, and walks her charges home.

We recollect that on Wimbledon Common, "five or six" children were "placed in one house" with their foster-mother, and in this domiciliary way came to be "many sisters and brothers". It is precisely the way Blake would put it, disregarding the reservations of office, and lining up his language with the children's. It is this bond of care in a community that makes the children "sisters and brothers" in Innocence. The only incongruous alternative would be to read "many sisters and brothers" as notional of large rural families.

In the second plate a boy carries his bat away from the green, one of a group of seven children (counting only those on the ground) and a nurse. The nurse is helped by "a man in a wide hat such as Blake wore".[25] He looks much younger and better dressed than Old John. The intervention of this central figure is interesting. The text makes no mention of male discipline. It seems to me that Blake is once more visually referring the visionary text to its matrix in reality. My guess is that, in lending his hat to the young man giving the helping hand, Blake is reliving a day of his own. We know the Governors often checked on the children at Wimbledon. But it is unlikely that the recollection of such a casual visit would lodge so vividly in Blake's imagination, and compel him, years later, to introduce this unique visitor to the contours of Innocence.

The third set of lines Blake transferred from An Island to Innocence was Quid's own inconsequential touch of sentiment, which, with the bounce of mockery taken out of it, becomes 'The Little Boy Lost'. Then for Innocence the little boy is "found" in the sequel by "God ever nigh", who leads the lost child back to his mother, "Who in sorrow pale thro the lonely dale / Her little boy weeping sought." The "vapour" which deceives the child from the outset is illustrated in Innocence as a "dancing meteor" or marsh light. It was a phenomenon Blake would meet in places south of

25. See Geoffrey Keynes, ed., *Songs of Innocence and of Experience* (Oxford: Oxford University Press, 1970), p. 132. Keynes uses the phrase in identifying a small figure playing a pipe, leaning against the I of 'Innocence' in the title-page. If Blake was piper, was he also participant? See Gardner, *Retraced*, pp. 46–49.

the Thames—over the "marshy bottoms" of Lambeth, or on Rush Common below Brixton Hill, by Vauxhall Creek towards Wimbledon, or along the Wandle or Beverley Brook nearby.

If the text recalls a familiar landscape, the presence of a divine Father in the illustration seems to reflect the Islanders' momentary solemnity ("nobody could sing any longer") on hearing the song in their "merry meeting at the house of Steelyard the Lawgiver". At the same time the Father moves among the heavy trees, anticipating his "forests of affliction" that were soon to possess Blake's imagination.

Time and again, both text and illustrations associate *Innocence* with the friends and neighbours Blake telescoped so vividly into the moon. It was in Steelyard's house that Miss Gittipin again put the Islanders into "such a serious humour" with her evanescent lament, curiously in line with the little lost boy's own distress:

> *Leave O leave to my sorrows*
> *Here Ill sit & fade away*
> *Till Im nothing but a spirit*
> *And I lose this form of clay*
>
> *Then if chance along this forest*
> *Any walk in pathless ways*
> *Thro the gloom he'll see my shadow*
> *Hear my voice upon the breeze.*[26]

In *Innocence* Blake surrounds the child, both lost and rescued, with trees which have no roots in the 'The Little Boy' texts. Again, however, they shade back into Blake's immediate past, into Miss Gittipin's arboreal distress. Then, from this congenial association, they convey the mind away from the years of *Innocence*, towards the barren trees that characterise the landscape of *Experience*; even towards "the forests of the night" through which the tyger burned. In these forbidding trunks and limbs we sense "the forests of eternal death" closing in already on Blake's imagination, across the muted recollection of Miss Gittipin, and of Miss Elizabeth Pinnard.

Then alongside these invasive trees in *Innocence* there is 'The Little Girl Lost' and 'Found'. Her salacious abduction in another forest, paraded in portentous symbolism and rhythm as an act of royal grace, ends in a family broken, and spiritual loss. Blake moved "lovely Lyca" out of *Innocence*, as soon as *Experience* was there to accommodate her; but her intrusion into *Innocence* suggests how close we come to Blake's rising grief at the change in human circumstance around him.

26. Phillips, ed., *Island*, p. 11. See Gardner, *Retraced*, pp. 69–75.

27. The name is not common. Richard Milward tells me that a 'Mrs Beal Schoolmistress' is recorded as living in a cottage at the Crooked Billet, Wimbledon, from 1776. She certainly did not teach at the charity school there, and may therefore have been one of the teachers employed to instruct the St James's children.

28. See Gardner, *Retraced*, p. 88.

As Blake finished putting the colours to 'Infant Joy', Miss Pinnard had left the King Street school. Her successor, Mrs Constantia Beale, brought over it appears from teaching the children at Wimbledon,[27] was in trouble with the Governors, as Miss Pinnard had never been, because "several children under her care were unqualified to render the usual Assistance for the making the Childrens Cloathing". She wrote in January 1790 that it was beyond her power to get the clothing made by Easter, as "other work may interfere". The "other work" that by this time raised the Governors' concern was no longer written in class, but in the ledger.[28]

And to the Contrary

When John Wesley mounted his tent, that popular pulpit set up close by the tabernacle at a country sacrament, the congregation of lambs in the field around him often rejoiced too enthusiastically. So much so, that on 21 January 1761, he noted in his *Journal* a gratifying maturity in one at least of his flock "who was as hot as any of the lambs at the tabernacle; but she is now a calm, reasonable woman".

One's mind goes back to the exuberance of the "multitudes of lambs", in the congregation that first fired Blake's imagination into his own concept of pastoral poetry; and then to the triumphant call, voiced for God by the Little Black Boy:

> *come out from the grove, my love & care,*
> *And round my golden tent like lambs rejoice.*

Wesley's portable wooden tent brought nothing to his lambs, to match the reconciliation the Little Black Boy achieves as he answers the psalmist's call, "Lord, who shall dwell in thy bright tent with thee?"[1]

The number of destitute negroes abandoned in London vastly increased during the years Blake was writing *Songs of Innocence*. In the 1770s there were already some fifteen thousand ex-slaves in the country, not many of them outside London. Then, to add to the influx, black recruits who had loyally fought for the crown were shipped to England at the end of the American war, where they fell derelict almost to a man. At the same time, the liberty of their kinsfolk who came over to escape slavery was more often than not denied. Given the contemporary respect for material wealth, they could find themselves still bound, as the property of previous masters.

Earlier in the century, ladies of the town sported a vogue for little black boys, dressed out as attendant toys. But by the 1780s fashionable boredom had more or less closed these cosy if precarious havens for black children. At the same time, we learn from Miss Gittipin's envy that Jacko and Maria Cosway still had "black servants lodge at their house", a touch of cheap out-dated exoticism among Jacko's silk hangings. But all this was the jester's cap on the head of skeletal black exclusion, like the moth eaten wigs that make grotesques of the diminutive chimney boys in Blake's engraving of their May day caper with the milk maids in Milk Lane.

1. 'The Little Black Boy', in *Innocence*, and Psalm xv. See *OED*, 'tent', 4, for the portable pulpit of wood. The crossing of ideas is interesting.

A pamphlet on police reform reported in 1784 that negroes in their thousands "traversed the town naked, pennyless and almost starving", a conspicuous regiment among Westminster's army of beggars. Issuing from the shambles, down-river from the chartered streets of the city, they frightened authority when their continuing bondage roused the ambivalent sympathy of the mob.

The fact that slavery had been abolished in rebellious Pennsylvania in 1780, if anything turned English justice truculent. "Getting christened or married", the immigrants often heard, "made them free",

though it has been decided otherwise by the judges. However it so far answers their purpose that it gets the mob on their side, and makes it not only difficult but dangerous ... to recover possession of them, when once they are spirited away; and indeed, it is the less evil of the two to let them go about their business.[2]

But "their business" then was to face the acrimony of the mobsters dispersed, whose earnings, if any, they were playing for. Compassion wore out with their boots, as the crowds walked home, and the immigrants' hope of base labour, much less advancement, was forlorn. Competition was innumerable and resentful.

It was the children of these negroes Blake knew round the streets, when the death of his brother in 1787 impelled his thoughts more directly to the true nature of Christianity. It was a time when the plight of the immigrant slaves, and their acceptance in a Christian community, were questions of topical concern. Jonas Hanway's newly formed Committee for Relieving the Black Poor in London had just transported some 450 negroes to Sierra Leone. They were applicants for a new life in what was promoted as "one of the most fertile and pleasant countries in the known world". Even the Government contributed £14 towards each departure. It also took the opportunity to provide for some fifty white prostitutes, by shipping them along as well. The endeavour was a catastrophe yet to come. Meanwhile Blake knew that concern for the plight of the negroes in the capital was official, if ineffectual. Coincidentally or not, his imagination moved to articulate the essential racial reconciliation. It derived from a Little Black Boy and his mother, in "one of the most fertile and and pleasant countries in the known world": "a southern wild".[3]

On 27 January 1788, about the time Blake was bringing the two boys, black and white, to the knee of their Saviour in *Innocence*, the Precentor William Mason was fingering his sermon on "the African Slave Trade", in the cold pulpit of his cathedral in York.[4] The Precentor was moved to preach in support of the Society for Effecting the Abolition of the Slave

2. Sir John Fielding, quoted in George, *London Life*, p. 140.
3. George, *London Life*, p. 143.
4. William Mason, *Works* (1811), vol. IV, p. 178.

Trade, then calling in its initial subscriptions, and "to promote the petition to Parliament, then under signature, for the abolition". When it arrived in Westminster, the petition was shredded by vested interests. The insistence of William Mason and others, that slaves were "of the same divine origin" as the legislators, "beings that have immortal souls like themselves, enshrined in a body which, though it has a variation of complexion, has hardly any in form or in feature", counted for nothing against the weight of business necessity. Meanwhile "God", the congregation in York Cathedral heard, was "the universal and equal Father of all Mankind". So in the words and colours of *Innocence*, Blake was epitomising a precept much in vogue up and down the land; but a precept which the pale skinned, commercial half "of all Mankind" found inconvenient to accommodate.

Topical as it now was, the dilemma was of ancient lineage. Even in the year of Blake's birth, John Dyer, as death approached, had published, "a poem in four books" on the wool trade in its widest perspective; so wide, it took in the question of slavery. Johnson "heaped on it the weight of his collosal contempt", while Wordsworth unaccountably found the work "a living lanscape fair and bright". For us, *The Fleece* enshrines the tone of its time in fascinating banality, and Dyer smooths into perspective his century's misgivings on "the sale of wretched slaves", shipped west, to

> *till our fertile colonies, which yield*
> *The sugar-cane, and the Tobago-leaf,*
> *And various new productions, that invite*
> *Increasing navies to their crowded wharfs,*

by commending those slave-traders, who

> *With just humanity of heart pursue*
> *The gainful commerce.*[5]

But the solace of such a compromise, between "just humanity" and "gainful commerce", brought little solace to some eccleciastical consciences. It was less easy to measure this compromise against the conversion of slaves to Christianity.

So, in a footnote penned as late as 1811, four years after the Slave Trade Bill made the traffic illegal, but did little for slavery, William Mason refers back to 1766, and "the masterly pen of Warburton". Warburton had, even then, written that "the Savages in the back settlements of America", should receive two benefits: "English working tools as well as English missionaries . . . Civilisation should always either precede or

5. *The Fleece*, IV, lines 194–200.

accompany conversion", if possible, *tools first*, an undertaking uncongenial to monopoly.

It was a proposition impossible to fulfil in America, and beyond credulity for negroes Blake saw in the "back settlements" of London, competing with a multitude, as the lowest resource of indigent labour.

In this context, the priority Blake gives to the Little Black Boy and his initiative in racial reconciliation is startling. Moreover his conclusion subsumes not only the sincere platitudes of the clergy and reformers, but also the literary travellers' reports of the self-reliant native, profitably transferred into pious and popular fiction.

Jacques Bernardin Henri de Saint Pierre's *La Chaumiere Indienne*, reprinted and bound with his *Paul et Virginie* in 1791, was one of the French texts much favoured as both 'liberal' in tone, and linguistic encouragement for beginners in the language the English middle classes aspired to speak, unseemly revolution or not. De Saint-Pierre has "*le docteur Anglois*" marvel at the equanimity of the native in a storm. Change the weather, substitute de Saint-Pierre's tempest for Blake's sun, and the French speaking native has assimilated the teaching of a parent, who could have been cousin to the Little Black Boy's mother:

Permettez-moi de vous faire quelques questions. Comment êtes-vous si tranquille au milieu d'un si terrible orage? Vous n'êtes cependant à couvert que par un arbre, et les arbres attirent la foudre. Jamais, répondit le paria, la foudre n'est tombée sur un figuier de banians. Voilà qui est fort curieux, reprit le docteur; c'est sans doute parce que cet arbre a une électricité négative, comme le laurier. Je ne vous comprends pas, répartit le paria . . . pour moi, je pense que Dieu, dans ces climats orageux, ayant donné au figuier des banians un feuillage fort épais, et des arcades pour y mettre les hommes à l'abri de l'orage, il ne permet pas qu'ils y soient atteints du tonnerre. Votre réponse est bien religieuse, repartit le docteur. Ainsi c'est votre confiance en Dieu qui vous tra[n]quillise.[6]

The Little Black Boy, and the Chimney Sweeper whom we come to later, are the two children in *Innocence* who exist outside the scope of nurture, the one by alien birth, the other by social exclusion and by belonging to the wrong parish. Already Blake's direction is changing; he beckons them from *Experience* into *Innocence*. Both boys, in different circumstances, are 'black'; both are redeemed by the Saviour, and apparently (only apparently) brought to paradise. It seems the resonances in texts and illustrations carry implications much closer to London than paradise could be. In 'The Little Black Boy', at first glance, the release from the clouds, which formed their divisive bodies, black and white, suggests a posthumous reconciliation of souls. Divine intervention, and

6. *La Chaumiere Indienne*, ed. cit., pp. 25–26. The Englishman speaks: "Allow me to put a few questions to you. How do you stay so calm in the middle of such a terrible storm? You are only sheltered by a tree, and trees attract lightning. It is unknown, replied the Indian, for a thunderbolt to strike a banyan-fig. Now that is very strange, went on the doctor, doubtless it is because the tree possesses a negative charge, like the laurel; to which the Indian replied, I do not understand you. For my part, I believe that God gave the banyan-fig dense foliage and over-arching branches, to protect us from the storms in this tempestuous climate, and, that being so, He will not allow them to be struck down. A very religious thought, said the doctor. In effect, it is your trust in the Lord, which reassures you."

heaven attained as so often promised, may have been the only freedoms for the dispossessed in their too transitory lives; but such a posthumous facility of freedom hardly fits Blake's thinking, given the provocative initiative allowed to the Little Black Boy, and the precision of Tom Dacre's vision.

If we set aside for a moment the 'obvious' resolution in paradise, and allow the illumination of Blake's language time to come through, the sense of 'The Little Black Boy' transforms uniquely. Circumstances, ideas and platitudes of the time, all familiar in *Experience*, are assimilated into the poem, cleared of their top-dressing of circumspection, and referred to *Innocence*. Doubtless Blake knew of the banyan tree, the Indian Fig Tree, specified in 1791 as "the most stupendous effort of vegetable nature", twenty trees rather than one, its branches drooping and rooting to form the shelter of arcades; or, as Blake would say, 'shady groves'. The words are virtually synonymous, in respect of an avenue of trees planted for shade, an undertaking particularly admired in the century.

In both de Saint-Pierre's India, and Blake's simile of "a shady grove" for negro skin, God does the planting and the shading, and both the Indian and the little black boy's mother hold the faith. From the purity of this faith Blake takes us towards a central theme of Innocence: unqualified reconciliation; and reconciliation in the face of intransigence. It is inconceivable that Blake proclaims a posthumous blessing, pitching God's "golden tent" as a "skyey tent" in the fields of the hereafter. If that other familiar preacher's tent in the fields, with the "lambs" cavorting round it, slips into the mind and at once away, we are left in England; with Christ, the boys and the lambs in the fields of Innocence. Then the Little Black Boy has made free both himself and his white friend from the racial degradation of their black and white skins. Initiative is reversed in a return to the fields of true Christianity, and Precentor William Mason need preach no more:

> *When I from black and he from white cloud free*
> *And round the tent of God like lambs we joy.*

The ambiguity of the poem is then given a direction home to Surrey in the illustrations. "In the southern wild" the mother nurtures her child under an English oak. The ideographic transition is made. This could be the same tree as shelters the mother and her infant in the first plate of 'Spring', among the Thameside flocks of Innocence.

Then, in the second plate, the Saviour sits as shepherd beside the waters of life, beneath a willow brought from the banks of the stream by which the children play in 'Nurse's Song'. The sheep graze safely in the fields, sustaining the signal which typifies Innocence realised among the living. The Saviour himself and the two boys at his knee directly recollect the nurse and her pupils on the title-page to *Innocence*. Christ is brought by simple faith in reconciliation from "the southern wild" to a place near London. God's people, black and white, are united by the initiative of the meek, there and then. It is a vision utterly worthy of Blake.

Both here, and in 'The Chimney Sweeper' in *Innocence*, Blake is essentially already facing and transcribing Experience. Extraneous atrocities are resolved into Innocence, in a way that becomes unavailable as the tragedy deepens. By then, the "contrary" to both Tom Dacre's poem and the Little Black Boy's is the capitalised alienation in 'The Chimney Sweeper' in *Experience*; until, finally, the only answer is 'The Tyger'.

It only seems ironic that the physical state of both Tom Dacre and his narrator in *Innocence* is worse than that of the boy sweep in *Experience*. Both Tom Dacre and his friend are sold of necessity by their parents into chimney sweeping. The boy sweep "among the winter snow" of *Experience* is out there not of need, but for parental cupidity. To dodge the law, his parents are exploiting the life of their own son while he is small enough. And while he sings and works the narrowest chimneys, "they are both gone up to the church", "to praise God & his Priest & King". In *Innocence*, Tom Dacre had his head that "curl'd like a lambs back" shaved against the fires of circumstance; in *Experience*, the master

Figure 6. Lady Dacre's Alms Houses, Westminster, whence, his name informs, Tom Dacre was sold to chimney sweeping.

sweep clothed his child "in the clothes of death", deliberately, literally, not figuratively, for money.[7]

Blake wrote the sweeper verses for *Innocence* against the background of the culminating Act of a long campaign to bring some protection to the climbing boys. It was a campaign familiar to Blake from boyhood. He wrote the poem for *Experience* as the master sweeps contrived to circumvent the same Act in the years after 1788.

In 1767 Jonas Hanway had already observed that master sweeps who took on apprentices, often "so young as seven years of age", used them up chimneys to put out fires. It was the best paid part of the undertaking. Hanway added his advice and an observation: "They ought to breed their own children to the business, then perhaps they will wash, clothe and feed them. As it is, they do neither". Blake knew it.

By the 1780s, public sentiment ensured that "few parochial officers place out their children to chimney sweepers". But unsurprisingly poverty and profit still combined to defeat sentiment. Like Tom Dacre, most climbing boys were now "orphans, or the children of poor parents, who cannot find bread for a numerous family".[8]

This meant that boys as young as four years old, too young for formal apprenticing, but more efficiently sized for work in narrow flues on fire, were sold into the work by drunken or desperate parents. Moved by the scandal, David Porter, a master sweep who had followed up Hanway's initiative, shamed Parliament into passing the Act (28 GeoIII) which, judiciously amended in the Lords, did a little, if not much, for the climbing boys.

It was 1788. Blake was illustrating his 'Chimney Sweeper' lines for *Innocence*. What was inconveniently legislated in Hanway's Act was soon ignored or avoided. The Act made illegal the hiring out of climbing boys by master sweeps, and no boy was to be employed under the age of eight. This left the industry with the problem of finding boys undersized enough to work the difficult flues. The employment of "orphans or the children of poor parents" being illegal, the master sweep's solution was to use his own son, to whom it was agreed the Act did not apply since he was not "employed".

Well regarded for a time was the requirement of the Act that each boy wear a leather cap, with his master's name on a metal badge on the front. However when later Blake came to colour the 'The Chimney Sweeper' in *Experience*, he left the "little black thing among the snow" bareheaded. The father, "gone up to the church to pray", had not thought fit, either to protect his son's head, or to establish his legitimacy with cap and badge.

The triumph of Innocence and the tragedy of Experience lie in rela-

7. See Gardner, *Retraced*, especially pp. 64– 68, pp. 112–13, and pp. 26–28.

8. Jonas Hanway, *Sentimental History of Chimney Sweepers* (1785), p. 25. See Gardner, *Retraced*, chapter 7.

tionships. The chimney sweepers reported in *Innocence*, are excluded from the community of Innocence. They sleep "in soot", mattressed and blanketed in sacks. The deprivation and hardships are related as aspects of existence to which their status inured the boys. To make a point, Blake takes into *Innocence* the consideration of ultimate social exclusion; Experience at its most desperate. The boys' only release from degradation lies in a transformation of relationships to match the concept of Innocence. To this end, Tom Dacre's dream is a seemingly forlorn hope, while the bounce of the account denies its likelihood in reality. Divine intervention is at hand, when all else fails, and, as in 'The Little Black Boy', our first understanding is of an outcome exclusively posthumous. But again, there is more to it, as Blake identifies the rescue in the living state of Innocence.

Being undersized, Tom and his friends were employed in the the most hazardous flues, as his dream recalls. At their widest, chimneys were difficult. After 1772 "a long and successful practice in building flues" decreed that "a flue as usually made for ordinary rooms in England is 14 ins. by 9 ins., and for kitchens 14 ins. square".9

By 1794 it was advised that "14 ins. square sufficiently answered for sittingrooms or bedrooms". Soon this was considered excessive, and, certainly before 1826, it seems "that 81 [square] ins. were thought enough for a common fire-place, though 126 [square] ins. had been adopted for the admission of climbing sweeps". The most hazardous problem, however, was not these officially notified appertures, but the flue which was the trigger to Tom's nightmare turned vision, when in sleep he imagined "That thousands of sweepers, Dick, Joe, Ned & Jack,/Were all of them lock'd up in coffins of black". These were the horizontal flues built, at times, over the fire itself, or over a false back, to connect with the ascending flue when a fire-place had been built under an opening. And then, as Revd T. Ridge reported to the Society of Arts in 1815, "if an elbow flue from a fire be carried into an upright flue, there will always be a large accumulation of soot below the elbow, and but little in the main flue". A single installation had long since solved this, to the comfort of householders: "where it is desirable to turn a flue at a very acute angle, a soot door should be placed at the elbow".

So, with the soot door in front of him, and behind it a box "stated not to be above 7 inches square", with the vertical bricks at the other end, Tom Dacre was facing a coffin of black. As he opened the door, no-one knew if the inevitable fall of soot was burning. As Blake wrote the lines, the protective leather cap was not yet mandatory; but Tom's master at least made sure by shaving, that the boy's hair was beyond catching fire.

9. An inch is, near enough, two-and-a-half centimetres. For details of the construction of the chimneys in which the boys worked, I am indebted to Ms Alison Shell, Curator of Rare Books at the British Architectural Library, RIBA.

Then, in sleep Tom has "such a sight": the "unlocking"[10] not of himself, but of "thousands of sweepers", from "coffins of black", in a general amnesty from suffocation, to "*wash* in a river and shine in the sun"—not bathe, swim, splash or play but "wash in a river". By using the little, unpretentious word, Blake unerringly refers the dream to the least hope of chimney boys in London.

Whenever Blake wrote the lines, either during the campaign for reform, or in 1788 as Hanway's Act became law, it was 1788 before Blake illustrated the poem, with the gowned figure of Christ supervising the dash for the water. Boy sweeps commonly went a year, four years, even five, without water touching their skin. The "better sort" of master sweeps took their boys once a year in summer to wash in waters like the New River Head. In Blake's illustration, the Saviour, a participant as always in *Innocence*, oversees the release to cleanness, in a "sight" stimulated by the hope of "good practice"; and maybe by considerations laid down in the new law, which decreed that the boys were to be "thoroughly washed and cleansed of soot and dirt", every Sunday at least.

It did not happen, as the years Blake chronicled in *Experience* occluded the land. And a century passed before sweeps were licensed, the police intervened, and the last Tom Dacre was helped down a chimney stack.

The Little Black Boy and the boy sweepers are the only children in Innocence directly to acknowledge divine provision, and Tom Dacre and his presenter are the only children of their age at work, "doing their duty", as their moral mentors so interminably required. As Blake moved the Little Black Boy and the sweeps in the illustrations towards the Christianity of Innocence, his mind was no longer possessed, as it had been, by the achievement of nurture he had so firmly recorded. The misgiving, the shift in conviction as times were changing, breaking through the layers of irony in the sweep's closing reassurance for his pals, echoing in Innocence the legislators of Experience: "So if all do their duty, they need not fear harm".

By the time Blake had the poems of *Innocence* ready for relief-etching, the legislators were well at work. The nursing at Wimbledon and the King Street school, so exceptionally conducted, were now recognised as philanthropic acts amounting to "impolicy", in the words of old Jonas Hanway, "in respect of teaching the indigent and laborious part of fellow-subjects more than belongs to their station". By now, Blake's neighbours, by whom his thoughts were always so powerfully moved, had come to realise that they had compounded the error even Hanway guarded himself against, in the way they had been running the King Street school, for children, not simply "indigent and laborious", but destitute.

10. *OED*, 'coffin', 8. There are the related old senses of a case in which articles were fired in a furnace, and of a chest, usually secured with a lock.

In those earlier years, the meticulous book-keeper who listed the haberdashery bills from the Blake family shop had recorded no complaints in his minutes about the expense of the school, or the fostering at Wimbledon. But on 29 May 1787, the Governors unanimously decided that a "difference should be made" in the lodging and "in the quantity and quality of the Provisions for the great number of Idle poor harbored in the Workhouse". And two weeks later they advertised for "a Sober Man Capable of Instructing a number of Boys in picking Cotton". They no longer enquired about ciphering, but now stressed, with an emphasis which turned learning into a threat, that the boys who were not picking cotton, or "employed making shoes for all the Poor of the Parish", were to be "kept constantly at school".

This was three months after Blake had watched his brother die, six weeks after he had signed up with Catherine in support of Emanuel Swedenborg and the founding of the New Jerusalem Church. It was for him a brief and unique recourse in distress to an organised church. Five months later, on 19 October, the book-keeper ominously made his first entry of the cash gain from the King Street school. For a year or more after this, some of the old habit of concern still lingered. The Governors of the school still took care to send out their messenger to check if tradesmen were fit to receive workhouse children into apprenticeships; and approval was never assured. As the decade came to its end all this changed.

With misgivings about Swedenborg already in his mind, Blake must have known that on 22 December 1789, the committee appointed by the King Street Governors, "to enquire into the Nature of the Manufactory near Manchester, and the propriety of binding poor Children Apprentice thereto", had reported most encouragingly. Children who were totally unskilled "could earn a sufficient livelihood" in the "northern Manufactories", after an apprenticeship which required no educational outlay.

In the temper of the times, six months after the Bastille had fallen, such facilities put serious questions against the "morality" of the expense of the extended schooling of destitute children. The expectations of the foundlings Blake had watched nursed and schooled in such "minute particulars" (as he put it decades later, shifting "duty" from the deprived to the affluent),[11] were reversed. And as Blake crowded the verses of *Experience* into his brother's *Notebook*,[12] the children who grew up behind Tilly Lally, Joe Bradley and their crew, found that "the minute particulars" of care in St James's parish had changed utterly.

So, in the New Year of 1790, three days after she complained of the difficulty she faced in marshalling the children's labour, Mrs Constan-

11. *Jerusalem*, plate 55.

12. Heavily worked drafts or fair copies of all but four poems ('Introduction', 'Ah! Sun-Flower', 'A Little Girl Lost', and the much later 'To Tirzah') appear in the Notebook which Blake took over from Robert and cherished. The pressure on space in the book was clearly a factor in the concentrated style of the poems.

tia Beale was summoned to explain to her Governors why "several children under her care were unqualified to render the usual Assistance for the making of Childrens Cloathing". And on the same day, her colleague, the Matron, "was called in and severely admonished" because she had failed to put the children "in Rotation to the Kitchen Laundry". To adjust matters, the book-keeper was instructed to make out a register "of the Names of the Children which are above the age of ten Years [with] the different Employment they are put to during the year entered in columns".

The Governors, who had rescued the children with such Christian magnanimity those few short years earlier, were now preoccupied with the conventional stock of "Christian" duty, and with the ledger. It is plain from the records of reprimands, that the staff had failed to anticipate the reimposition of historical Experience on the discredited initiative of Innocence.

Further, having disposed of the expense of "sweet instruction" for the children from Wimbledon, the Governors, still in 1790, turned their minds to a plan

[that] was suggested for employing all the able poor in the workhouse [and] ... contracted with Messrs Gorton and Thompson, tenants to Lord Bathurst at Cuckney in Nottinghamshire, and very considerable manufacturers, that the Governors should build a workshop capable to hold 90 looms at the least, and keep the same in repair, and that Gorton and Thompson should ... build and set up that number of patent looms, and all other machinery, wheels etc ... useful and proper for carrying on the business of spinning, winding and weaving.

The set-up was contrived by wheels within influential wheels. Cuckney, of all places, came to St James's, Westminster, because Henry, the second Earl Bathurst, was Visitor to the King Street school and the workhouse. He had also pressed the woolsack as 'one of the weakest, though one of the worthiest" Lord Chancellors of his century.

The proposal to add one more to the "dark Satanic Mills" of Thameside, built in a workhouse, across a graveyard, based on the takeover of the destitute by the Lord Chancellor and his associates, exemplifies the conspiracy of title and commerce which was for Blake implacably tragic. Times had moved on from Mr Becknel's frustrated attempt in the years of Innocence, to persuade the Governors to install spinning-wheels in their school, and make the children work for his profit.

Not surprisingly, the book-keeper no longer minuted the Governors' gratification at the improvement the Committee reported in "the Boys writing & ciphering books", as he had on 4 May 1784. A decade later, reassurance lay elsewhere: the school now exceeded

the most sanguine expectations of its patrons. All the children are taught their duty as Christians. The girls make and mend . . . all their clothes; knit their own and the boys' stockings, and make the boys' linen . . . The boys make their own clothes and clothes for hire; they also mend their own and the girls' shoes; the rest are employed in the heading of pins.

These shifts in priority, told by the book-keeper's continuing quill, are familiar and cold; and they epitomize close at hand the wider social atrocities, polite and crude, which Blake was writing into *Experience*. The children's "duty as Christians", impressed now, as of old, in relation to cobbling, knitwear and the heading of pins, was never mentioned alongside "writing and ciphering", when Joy was a foundling's name. In those years of Innocence, Christ was not preached; he was present. It is easy to comprehend the tenacity with which Blake etched this lately abandoned State of the Human Soul, as its Contrary once more closed in. Experience was an ancient dispensation, fondly revived in a restored normalcy.

Songs of Experience is a report of the intimate corrosion of the soul, destructive of personal and social relationships. The book has nothing directly to do with the impressive issues of revolution bred from the fall of the Bastille in 1789, and fought over in the Corresponding Societies; or with the model of freedom in America, which was seen by some to disturb the dominance of English oligarchy. Blake considered these themes profoundly elsewhere;[13] but in *Experience* we move into the brick-fields, chapels, bedrooms, nurseries, ditches and secret gardens of people's lives. The distortion of swaddling, the wreck of a prostitute, the jealousy of a father, the manipulation of a nanny, the murder of a friend—it is intimacies such as these, the consequential evils of privileged misgovernment, which overwhelm our imagination with their sustained immediacy.

So even the radical challenge of writers such as Tom Paine and Mary Wollstonecraft is irrelevant for us. Blake doubtless shared their thoughts; but he alone never compromised. Tom Paine, having demonstrated from the Bible that "all men are born equal", could still approve of "natural subordination", and go on to consider the poor to be "dissolute", and "bred up in the world without morals". It was a conclusion very close to the hearts of the founders of the Philanthropic Society, instituted in 1788 on an old-fangled notion of charity, anathema to Blake: "for the prevention of Crimes, and the Reform of the Criminal Poor", without reference to general cause and particular effect.

13. Blake's reaction in the Lambeth Books to political themes during the 1790s is covered substantially by other writers. Among them, David Erdman's *Blake: Prophet Against Empire* is comprehensive. Gwyn A. Williams's *Artisans and Sans-Culottes* (London: Libris, 1989, 1st edn. 1968), and Albert Goodwin's *The Friends of Liberty* fill in the background effectively. David Erdman's *Commerce des Lumières: John Oswald and the British in Paris, 1790–1793* (Columbia: University of Missouri Press, 1986) is full of local detail, and the interchapters summarise the early years neatly.

Mary Wollstonecraft, in her turn, italicised her approval of "the little indirect advice that is scattered through Sandford and Merton", not for the delectation of *ladies*, but for the guidance of *women*, at whom she aimed her book. As she put it in her Introduction,

addressing my sex in a firmer tone, I pay particular attention to those in the middle class, because they appear to be in the most natural state. Perhaps the seeds of false refinement, immorality and vanity, have ever been shed by the great.[14]

But disconcertingly these seeds are shed in *Experience*, by "those of the middle class . . . in the most natural state".

This being so, *Songs of Experience* responds to the meanness of social pretentions, and from there to the invasive social and personal animosities visited on the poor and the dispossessed, as a frightened hierarchy watched the blood-letting of chaos in France. But the malaise predated, and went deeper than, evils generated by political dread, as Blake could see in the collapse of neighbourhood care before 1789; and he could see that his own parish once more simply and tragically epitomised all London.

This being so, it seems that in the illustrations he was putting to *Songs of Innocence* at this time Blake was recording quite objectively the common kindness of nurture, which, however transiently, had brought deliverance to Westminster children as familiar and actual as the circumstances of Experience closing around him. Any promising venture into children's literature from his early days in the print shop with James Parker was long superseded. He was illustrating a moral awakening he had known, the "State of the Human Soul" called Innocence, which had transformed a local reality: a substantial record against which to match *Experience*.

With *Songs of Innocence* published, Blake reacted to a neurosis of alienation that became endemic in the early 1790s in a way which was always specifically generalised, never class-contrived, never egocentric. It was to be 1796 before it belatedly occurred to Pitt that, since historic "experience had already shown how much could be done by the industry of children", Parliament should consider "the extension of schools of industry", in line with precedents a century old. Maybe; but the temper of the times had changed utterly, as Pitt must have noticed, had someone put in front of him the ebullient lines John Dyer wrote back in 1757. With mid-century assurance, they celebrated the gaiety "in the mind employed . . . on swiftly circling engines", round which the children at their task "Warble together, as a choir of larks". It was with none of the old poet's gladness of heart that Pitt now put the same question: why not more?

14. Paine, *Rights of Man*, pp. 66, 218, and 246. Wollstonecraft, *Vindication of the Rights of Woman*, p. 81. The book has the revealing, but mostly ignored, sub-title: *With Strictures on Political and Moral Subjects*, a nod towards the expectations of the age that Blake never quite managed.

Houses of labour, seats of kind constraint,
For those who now delight in fruitless sports,
More than in cheerful works of virtuous trade,
Which honest wealth would yield, and portion due
Of public welfare? Ho, ye poor, who seek,
Among the dwellings of the diligent,
For sustenance unearned; who stroll abroad
From house to house, with mischievous intent,
Feigning misfortune: Ho, ye lame, ye blind;
Ye languid limbs, with real want oppressed,
Who tread the rough highways, and mountains wild,
Through storms, and rains, and bitterness of heart;
Ye children of affliction, be compelled
To happiness: the long wished daylight dawns,
When charitable rigour shall detain
Your step-bruised feet. Even now the sons of trade,
Where'er the cultivated hamlets smile,
Erect the mansion:* here soft fleeces shine;
The card awaits you, and the comb, and wheel;
Here shroud you from the thunder of the storm;
No rain shall wet your pillow: here abounds
Pure beverage; here your viands are prepared;
To heal each sickness the physician waits,
And priest entreats to give your Maker praise.
. . . . Nor less they gain
Virtue than wealth, while, on their useful works
From day to day intent, in their full minds
Evil no place can find.

[*Dyer's footnote: Erect the mansion: this alludes to the workhouses at Bristol, Birmingham, &c.]

Little of old Dyer's yo-ho, running uplift was still around when the Home Office in the 1790s hit upon industrial conscription for potentially disruptive commoners; but the last nine words of the poem resounded still.[15]

No Act was passed at Pitt's behest in 1796; but then, no Act was needed. Four years earlier the irrepressible Sarah Trimmer had already taken in hand the matter of keeping the poor in their place. As she explained,

Day schools of industry have as yet made little progress among us; but from the happy success of an experiment at this time making in one of the most populous parishes in London, we may reasonably hope to see in the course of a few years

15. *The Fleece*, III, lines 234–58, 272–75.

Parochial Schools of Industry

set up everywhere. The "happy success" was the school established eighteen months earlier in St Marylebone, where "the boys put heads upon pins, and close shoes and boots for exportation. The girls spin wool for blanket manufacture", occupations, Mrs Trimmer adds, for which there was "no time to be found in charity schools". In John Mossop's day, there had been no time for Mr Becknel's looms, or for boys to "put heads on pins", in the "happy success" of the King Street school.[16]

It is difficult to exaggerate the measures of oppression laid upon people as the revolution in France bred mounting trepidation among the priviledged. As we have seen, in "the years of toleration" the Sunday School Society had been founded, on such "liberal and catholic principles" by Hannah More and her friends, that it had the encouragement of radical people like Joseph Priestley. Yet within a decade "the psychological atrocities committed upon children" in these same Sunday Schools were extreme, to breed them to an unfaltering respect for authority, in "patience and submission to poverty".[17] And Hannah More, besides taking her own initiative in required constraint, was commissioned by the Home Office to counter the threat of Tom Paine.

It was in 1790 that Joseph Johnson thought twice about publishing Blake's first political long poem, *The French Revolution*, and Tom Paine's *The Rights of Man*. Blake's poem remained in manuscript. The first part of Paine's book, out in March the next year, sold fifty thousand copies in weeks, even with its price at three shillings, and ran into three editions in a fortnight. Despite an attempt by Pitt to bribe the publisher into withdrawal, the second part of the "most masterly book" was as widely distributed as the first, both through the political clubs. A cheap edition ran into hundreds of thousands. To the consternation of the authorities, *The Rights of Man* bit deeply "into British reality", penetrating "every hidden corner of society".

But even the free distribution of this socially worrisome book did not match the circulation of Hannah More's *Village Politics*, put abroad in a panic by the Post Office to counter the spread of subversive and dangerous expectations. Since 1789, Hannah More had restricted access to the Bible, in case its knowledge "should lay men open to the delusions of fanaticism on the one hand, or of Jacobinism on the other". She also reassured the Bishop of Bath and Wells that, from that date, she had required the Sunday schools she inspected "to train up the lower classes in habits of industry and piety", and to confine Christian encouragement for "the little ones" to the repetition of "Watts' Hymns". With emphasis, she added: "I allow of no writing for the poor".[18]

16. See Gardner, *Retraced*, chapter 8, for these oppressive measures.
17. Williams, *Artisans*, p. 67.
18. Goodwin, *Friends of Liberty*, pp. 264–5. Gardner, *Retraced*, p. 92.

Clearly Blake went along intellectually with the radical measures
which engaged Tom Paine and the Corresponding Societies. But it is
the familiar, insidious neurosis of intimidation—official, class and clerical—that breeds and characterises the state "of the Human Soul",
"contrary" to *Innocence*. It was a suppression invariably delivered with a
conniving sleight of hand. Lifelong it appalled Blake's imagination, and
against it for him intellectual adjustments were out of the question.

By 1792 the Government had begun to buy up the London press, and
bribe the provincial papers. Mail was intercepted. Soon the Home
Office was infiltrating its spies into the radical clubs; but even closer to
home, through an undertaking we see reflected directly in 'The Little
Vagabond' in *Experience*, suspicion and mistrust were instilled into
neighbourly relationships. Blake knew that "respectable" Government
informers were planted around his familiar streets. House-to-house
visits were made in the contingent parishes of St Anne and St James to
check on occupiers and servants. Neighbours were required to report
Masters who neglected to enforce declarations of loyalty from journeymen and apprentices. Innkeepers who failed to name "suspected
persons" lost their licences. The Home Office was nervously and effectively generating the enmities of *Experience*.

By February 1793, England was at war, and Blake watched the Hessian
mercenaries settle into unwelcoming billets. As he worked through his
poems of Experience with copper and acid and colours, the air was
loaded with the intimacies of the oppression he was immortally illuminating. The next year, the middle of three seasons of crop failure and
famine, Pitt talked his Committee of Secrecy into suspending Habeas
Corpus, and the first Treason Trials were set up.

It was the year Blake issued *Songs of Experience*, and in them reported
not only on the the misery and tyranny of the decade, but also on the
delicate and introspective nannying which prepared the children of
privilege, as impeccable directors of sexual, social and spiritual manipulation.

It was some years since Blake had moved his belongings over Westminster Bridge, and settled in Lambeth.

Experience Invasive

By leaving Poland Street for Lambeth early in 1791, Blake had escaped the peril of the fire of the century. Across the street from his old home, in the small hours of Saturday 14 January 1792, the Pantheon went up in flames. This "finest of modern temples with its scaglioli columns" was engulfed. The chandeliers gyrated to the floor, and the vast curtains of damask caught fire, and blew around like flags in triumph. If Blake was roused from his bed in Lambeth, the sight across the river was worth a cold night's walk on to Westminster Bridge, especially if he timed it as the pillar of smoke and flame exploded through the domed roof.

Blake's lifelong preoccupation with fire is understandable. Conflagrations regularly diverted Londoners. The old King's Theatre in the Haymarket, five minutes from Golden Square, had been gutted at dusk on 17 June 1789, weeks before the Bastille was fired. So the name was available for reissue. James Wyatt, the architect, was at the time converting the Pantheon into an opera house, and acquired the redundant royal title. So the Pantheon in flames was another prophetic royal fire. When this new King's Theatre was ablaze, seeing the glow in the sky, Wyatt stopped his post chaise on Salisbury Plain. He first thought that all London was burning.

At the back of the Pantheon, the fire terrified the wild beasts which Joshua Brookes, the anatomist, kept caged in his garden. Roused to sympathy for the animals panic stricken among "large masses of the Rock of Gibraltar", the crowd enjoying the excitement turned into a mob. They threatened to pull up the railings, until the state and strength of the animals bred second thoughts, and instead they moved to ransack the anatomist's house. Among the buildings nearby, Blake's recent home was no further away than Joshuah Brooke's 'Rock of Gibraltar', within licking distance of the flames.

Before he left the stimulating neighbourhood of the Pantheon, Blake had included in *Songs of Innocence* two poems, 'The Little Girl Lost' and 'The Little Girl Found', together with their three illustrations; simply, it seems, because they were too good to leave out, since they were later conclusively transferred to *Experience*.

The lines have their origin in a commonplace fiction—the dominance of chastity over beasts of prey. Swift had told, in the fifth issue of *The Tatler*, how his maid servant left her story book by his bed "full of strange impertinences, fitted to her taste and condition . . . among other things . . . this sage observation: That a lion would never hurt a true virgin". As Blake knew, Milton made use of the same "sage observation" in *Comus*. Starting from this initial "strange impertinence", Blake takes the reader, in words and pictures, through a landscape of trepidation, to a conclusion settled in the submission of virginity to royalty, and seclusion under the protection of a spiritual predator. 'Lovely Lyca' and her parents, deceived and baffled by regal condescension, finish in isolation typical of Experience. And we have reached this state of Experience by way of so many concepts alien to Innocence, that they defy listing; among them, virginity, fear, awe, separation, loss, power, fantasy—and the garden.

Set first in *Innocence*, these plates present a disturbing, ambivalent consequence to errors of Experience. We see the way Blake's mind was moving, already in 1789, both in style and concept. It is easy to see why the move of 'The Little Girl' plates to *Songs of Experience* was permanent, especially after Blake's time with a garden to tend, among the neighbouring but excluding gardens of Lambeth.

Among all the drudgery, 'Social Love' and diversions of Lambeth's Vale, it is these little gardens which move most unexpectedly into *Experience*. The withdrawal from the responsive neighbourliness of Innocence into a contingent privacy leads in *Experience* to an invasive sense of suspicion, and murderous consequences. In the exclusive gardens of Lambeth, Blake sensed a counter symbol to the communal greens of Innocence.

Number 13 Hercules Buildings, Lambeth, was a comfortable two storey house with a garden front and back. The Blakes lived there, at least from the summer of 1791, until they moved to Felpham on the South Coast in September 1800. The first three years in Lambeth redirected Blake's thinking on the follow-up to *Songs of Innocence*, and from here he launched his attack on the broader conspiracies of place and power, which perpetuated oppression and conflict. The denunciation came not only most tragically in *Songs of Experience* and the verses crammed into his Notebook, but also in *The Marriage of Heaven and Hell*, and the Shorter Prophetic Books, known as the Lambeth Books. The themes of these shorter epics, particularly *Visions of the Daughters of Albion, America* (1793), *Europe* and, above all, *Urizen* (1794), are in many ways an extension, both of the tyrannies and of the more intimate alienations, which generate in the nurseries and gardens of Experience.[1]

When Blake moved to Lambeth, the Surrey Hills and the villages around, which he had known since boyhood, were still rural. Clapham, Peckham, Dulwich, Camberwell and Brixton would catch the builders'

1. The nurseries and gardens are discussed in Gardner, *Retraced*, pp. 125–33, chapter 13, pp. 149–52 and *passim*.

eyes in the next century, and only the thousand acres of Wimbledon Common would survive to the present day as "the wildest, most beautiful and most invigorating open space near the metropolis". But, even in the Kent and Surrey countryside unclaimed by speculators, the spirit of Experience survived in the tolls, enforced on average along every two miles of mud track. "To the complaint and jest of foreigners", turnpikes punctuated the hundred miles of roads south of the Thames, well into the 1870s. Despite the coins paid to turnpike keepers, the roads still "constituted an intolerable grievance". It was simply that respect for tax gathering and sinecure, however extortionate and troublesome, was rooted deep.

Lambeth itself, convenient to Westminster Bridge, had long been a place of commercialised charity, tough factories and seedy pleasure. The land downstream from the bridge, between the river and the marsh, was lined with a half mile of timber yards, Lambeth Waterworks, barge makers and a patent shot manufactory. Across and around the marsh, on twenty-nine acres leased from the Prince Regent, were dye-houses, storehouses, cranes, brewhouses, stables, Mr Beaufoy's vinegar manufactory, and among the ponds and water courses across the marsh, seventy dwelling houses. Sentinel over all, the new shot-tower was dropping into wartime production as Blake pulled together *Songs of Experience*.

For ten years after 1779, the London Botanic Garden had brought some relief to Lambeth Vale. William Curtis had established his garden between Green Lane (now Cornwall Road) and Broadwall. "The situation", it was said, "being low, renders it peculiarly favourable to the growth of aquatic and bog plants".[2] By the time Blake moved into Hercules Buildings, however, all that was left was an insignificant nursery. Two years earlier Curtis had given up fighting the elements, and moved his garden out to Brompton, complaining of

the smoke of London, which, except when the wind blew from the South, constantly enveloped my plants ... the obscurity of the situation, the badness of the roads leading to it, with the effluvia of surrounding ditches being at times highly offensive.

During Blake's time in the Vale of Lambeth, some roads perforce were strengthened to serve new industry. Sections of the Narrow Wall through the timber yards east along the river became Belvedere Road, where Messrs Phelps & Co established a large soap and candle manufactory. It was demolished in 1826, having failed "for want of a sufficiently extensive connection"; and in competition were Messrs Hawes & Co, trundling out sixty tons of tallow and soap a week from the site of the Old Barge House, now Barge House Street, near Blackfriars Bridge.[3]

2. *Survey of London* (London County Council, 1930), XXIII, pp. 16–17. The *Survey* gives much information on London and Lambeth.

3. *Surrey County History* (1967), vol. 2, p. 404.

This candle making may have been an extension of a less respectable Lambeth initiative. The local press reported that

a society of persons did exist at Lambeth in the year 1793, who made a trade of digging up the bodies of the dead: they made candles of the fat, extracted volatile alkali from the bones, and sold the flesh for dogs' meat.[4]

If Blake knew this as fact, he would hardly raise an eyebrow, familiar as he was since childhood with the burial ground in Pawlett's Garden. Similar atrocities there were not often worth press report, but regularly made the parish records.

Good works and self indulgence made the west side of Westminster Bridge Road, approaching Lambeth Palace, ostensibly more desirable than down-stream. Just round the corner from Hercules Buildings, "near the second turnpike on the Surrey side of Westminster Bridge", a group of "noblemen and gentlemen" had converted the old Hercules Inn into the Female Orphan Asylum, to save girls between the age of nine and twelve from "the guilt of prostitution".

The age range was deadly accurate. The alternative to the Asylum was an informal apprenticeship "thro' each charter'd street" in London, as fatal as chimney sweeping was for their brothers; but far more competitive, and more intimately brutal. As *The Observer* reported, many a west country gentleman was surprised "at the flocks of chicken prostitutes which he observed before Somerset House, and which he actually mistook for the pupils of some large boarding-school". And few of these desperate and tragic children survived into their twenties to join the sophisticates in The Dog and Duck.

Complementary to the Asylum, the Philanthropic Society had built sixteen almshouses, complete with the customary chapel and workshop, all "surrounded by a very high wall", within which "the criminal poor" should become "honest and useful members of the community".

Blake saw the philanthropy one way, and crammed the reaction into his Notebook:

There souls of men are bought & sold
And milk fed infancy for gold
And youth to slaughter houses led
And beauty for a bit of bread.

Nonetheless for concerned philanthropists these institutions fulfilled "Social Virtue's liberal plan": to rescue the poor "from Vice's horrid train", and to apprentice their children as "bulwarks of our wealth and

4. *The Cabinet*, Norwich (1795), quoted in Erdman, *Prophet*, p. 288, n. 17.

trade". And though some "liberals" (among them, interestingly, even Anna Barbauld) expressed misgivings at "the design of making religion an engine of government", few indeed could bring themselves to buy Blake's unqualified indignation. While attempting the impossible rescue, they all, including Mrs Barbauld, respected their dying century with the old advice to the poor: "Bear, bear thy wrongs–fulfil thy destined hour", and in the end

> *Prepare to meet a Father undismayed,*
> *Nor fear the God whom priests and Kings have made.*[5]

Neither injunction, we find, would satisfy Blake's little vagabond.

Around the crossroads at the end of Hercules Road, conveniently sited at that second turnpike from Westminster Bridge, and refreshingly adjacent for visitors leaving the Female Orphan Asylum, by this time taken under the ubiquitous Royal title, were three places of pleasure: the Temple of Flora, the Flora Tea Gardens and Crispus Claggett's moated Apollo Gardens. Less pretentiously disreputable than Vauxhall, but profitable enough, the last two matched the aspirations of Miss Gittipin or Elizabeth Pinner, rather than Maria Cosway and her circle. The Temple of Flora here, and the Dog and Duck, where the tracks across St George's Fields met the Lambeth Road, were for more hardened souls, "certainly the most dreadful places in or about the metropolis . . . the resorts of women, not only of the lower species of prostitution, but even of the middle classes"—ladies of class beyond even Mary Wollstonecraft's recall. Hanging about the Dog and Duck as a boy in the 1780s to see the highwaymen collect their horses, Francis Place had watched these "flashy women come out to take leave of the thieves at dusk and wish them success".[6]

Philip Astley, the 'Riding Master for the Royal Grove and Amphitheatre', celebrated for exploiting Jacko, the intellectual monkey Blake knew so well, ran the Royal Saloon on "a large piece of ground of a timber merchant, near Westminster Bridge, on the Surrey side".

The seal of royalty seemed to attract combustion. Almost as Blake arrived in Lambeth, Astley's amphitheatre collapsed into his Royal Grove in yet another fire of inperial grandeur. Astley, however, stayed on as a neighbour in Hercules Hall, on a triangle of ground at the back of Blake's garden while his associate, Crispus Claggett, acquired the contract to rebuild the burnt out Pantheon in 1794. He prefabricated the timbers for the roof in the field alongside his moat, and carted them over Westminster Bridge to Poland Street. He disappeared in 1796. His bones came to light forty years later, still in the Royal Theatre, when

5. *The Observer*, 11 December 1791, and see Anne Penny and Anna Barbauld in Roger Lonsdale, ed., *Eighteenth Century Women Poets*, (Oxford: Oxford University Press, 1989), nos. 192, 200. The book gives a refreshing new lead into the century.

6. George, *London Life*, p. 296.

they lifted the stage that someone no doubt long dead had nailed down.

A mile to the east, the Rector at Newington Butts lived even more defensively than Crispus Clagget, opposite the butts and alongside the Fishmongers' Almshouses, at the turning into the road to Camberwell. The Parsonage House, on the edge of St George's Fields and within pistol shot of the Dog and Duck, was "a very ancient wooden building, surrounded by a moat, over which were four bridges".

Withdrawn among "rotten wood", behind his defensive ditch and bridges, within earshot of the ground where killings were anciently practised, adjacent to the hospital, yet handy for the archbishop's palace, the Rector typified a "parochial minister" of "the God whom priests and Kings have made". It was while he lived in Lambeth, that Blake named the deity Urizen.

Expedient, profitable, and sanctioned under Urizen by the Rector of St Mary's, from his parish church alongside Lambeth Palace, was the undertaking to build a chapel on a green near Vauxhall. It was precisely the kind of 'experience' Blake reflects upon in 'The Garden of Love'.

To protect the status of their New Bond Estate around the green, it was essential for the speculators to control access to the sacrament. Consequently, "on 9 January 1793, John and Sarah Bond, granted a lease for 99 years of land fronting South Lambeth Road, to certain inhabitants for the erection of a proprietary chapel." Money was raised by the issue of sixty shares at £50 each, every shareholder being entitled to four seats. Beyond this the congregation of six hundred paid rent to pray, and required the approval of the proprietors who shared profit and authority with the Rector. Against anyone else, as Blake put it, "the gates of this Chapel were shut". Such monopolies were commonplace, not only in Lambeth. The Bond consortium took this initiative six years after Mrs Sarah Trimmer had faced the disadvantages that arose from mustering the poor at the lich-gate, in a book with the infallible catch-penny title of *The Oeconomy of Charity*. Her concern was not the reclamation of souls, since the "lower classes" were already seen to have a redeeming advantage over their affluent neighbours, in the fulfilment of service and the release from temptation their station conveyed. Mrs Trimmer's purpose was supervisory.

She had pointed out that the poor, if they contemplated church, too often found the doors "shut against their entrance . . . where the pews are let for the emolument of private individuals (as is the case in many chapels)". Her solution was simple and in italics—separate and supervise: "How easy would the task of the parochial minister become, by having his flock divided . . . into *separate congregations*". So, in 1787, as Blake

had been addressing his mind to relief-etching the neighbourly togetherness of Innocence, Mrs Trimmer was advocating mustering the poor
under the divine authority of Urizen's church. It was a task that need
not even fall to the "parochial minister", she exclaims, but to "assistants,
acting in strict conformity to the doctrines of the Church, and subject
to his immediate inspection!" This solution of separate altars, strictly in
the spirit of Experience, would end "the great estrangement which has
taken place between the lower orders [and] the parochial clergy".[7] But it
seems even Mrs Trimmer's proposed reorganisation of the poor lacked
"the oeconomy of charity". It was ignored.

A decent way from Lambeth Palace, nearer to the South Lambeth
Chapel, the long walks of Vauxhall Gardens, more pretentiously disreputable than the temples round the second turnpike, were the settings
for assignations both as common as Milk Lane, and as elegant as
Piccadilly. Among ionic columns, transparencies, fountains, statues and
in company with "Britannia, holding in her hand a medallion of his
present Majesty, and sitting on the right hand of Neptune in his chariot
drawn by sea horses", as Dr Johnson observed, nightingales were out-
numbered by prostitutes. They were also outsung in soprano by Elizabeth Billington, celebrated unprofessionally as "the Poland Street
man-trap" when she lived at number 54, across the road from Blake.

The landscape which nourished Blake's thinking in these years of
Experience extended across and beyond the Vale of Lambeth, into what
he called the Vale of Surrey. The weight of industry supported by indigent labour and the waters of the River Wandle, east of Wimbledon
Common, was formidable. "Mr Coleman's calico printing works" was
followed in the ten years after 1792 by some forty more industrial undertakings along this Surrey Vale, including no fewer than twelve more
"manufactories for the printing of calico", in competition with Mr
Coleman.

The Wandle fed three bleaching works, and from his favoured site
along these pastoral meadows, Mr Heath of Garratt Lane rolled out
twent-five thousand lengths of printed dress material a year.[8] Unsurprisingly Blake's initial working of his symbolism of the mill towards his
later epic poems coincides with this local industrial development. As
we shall see, the matrix of his symbol of the furnace, predominant in
his work towards and after 1800, is even more dramatically identifiable
along the Wandle in the 1790s.

In line with standard practice, Mr Heath's associate owner of the
stocking weaving mill in Lambeth itself employed some sixty or
seventy apprentices from the workhouses in the Surrey Vales. Discipline was exemplary:

7. See *Survey of London* (1956), XXVI,
p. 71, for the New Bond Estate,
and Gardner, *Retraced*, pp. 139–41,
where the chapel is illustrated. It
is now rebuilt as St Anne's
Church.

8. *Surrey County History*, pp. 376–7.
Garratt Lane still follows the
course of the Wandle.

*An apprentice at this establishment was brought by his friends to Bow Street to show
one of the modes of punishment adopted by the master . . . It consisted of an iron
collar, fastened round the neck with a padlock. The lad said he had worn it above a
month, and that he understood it was his master's intention that he should wear it
till he was out of his time.*[9]

Such severity was not simply managerial. It extended to the familiar relationships underlying *Experience*. We are reminded of Frederick Tatham's
well known report of Blake's fury at seeing, from his back window, the
boy in Philip Astley's garden, "hobbling along with a log to his foot such
an one as is put to a Horse or Ass to prevent their straying".[10]

Blake had long known the innumerable one room, domestic mills in
which the Spitalfields weavers hardly breathed, years before the trade
crisis of 1792–93 broke most of them into even deeper distress. Now the
oppression was industrialised, though not augmented, in "these dark
Satanic mills" between the gardens of Lambeth and the wild thyme on
Wimbledon Common. So the contours of the prophetic symbolism
shaping in Blake's mind were all around him. Mankind was turned
against mankind, "As cogs are formd in a wheel to turn the cogs of the
adverse wheel", exemplified in the apparently inexhaustible "labours at
the Mills which seem everything".[11]

But in *Songs of Experience* Blake traces the social attrition and manipulation far back from the mills on the River Wandle; back even to the
midwife's swaddling bands. The seed of Experience strikes root in the
turmoil and stress of that claustrophobic birth in 'Infant Sorrow', even
before the infant is cradled:

> *My mother groand! my father wept
> Into the dangerous world I leapt.*

Then, in a conclusive juxtaposition, Blake consigns the manipulative
binding of the infant, not to the unmentioned midwife, but to the father.
This improbable *accoucheur* fights for control of the child, the swaddling
anticipating the "stern commands" of the Omnipotent Father, Urizen.

So the initial rebellion of this child of affluence is against his "fathers
hands", as they bind his limbs into historic shape, and his head into
proper thinking, in ten feet of tight bandages. This 'contrary' to the
gracious redemption of the foundling in 'Infant Joy' could not be more
intimidating. And again at a nativity Blake derives his spiritual and
social analogies from a place and practice he familiarly knows.

It was as long ago as the August issue of 1748, that *The London Magazine*
had printed

9. *The Times*, August, 1795, quoted
in George, *London Life*, p. 380.
10. Bentley, *Blake Records*, p. 521.
11. See Gardner, *Retraced*, pp.
91–98, 140–46, 153–57 and index;
Gardner, *Blake*, pp. 41–61; and
Milton, plates 4 and 27.

Figure 7. The image of the swaddled child was familiar through the centuries from the Innocenti of Andrea della Robbia outside the Foundling Hospital in Florence. Blake turned it to devastating effect, and it survives as the bands fall away in the headquarters of The Children's Society. *Photograph by Mary R . Gardner.*

[the] substance of an essay upon the nursing and management of children, from birth to three years of age, in a letter from a physician to a governor of the foundling-hospital. Published by direction of their general committee.

Mothers and nurses were recommended to abandon

the superstitious whims and customs transmitted to them by their great grandmothers . . . no swathes or bandages either for the head or body . . . children should be kept clean and sweet, tumbled and toss'd about a good deal . . . play with it and keep it in a good humour.[12]

The old writer of this advice, presaging Innocence, was clearly Dr William Cadogan. Having put his revolutionary views into a book which went into twenty reprints in ten years, he became physician to the Foundling Hospital in 1754, and at once sent out printed notices to his nurses in the country forbidding swaddling, insisting on loose coverings and prescribing good diet. Paradoxically it was the Foundling Hospital, and the nurses at Wimbledon from St James's parish, who were ahead of their time and most middle ranking parents in child care.

12. The whole article is remarkably before its time in the quality of the advice on dress, care and nutrition.

During Blake's working years, it was Dr William Buchan who followed up and extended Cadogan's initiative. Twenty one years after the Governors of the Foundling Hospital had engaged *The London Magazine* to publicise the new approach, Buchan brought out the first ever book on *Domestic Medicine*, which was thumbed to destruction in countless reprints. In his first edition, Buchan could already report that Cadogan's common sense had been effective, and that "the practice of rolling children with so many bandages is in some measure set aside". At the same time, "in many parts of Britain to this day, a roller, eight or ten feet in length, is applied tightly round the child's body as soon as it is born". By 1784 visitors from abroad worried that English children "are not swaddled", and the next year *The Ladies Magazine* wrote that there were few gentlewomen who would know how to swaddle a child. Clearly Cadogan's message had reached the nurseries of gentlefolk, where the midwife or nanny could do the tugging.

So Blake had it both ways when he used the image of swaddling to such fearsome effect. Buchan writes, as it were, an authoritative footnote to the poem, when he explains that the purpose of the nannying in "bracing and dressing an infant . . . as soon as it came into the world" is to "mend the shape" of the child, an effort always "seconded by the vanity of the parents". It was a "mending", we notice, that Blake knew extended to the head. Experience was as old as swaddling.

Buchan takes the "footnote" further in the 1786 edition of *Domestic Medicine*. He reports there that he had "known a child seized with convulsion-fits soon after the midwife had done swaddling it [and] loaded with too many clothes . . . laid in bed with the mother", both mother and child in a fever. As we read it in *Experience*:

> *Bound and weary I thought best*
> *To sulk upon my mothers breast.*[13]

Buchan's advice and observations are not only to the point Blake was making here. He also, as it were, authorises the "contraries", 'Infant Joy' and 'Cradle Song', in *Innocence*. "England", the doctor wrote, "would hardly know such a thing as a deformed child", should parents stop "manacling their children", adding "nature knows no use of clothes to an infant but to keep it warm". It is as if Blake illustrates Buchan's observation in 'Cradle Song' in *Innocence*.

The manipulation of the child until thought and conduct "have been cramped and twisted and swaddled into deformity" in old and begrudged bandages is the initial act of Experience. The sophistication in the nurseries where the doctor's book could be well afforded, the

13. *Domestic Medicine* (1786 ed.), pp. 10–17. See also Gardner, *Retraced*, pp. 125–28.

suspicious self-regard in the gardens, social antipathy and even murder—all derive from this initial claustrophobic discipline. It is the birthright of Experience. Its contrary in Innocence was 'Infant Joy', far more than in name only.

In 'Infant Joy' Blake recalled the lavishing of Christian care on a foundling, and a girl at that. Accountably, "not two days old", she should have been left to fend for herself by chance, or to relieve the rates by dying. Her rescue is the essential gesture of Innocence. From this principle of salvation follows all the organisation of Innocence, the secure and correct cradling, the selfless calm, "sweet instruction", the social cohesion and finally the acclamation in 'Laughing Song'.

The realisation that in 'Infant Joy' we have a symbolic question and answer, not between a natural mother and her child but between a nurse and a foundling, is established by the first question, "What shall I call thee?" The words would hardly come convincingly from a mother, after long months of contemplation, and two days after a birth; but the spontaneous question rings true on the lips of a nurse, at the rescue of a

Figure 8. The Foundlings, engraved by Mills (1798) after Hogarth's design (1739). Blake was aware that everyone knew Hogarth's design, reissued season after season from 1740 by The Foundling Hospital, "as a headpiece...for collecting subscriptions". Blake's appalled reflection of the "dropped child" draws the eye again in 'Holy Thursday' in *Experience. Reprinted with permission of The Master, Fellows and Scholars of Christ's College, Cambridge, to reproduce their copy in The Fitzwilliam Museum.*

"dropped child", such as shocks the passing lady in 'Holy Thursday' in *Experience*. The recognition resonates through the text.

'Infant Joy' is not simply a sweet thought. It is the uncompromising statement necessary to outface its "contrary". The infant's deprivation and salvation are measured in the voiceless question and answer, echoing the initial greetings. The child is christened with her identity, startling in destitution, since girls in the century, of any social class, were rarely, if ever, named Joy. The name arises here, as it commonly did for foundlings like Tom Dacre, from circumstance. The circumstance of the infant named Joy, however, is not an institution, but caritas realised. She has escaped both death and "the incarceration of the swaddle" of the soul.

The continuity of care in *Innocence*, always outgoing, whether individual or communal, has its contrary in the introspective sequence of nannying in *Experience*, beginning with 'Infant Sorrow', where the illustration becomes an extrapolation of the text. It is a technique we find everywhere in the *Songs*. So, in 'Infant Sorrow', the illustration transfers the conflict from the "fathers hands" to the nanny, and adds muscular years to her charge. Her struggle is on.

In the design to 'The Fly' she attends the first steps of a toddler, beneath the leafless tree, while at her back the indifferent sister plays aimless shuttlecock, with no-one to respond. In 'Nurses Song', she has shaken her hair free from her cap, and her solicitude for the boy takes on the gestures of a dance. The maturing youth acknowledges the approach by stepping away and crossing his arms, a gesture in both sensual play and self-inclusion. The youth is learning to appreciate "woman, lovely woman", submissive to the purposes of Urizen. The next steps are towards "dark secret love" in the garden of Experience. The sister knowingly reads her book. The book she is reading will conduct her, discreetly, indirectly, the same way.

"The inferior Classes", as we shall see, took what they could in the way of recreational reading from the Cheap Repository. Readers "in the middling stations of life" were fed in their youth on an encyclopedic diet of good breeding, educational and moral. As the century fell away in conflict and apprehension, countless writers of anonymous merit worked the rich vein of liberal culture, bringing profits for booksellers, and the distinction of class for the customers.

Books like *The Little Emigrant*, which appeared anonymously five years after *Songs of Experience*, and which justified its blurb claiming "no merit superior to the generality of works published for the amusement and moral instruction of youth", peddled an impressive curriculum of improvement in stock format. Mythology, "certainly a very dark and mysterious path", is explained on page 78. The venerable recreational reading from the classics is formidably reinforced with extracts from Voltaire, Rousseau, Montaigne, and Hume. Annette, *"une pauvre Orphe-line Francoise"*, converses instructively in French. The war with Napoleon, which confined the literate poor of England in the Cheap Repository, did nothing to diminish the fashionable respect for anything French. Annette, being French, though an orphan nonetheless recognises anything composed by "Purcell, Handel, Arne, and Corelli"; but she very properly "knew little of Clementi, Pleyel and other fashionable composers".

The wrecked and rescued orphan joins Louisa in the topical study of Geography, and in instructive country walks, frequently past cottagers, deserving either by their labour or ill-fortune. Artistic impressions of these expeditions are recorded in portfolios, and anything may lead into the genteel moulding of character. So Annette, found by the Curate to have touched up Louisa's indifferent effort, is caught in deception: "Ah, Annette, you have certainly shaded that tree, and the thatch of the cottage looked very different when I left it". Correction was rarely more severe for the young reader already born to right think-ing, who graduated to journals and newspapers, presenting intellectual refreshment diluted in ink.

There was *The Microscope of Fashion*; *The Witticisms, Jests, and Sayings of Dr Samuel Johnson*, "embellished with a Representation of Dr Johnson in high Glee at the Breakfast Table of Mrs Thrale"; *The Bonton Magazine*, "containing Anecdotes of the Amour between Royal Tar and Little Pickle"; *The New Universal Traveller*, "by a Gentleman of the University of Edinburgh"; *The Conjurer's Magazine*, including "Sympathetic Secrets in occult Philosophy"; and a couple of histories of France, alongside dance and song books by the dozen. And to carry into old age, the universal assurance of *The Companion* or *Little Library*:

> *Seek here, ye Young, the anchor of your mind;*
> *Here, suffering Age a blest provision find.*

Topping them off were the challenges of a "New and cheap Edition of Lavater's celebrated *Essays on Physiognomy*", and *The Philosophical and Liter-ary Register*, superintended "by several of the Literati of the Universities of Oxford, Cambridge, Edinburgh, Glasgow, Aberdeen, &c." The issue of *The Observer* which carried these notices on Sunday 4 December 1791, ran an editorial, balanced for its day, commending:

the modulation of truth, of justice, of indispensable subordination, of necessary obedience, and of equitable right ... and next in succession to those great universal attainments, is the colonial and domestic prosperity of the BRITISH EMPIRE.

It was a balance of "equitable right" that the government came less and less to share, as it doubted the general acceptance of "indispensable subordination" with mounting apprehension. While few among "the inferior classes" could afford the price of *The Observer*, and fewer still the magazines it advertised, many among them could now dangerously read. And publishers, as ever, were spicing the market.

So by 1787 Sarah Trimmer had already expressed concern that the under-class might set hands on "the wrong books". Her interminable tract called *The Servant's Friend* was written to wean "the literate poor" from the ballads they might purchase and pass round, and from novels they might pick up by the way. A year later she went further, with *The Family Magazine*, "to counteract the pernicious Tendency of immoral Books etc. which have circulated of late years among the inferior Classes of People".

In 1795, as fear received its official seal, the establishment reacted in line with these sentiments. John Marshall had made such a success of selling books free from "prejudicial Nonsense", that he was appointed, uncontested, as "Printer to the CHEAP REPOSITORY for Moral and Religious Tracts". The post guaranteed Marshall a fortune, the oligarchy of government peace of mind, and the poor a pittance of words. Just as the re-institution of the schools of industry was set to bring their bodies, minds and expectations into line, so the Cheap Repository was to confine their aspirations and imagination. Any stimulus to the imagination, in any book, was imprudent, wrote Hannah More.

It is a lion which though worldly prudence indeed may chain so as to prevent outward mischief, yet the malignity remains within; but when sanctified by Christianity, the imagination is a lion tamed; you have the benefit of its strength and its activity divested of its mischief.

The template for all the Cheap Repository tracts which debilitated the country after 1794 was Hannah More's over-sold answer to Tom Paine, as down-market as its contrived mis-spelling: "*Village Politics. Addressed To All The Mechanics, Journeymen And Day Labourers In Great Britain. By Will Chip, A Country Carpernter*". Tom Paine had remarked in a line reminiscent of Blake, but more cool, that all national institutions and churches were established "to terrify and enslave mankind, and monopolise power and profit". "To teach the poor to *read*, without providing them with safe books", Hannah More countered, "was a dangerous measure".[14]

14. Hannah More, *Strictures On The Modern System Of Female Education* (1799), pp. 237–38. Tom Paine, *The Age of Reason* (1794), pp. 2, 22, 27.

To provide the poor with "safe books", and to "monopolise power", William Pitt, many lords, the Archbishop of Canterbury, and a roll-call of bishops, financed the Cheap Repository. Marshall's initiative was simple and a model of commercial know-how. He fed the appetite of the newly literate poor for reading matter, by marketing it at a price they could barely afford. To do this, having censored out the native scurrility, he revived the fashion for chapbooks which refined taste had discarded twenty years earlier. Samples were generously made available to fairground stallholders, schools were circulated, and local agencies established. Embellished with dialogue, verse and woodcuts, with Marshall as entrepreneur and subsidies from the top in the land, the Cheap Repository distributed some two million tracts of moral exhortation and intimidation a year, not counting shipments to Ireland. The advertisement on the title pages ran:

Sold by J. Marshall,
(Printer to the Cheap Repository for Moral and Religious Tracts)
Great Allowance will be made for Shopkeepers and Hawkers.
Price one halfpenny, or 2s/3d per hundred, 1s/6d for 50, 9d for 25.
A Cheaper Edition for Hawkers.

So the cost to the hawkers was about a farthing a pamphlet.

Though it has merited hardly a footnote in history, the deprivation imposed through this tendentious undertaking was unique. The age-old crudity of conduct management through print intensified into the debilitation of a generation. It was tragic. These sales by the million recorded the success of the Cheap Repository in the years of suspicion and war. But, more effectively still, these sales by the million testified to the intellectual hunger of the poor who had mastered literacy. As Blake set *Songs of Experience* against its "contrary", since the poor could afford no better, they picked up the scraps dropped to them from the Home Office and the episcopacy, through the fingers of John Marshall. So constraining were the pamphlets of hell fire and submission, that even Mrs Anna Barbauld's improving best-sellers, even her *Early Lessons for Children*, failed to qualify for the Cheap Repository. They lacked cohesive recrimination. So intense was the fear that the French were at work undermining "the moral and religious advantages of society", that even Hannah More was accused of "evangelical sympathies" by the "virulent conservative faction of the church".

All circumstances must have conspired to make it plain to Blake that his *Songs* was hopelessly unmarketable. But circumstances also made the publication an irresistible challenge to his integrity. The most

pitiable victims, who are given a voice in Experience, existed beneath
the notice of the oligarchy; beneath Tilly Lally and Joe Bradley; beneath
the reach even of the Cheap Repository. Even "Will Chip, the Carpernter", had nothing cheap enough for the cripple and the street boy to
read in the light of the reverberators, for the families round the fires in
the brick-field across Oxford Street, or for the mother who has laid
down one child to die on the grass, and hopes not to discard a second.[15]

Perhaps it is these people, before all others, who moved Blake to
work so hard on getting the text of 'The Tyger' right. He covered invaluable space in his Notebook with two drafts and repeated crossings out
before he settled on the incomparable fair copy. It was a commitment
to which he must have returned repeatedly, while, at the same time, he
was writing the Lambeth Books, in which the symbolism concentrated
in 'The Tyger' is extended.

Issues of freedom, political and personal, and the struggle against
"the starry hosts" of tyranny, in history and pre-history, predominate in
these books; and primevally in *The Book of Urizen*. Here, initiating a bitter
summary of oppression, we read back into Urizen's act of "creation",
which broke the flowing order of eternity into chaos; but a chaos of
deprivation and isolation.

> *Times on times he divided & measur'd*
> *Space by space in his ninefold darkness.*

until mankind is forged in

> *Forgetfulness, dumbness, necessity!*
> *In chains of the mind locked up,*
> *Like fetters of ice shrinking together*

and condemned to perpetual separation, brother from brother;

> *And their eyes could not discern,*
> *Their brethren from other cities.*[16]

Blake's second name for Urizen points back to the god's genesis in
Newton's incredulous temerity about gravity. He himself felt bound to
give a name to the creator and manager of his wheeling universe. Blake
took it over bluntly: "Newton's Pantocrator" is Urizen, a pseudo divinity
fathered by expedient doctrine on magazine science. We can watch the
mastodon gestate through decades into Blake's lifetime.

In 1684 Newton had completed his calculations. One year later,

15. See illustrations to 'London', 'A
Little Boy Lost', 'The Little
Vagabond' and 'Holy Thursday'
in *Experience*.
16. *Urizen*, plates 1, 10, 28.

Robert Boyle was already adding authority to the "Cosmical Mechanism, that is a Comprisal of all the Mechanical Affections (Figure, Size, Motion, & c) that belong to the matter of the great System of the Universe". The Pantocrator received royal approval from Queen Anne, and by 1712 Sir Richard Blackmore, her physician and enthusiastic epic poet, had formalised the thinking of his century, to the commendation of his coarse queen and of the literary establishment, when his rhetorical questions declared how the projenitor of Urizen mechanised infinity:

> *Did this your Wise and Sovereign Architect*
> *Design the Model and the World erect?*
> *Were by his Skill the deep Foundations laid,*
> *The Globes suspended and the Heav'ns display'd?*
> *By what Elastic Engines did he reer*
> *The starry Roof, and roll the Orbs in Air?*[17]

Centuries back, there had been a "divine Architect", who was now usurped. With equally sovereign authority, if fallibly to Georgian minds, he had then required "commonwealths" to be created, "wherein the governors seeke the publike profite of the citizens, and the benefite of the whole civill societie", to the exclusion of any "corrupt common-wealth which seeketh onely the increase of private commoditie, having no care for publike profit".[18]

As Blake grew up, the "exclusion" was erased, as the Pantoctrator was proclaimed by politicians, philosophers and poets. And the deity was sold down to generations of children, having almost become John Newbery's "private commoditie". Here, and in every pulpit, it was a comfortable step from "God", the Pantocrator, "the builder of the universe" to his "ruling the universe he built", and from there to the uncompromising social gradation, buttressing "private commoditie" and its imperial merchants, who receive "the clearest sense of Deity", "weighing out, and dispensing the fates of men".

So the dispensations of the "political church", which Tom Paine later reviled, was fashioned down the century on the laws of the Pantocrator, "Prince of the Starry Hosts/And of the Wheels of Heaven," which became "a mighty circle turning; God a tyrant crown'd".[19]

By 1790, the Pantocrator had aged into Urizen—"so his eternal name". And, consequent upon his initial act of Satanic creation, during "Ages on ages he lay clos'd, unknown,/Brooding, shut in the deep," in "the forests of affliction", "compassed round/And high roofed over with trees." Under "the iron law", "barr'd and petrify'd against the infinite", "that which pitieth" becomes "a devouring flame", and mankind's only

17. For the Boyle quotation, see *OED*, 'mechanic', 1a. Sir Richard Blackmore, *Creation. A Philosophical Poem* (1712), IV, ll. 110–15. For commendation by Addison, Dennis, Ambrose Philips, "Mr Draper, an eminent bookseller" among others, and Johnson himself, see Blackmore in *Johnson's Lives*.

Blake displays the influence of the Pantocrator in *Milton*, plate 4, where his powerful symbol of the mill (famously, "these dark Satanic Mills") exemplifies the firmament of oppression. Satan, "The Prince of the Starry Hosts / And of the Wheels of Heaven" turns his "Mills day & night". Satan is "Newtons Pantocrator weaving the Woof of Locke / To Mortals thy Mills seem Everything".

18. Pierre de La Primaudaye, *The French Academy*, tr. T. Bowes (1586), quoted in James Winny, ed., *The Frame of Order* (London: Allen & Unwin, 1957), p. 109. For 'the Architect's understanding' see also p. 207.

19. Augustus Toplady, *Sermons and Essays* (1819 ed.), pp. 101, 103. The sermons were preached in the 1770s. Paine, *Rights of Man*, p. 42.

consolation is concealment under Urizen, in his "forests of dark soli-tude"; "the forests of the night".[20]

From this, to 'The Tyger'.[21] The irresistible sequence of questions, implying so much more than they enquire, fetch the wings of divine aspiration down to a physical endeavour of direct and sinewy toil. The labour of the particular enforcement of a divine initiative is for Blake the only way to clear the ageless, "endless labyrinth of woe", "enrooting itself all around", in Urizen's "forests of affliction".[22]

The first draft of 'The Tyger' in the Notebook consists of five verses; that is, the finished poem less the fifth verse. Read as such, it is complete. To put it in banal terms: the Immortal seizes the fire of aspiration and revolt, still unquenched in Urizen's "forests of the night", and with labour directed by the imagination frames it into the symmetry of action.[23]

In this early five stanza form the poem anticipates, symbolically in brief, Blake's later and long exposition of the conflict and labour needed to build Jerusalem in the social wreckage along the Thames. Had the present incomparable fifth verse never been written, we could never have noticed its absence.

In 1787 John Rennie had built the Albion Flour Mill by the south end of Blackfriars Bridge, using cast iron for the machines instead of wood. By the time another spectacular fire destroyed it in 1792, Rennie had used his technique to set up the extensive iron foundry for Mr Henkell among the textile mills along the Wandle. Rennie's momentous cast iron brought heavy industry, categorised for war, to the Lambeth side of Wimbledon Common.

Of "Mr Henkell's iron mills", it was reported that:

here are cast shots, shells, cannon and other implements of war ... the splitting of iron bars of prodigious lengths, on a pair of shears which will cut asunder pieces of iron more than two inches in thickness, and in working of a hammer which weighs from five hundred and a half to six hundred pounds ... the wonderful power of all the elements are here made subservient ... in the name of war and peace.[24]

It can have been no smithy on a corner in Lambeth, with a boy's foot on the bellows, that generated in Blake's mind the cosmic foundry in which the tyger is forged. As the hammer beats on the anvil of infinity, the matrix is specified in the chain round the pulleys by the furnace:

> *What the hammer? what the chain,*
> *In what furnace was thy brain?*

This is the chain hauling breath from bellows to furnace, part of "the

20. *Milton*, plate 4, *Europe*, plate 10; *Urizen*, plates 3 and 10.

21. Tyger: simply a common variant spelling in the eighteenth century, best retained, since it identifies Blake's symbol against the living animal. For 'The Tyger', see Gardner, *Retraced*, pp. 149–58.

22. *Ahania* (1795), plate 4.

23. Art: Blake associated the word with labour, and would endorse the original sense of the word. See *OED*, 'art', 1: "skill in doing anything as the result of knowledge and practice". A component in the meaning has diminished in time. See Gardner, *Retraced*, index under 'Illustrative technique'.

24. *Surrey County History*, p. 414.

wonderful power of all the elements" harnessed by Mr Henkel on the Wandle, as Blake was working and reworking 'The Tyger' in his Notebook.

Above Blake's roof, Urizen, the Pantocrator, marshalled in celestial rank and order his army of stars, for the wars to which Mr Henkell made the elements "subservient". Blake had heard this "Lord of the armies of the sky" saluted in hymns since his boyhood. And at some immortal moment his mind clearly turned from "the armies of the sky" to "Wimbletons green & impurpled Hills"[25] beyond the Wandle, where his neighbours had recently cherished pity so conclusively, that it seemed Urizen's tyrannic regiments were routed. And, in tranquil release from the beat of the cosmic foundry, the transforming question asked itself:

> *When the stars threw down their spears*
> *And water'd heaven with their tears*
> *Did he smile his work to see*
> *Did he who made the Lamb make thee?*

In this incomparable after-thought, the laborious act of revolt is super-seded in a revelation of reconciliation briefly achieved, yet indelibly recorded in *Innocence*. The recollection and the questions recall the circumstance of social grace, when the Immortal, "who made the Lamb", went on to give it "softest clothing", and to bid it feed. When the birthright of a foundling "but two days old" was assured against all the odds, Christianity was truly realised in "the terrible desart of London", and the Saviour walked with destitution. Before the tyger's immortal sinews were tempered to conclusive insurrection, there had been another way: *cherish pity*.

The symbol of the cosmic furnace came to Blake as metal first ran liquid by the Wandle, and stayed with him as long as he was writing. Alongside this, to the end of his days he recalled the "ancient time" when the reality of Innocence drew "the Holy Lamb of God" to the "pleasant pastures" west of the river.

25. *Milton*, plate 42.

From Lark-Rise Across Tyburn River

For we contend not with the flesh and blood, but with dominion, with authority, with the rulers of darkness in this life, with spiritual malice from on high.[1]

From 1794, the year he linked *Songs of Experience* to *Innocence*, Blake's circumstance changed utterly with the times. In that year, Horne Tooke, with others faced trial for sedition, and were relieved to walk away. Tom Paine was jailed in Paris, an imprisonment that lasted nine years. Joseph Priestley escaped to America, where he died. In Westminster Lord Abingdon measured the times, and routed the Abolitionists with one parliamentary question: "What does abolition of the slave trade mean more or less in effect than liberty and equality?"

The aspirations which had fed Blake's earlier expectations were buried. For the next twenty years the country was at war, not simply in Europe, but in defence of an empire chartered to commerce. So, during five years at the start of the wars Whitehall laid out the collosal sum of £4 million, solely to regain San Domingo, and secure London's investment in the slave trade. Such profligate commitment to charters and conflict meant famine at home and relentless oppression.

In the earlier years, Blake's vision was fired by people around him, people he intimately knew. Into *Experience*, he seems to recognise the the perpetrators and their victims as neighbours. In later years, the intimacy of the *Songs* is dispersed in an intellectual cosmos fought over by figures of the mind, a mythology of shifting concepts, in an epic trilogy: *The Four Zoas*, never etched, *Milton* and *Jerusalem*.

Now it is places, symbolic, mythological or actual, not the influence of intimate society and experience, that generated his poetry: Felpham, the South Downs, Tyburn, Jerusalem, South Molton Street, the sea, the cave, the forest, Golgonooza—even that material world, Ulro. The list is endless. And to inhabit these locations of the mind, within his steady symbolism, Blake generalised his implacable sense of human desolation in a personal mythology of shifting concepts: Urizen, Orc, Vala—again, countless. It was a smoke-screen behind which he was safe with his truth. He had brushed against authority already. He was to come up against authority again, and the age was perilous. But the epic writing was still generated in an irreconcilable tragedy:

What is the price of Experience do men buy it for a song
Or wisdom for a dance in the street? No it is bought with the price

1. Preface to *The Four Zoas*.

Of all that a man hath his house his wife his children
Wisdom is sold in the desolate market where none come to buy
And in the witherd field where the farmer plows for bread in vain.[2]

Blake's change of poetic track is epitomised in the symbolism of 'The Tyger'. Six years after she had helped her husband to release 'The Tyger' from the thicket of alterations in the Notebook into *Experience*, Catherine Blake announced a move. It seemed providential. On 2 July 1800, Blake had written to George Cumberland that he had then begun to "to Emerge from a Deep pit of Melancholy". On 14 September, Catherine wrote to Nancy Flaxman, to say that she was to put one hundred and sixty miles between herself and "the terrible desart of London" on the following Tuesday.

Nancy was the wife of Thomas Flaxman, now a man of substance, and Blake's friend from the years of *An Island in the Moon*. Flaxman and Thomas Butts, whose more or less single-handed friendship kept Blake alive through difficult years, knew that William Hayley wanted an engraver close by him in Sussex. Hayley was a poet of equal fortune and self-esteem.

On 19 August 1800, the grit of future friction for Blake between each deferential line, John Flaxman had written to Hayley, looking forward to his overseeing Blake's work.[3] What is more, Hayley wanted Blake as "a Miniature Painter", an occupation which helped to land him with a charge of sedition as "a Military painter", in the pay of France. Blake was the last person to find "Mutual Comfort" in working with an eye by his shoulder, or to appreciate for long the exertion of Hayley's "usual Benevolence", or to accept the advice that he might gain "by making neat drawings".

Blake set out from Lambeth for the cottage at Felpham on the Channel coast, "between Six & Seven in the Morning" of Thursday 18 September 1800, with his wife and sister among "Sixteen heavy boxes & portfolios full of prints". "And Now," he wrote, "Begins a New life".[4]

By Hayley's "fortunate advice" as was proper, they took their "journey thro the Petworth Road". Travelling "thro most beautiful country on a most glorious day", Blake brought his family and mobile print shop to the sea. The man for whom Muswell Hill was "mountainous" had traversed "the vast range of mountains known as the Sussex Downs".[5] But by September 1803 Blake was shifting from coach to coach back along the Petworth Road. He was leaving behind an idyll of three years, which intrusive relationships, sickness and a charge of sedition had soured. He was on his way back to places and people he knew so well.

It was during his three years at Felpham that Blake worked intensely

2. See *The Four Zoas*, plate 35.

3. Bentley, *Records*, p. 72.

4. Letter to Flaxman, 21 September 1800.

5. So Gilbert White, Blake's contemporary, described the South Downs at the beginning of *The Natural History of Selborne*.

on his epic, *Milton*. He put *Finis* to it, or to part of it, after he had been back in London for a year at least.[6] It is convenient practice to add a preface to a book after the book is finished. So it seems that the universally recognised 'Jerusalem' verses, "And did those feet in ancient time", were written into the Preface to *Milton* as Blake settled once more among "*these*" familiar "dark Satanic Mills". "These" sets the mills around the writer. And they are obscured by "*our* clouded hills"—that is, "the awful gloom Of London City on the Thames from Surrey Hills to Highgate".

As Blake finished *Milton* in his rooms beneath the "clouded hills" of London (and, we take it, turned to the Preface), his thoughts went back to the song of the morning lark among the green mountains of Sussex; and from there, we shall see, to the "ancient time", twenty years past, when the Lamb of God walked among the children of *Innocence* on Wimbledon Common. Then it is from here that the immortal, affirmative questions lift the imagination towards the prospect of Jerusalem known, and to be regained:

> And did those feet in ancient time,
> Walk upon Englands mountains green:
> And was the holy Lamb of God
> On Englands pleasant pastures seen!
>
> And did the Countenance Divine,
> Shine forth upon our clouded hills?
> And was Jerusalem builded here,
> Among these dark Satanic Mills?

In Blake's mind, the presence of the Lamb of God in "ancient time" is related, with a simple conjunction to "this" London, still burdened with grief. Almost invariably, when Blake writes as incisively as this, the impulse is contained within his lifetime. Such an impulse generates the reaction to "the rulers of darkness in this life", to make England a "pleasant land".

The ramifications Blake later pursued on the Jerusalem symbol in his epics are an intrusion here. They are devised by a poet with a changed objective. Here the trenchant stimulus for these cohesive lines is familiar circumstance, to be identified in Blake's own words, if we hesitate to allow the word "ancient" to trail us back to the druids and beyond.

If we simply take "ancient" with reference to recent time, a sense common to Blake, we resist a superimposed mythology, and the lines move with the familiar Blakean immediacy. The light in the lines is

6. See Erdman, ed., *Poetry and Prose*, p. 806, for the complex problem of dating *Milton*.

both the South Downs, and the manifestation of the Lamb of God on the "pleasant pastures" of Innocence—the light that shone for Blake across his lifetime.[7]

Before the camera fore-shortened time, the past effectively became "ancient" in living memory. So a resolution no more than eighteen years old was an "ancient vote" in 1792 for Thomas Jefferson, who went on, a year later, to compliment a contemporary by recollecting his contemporary, yet ancient, past: "profound arguments entitle him to his ancient signature". Then Blake himself referred to renewing "the nerves of youth", alongside the "desires of ancient [sc. youthful] times"; and he even conclusively replaced a first reading "former", with its synonym, "ancient".[8] Then, the Concert of Ancient Music (1776–1848), of which George III became patron in 1785, only registered, as truly ancient, music over twenty years old.

Comprehending this royal and colloquial sense of "ancient" in "And did those feet" fetches us from patriarchal mythology to face a series of questions contemporary in reference; and intuitively, they are restored to Blake, as he takes us back those twenty years, to the "ancient time" of *Innocence*, when Jerusalem became a visionary reality.

Blake himself clinches the issue. He links the pastures of Felpham by name to Wimbledon. And this is not casual, but a visionary transition.

As he arrived on the coast, Blake wrote in proper style to assure John Flaxman that Felpham was "more Spiritual than London Heaven opens here on all sides her golden Gates . . . voices of Celestial inhabitants are more distinctly heard & their forms more distinctly seen". The "Celestial inhabitant" that fired Blake's imagination with its flight and song was the lark, which developed as a controlling symbol in *Milton*, "the Grand reason" for Blake's being "brought down" to Felpham. The song of the morning lark was a moment which became eternity. As the lark "mounts upon the wings of light into the Great Expanse",

> *all Nature listens silent to him & the awful Sun*
> *Stands still upon the Mountain looking on this little Bird.*

It is the angelic messenger, singing of inspiration as it brings the Lamb of God to walk on earth. Associated with the lark are the "morning odours", rising "first from the Wild Thyme", the flower of hope in folk lore. At the end of *Milton*, Blake resolved his vision in a conclusive transition, local in place and time. As his mind turned home to "the Hills of Surrey", "the Vales of Lambeth" and "the Cry of the Poor Man" across London, Jesus himself, he recollects, "walked forth from Felphams Vale" beneath the "mountains green".

7. "Pleasant": otiose today, the word was favoured by Blake. The little vagabond (plate 45) demanded the unthinkable from the patriarchs of *Experience*—a 'pleasant' God. England's "pleasant land" *records* an observation, and acknowledges a transformation. The word is climactic.

8. See *OED*, 'ancient', 1(a). The primary sense is given: "Of or belonging to times past, former, earlier, bygone". See also *America*, plate 15, and *The Four Zoas*, plate 7. Erdman, ed., *Poetry and Prose*, pp. 57, 369, and 839.

Immediately the Lark mounted with a loud trill from Felphams Vale
And the Wild Thyme from Wimbletons green & impurpled Hills.[9]

Wimbledon: we comprehend a unique social rescue, to which Blake was neighbour. Jerusalem, "Friendship & Brotherhood", had been "builded here" when, "in ancient time" some twenty years earlier, the Lamb of God had graced the "pleasant pastures" that were the ground-base of Innocence. With antiquity returned to its mists, the past makes the present retrievable.

Back in London, Blake had loaded his boxes into rooms at 17 South Molton Street, where he heard

The Shuttles of death sing in the sky to Islington & Pancrass
Round Marybone to Tyburns River, weaving black melancholy as a net.[10]

Not all the mills matched in range the stocking mill in Lambeth or the textile mills along the Wandle, shadowing "Mr Henkels iron mills", now casting shot and cannon on the way to Wimbledon, to sustain habitual war. None of these was as entrenched with exclusive dogma as the "Mills of Satan", in which the priesthood enforced the divine dispensation of duty to state and commerce. And none of these was as pitiful as the countless shuttered one room mills, each a workplace and home awash with sewage.

Though back among places he knew so well, Blake was settled among yet another new set of circumstances. There are two Tyburns, River and Brook, as the name ("two burns") implies. The streams, with Tyburn Hill, became potent symbols of oppression in his later writing. He was now living close to the "hill", and closer still to "Tyburn's bloody river", over which he lived in his South Molton Street rooms for the next eighteen years.

The land round the marshy banks of the river, which split the fashionable Mayfair estate, was useless for the speculators' "grand design". It went to housing for trades-folk who served the great estate. By the time Blake moved there, South Molton Street had been built up for some sixty years or so, with the Tyburn River buried in a culvert under its houses.

Tyburn Hill, the abandoned hanging-field, a rise hardly enough to divert the Tyburn Brook which flowed past it, was a few minutes' walk west along Oxford Street. Tyburn Tree, hauled out of its mud from place to place down the years, had been the Middlesex gallows since before William FitzOsbert was hanged there in 1196. The gallows tree had been transplanted permanently in Newgate Jail along Holborn,

9. *Milton*, plate 42.

10. *Jerusalem*, plate 37. *Jerusalem* ends in an extended reprise of the symbolic call for social restitution in "And did those feet", appropriate to the status of the epic. When Blake turned his mind to pre-Roman times, he never set them in England, "pleasant" or not. The Druids, correctly and invariably, walked in Albion (Britain), among Britons, not among the English. Jesus came later to England.

back in 1783. But for all Londoners shades of the hangman's victims still walked Tyburn.

The two decades, from that time to Blake's presence above Tyburn River, were trivial against ancestral fears. So many voices had "preached at Tyburn"; so few feet, by local counting, had yet "danced the Newgate hornpipe"; so ingrained were six centuries of ceremonious retribution, that the dread of the name still hung round Tyburn into the twentieth century.

Tyburn was Blake's local emblem for the ultimate sanction of *Experience* as he worked on *Jerusalem*. The "endless labyrinth of woe" that flourished around him was seeded from one "deadly Tree" named "Moral Virtue", first rooted in Tyburn water.[11] And in common with all Londoners, he assimilated both Tyburns, river and brook, in one symbol of oppression.

Both rise on Haverstock Hill, and join to flow down the valley west of Primrose Hill, through meadowland Blake walked so often on his way to Hampstead in his later years. By the 1660s, the lower reaches were already sewers. South of Primrose Hill, Tyburn River flows down Marylebone Lane (turned east at Wigmore Street, "by order of the City" in 1738), and across Oxford Street into South Molton Street. From there it runs through Green Park and under Buckingham Palace, then known as the Queen's House, where it branched to take in the destitute camps in Tothill Fields, then Whitehall, and Westminster, and into the Thames. So Blake shared his subterranean river with the loftiest and lowliest in the land.

From south of Primrose Hill, the other stream, "Tyburns awful brook" ran past the gallows at Tyburn Hill, to join the Westbourne in the Serpentine. By the end of Blake's life the lake was a cess-pit. From here, the fetid water fed Five Fields, the rubbish filled swamp, between the suicides' burial ground in the gardens of the Queen's House and the Thames. In 1827, the year Blake died, Thomas Cubitt cleared the swamp and buried the brook, for residences to "ease the magnates of the land". For the vision of *Jerusalem*, Blake did not "fondly construct a fictitious city", but "built Jerusalem on historical minutiæ that come into his ken as an inhabitant of the northwest regions of London".[12]

Already by 1791 Lord Camden (Lord Chancellor when Blake was young) had sold land for development in Kentish Town, and before Blake left for Felpham, the place was becoming Camden Town, with 1,400 dwellings across the fields. Then, while he watched from South Molton Street, the titled owners capitalised on their domains. in a dramatic architectural march into a sequence of residential squares north of the city.[13]

11. I am indebted to Ms Alison Shell, The British Architectural Library, for information on the Tyburns. For the deadly tree rooted in 'Tyburns brook' see *Jerusalem*, plate 28. In David Erdman's telling phrase, Blake's Jerusalem is "peace with a vengeance".

12. Erdman, *Prophet*, pp. 473 et sq.

13. Information on the London squares is from Edward Jones's and Christopher Woodward's indispensable *A Guide to the Architecture of London* (London: Weidenfeld & Nicholson, 1983). Bedford Square is the one square in London which "remains a magnificent unscathed example of Georgian planning".

In 1811 it was Bryanston and Montague Squares, within cheering distance north of Tyburn Hill; and beyond them, in 1815, Dorset Square, with its new style, colonial cast-iron verandas. Three years earlier Nash had already built Park Crescent, at the entrance to Regent's Park. By 1815 Macclesfield Bridge delicately spanned his canal, north of the park; they tossed the soil dug out of the canal on to Primrose Hill nearby, making it even more "mountainous" for Blake. Three years later, Nash's six villas round the Inner Circle were occupied. By 1822, a year after Blake had finished *Jerusalem* and left South Molton Street, Sussex Place and Hanover Terrace were complete, and Nash was moving his builders round the rest of the Outer Circle.

The transformation of the royal rough heathland beyond the Marylebone Road into Regent's Park occupied the years of Blake's old age. He would know the plan had been tabled since 1793. He died only months before Nash completed it. And while the grand squares, gated and padlocked, assured their residents' social separation, other builders were speculating as profitably in more modest bricks. Lord Camden's old initiative was extended round Kentish Town. The historic rubbish mountain at Battle Bridge, Pancras, was shovelled away, and by 1819 the desirable St Pancras suburb needed a fine new church in Greek Revivalist style. And there was still the breath of open country round Willan's Farm up towards Primrose Hill. But, "Friendship & Brotherhood", the promise Blake sought to proclaim, was as insubstantial as ever. Old Experience possessed the minds of the "golden builders", and John Nash was still right in line with old Mrs Sarah Trimmer, when he planned Regent Street to form "a boundary and complete separation between the streets and squares occupied by the nobility and gentry, and the narrow streets and meaner houses occupied by mechanics and the trading part of the community." Nash was not paving Jerusalem, either round Regent's Park or along Regent Street. This new road was bullied through the relentless clutter of common housing and trade round Swallow Street, only to ease the carriages from the palace of St James to Regent's Park. Under his carriage-way Nash buried the King Street school.

Blake's bitterly expressed reactions to the dispensations of Experience, which still prevailed, ran as a base-line through *Jerusalem*. Then, arising from this with startling insight, his message from those who "labourd at the furrow", recollects Innocence with its subversive slant on "duty",

> *Saying: It is better to prevent misery, than to release from misery*
> *It is better to prevent error, than to forgive the criminal:*

Labour well the Minute Particulars, attend to the Little-ones:
And those who are in misery cannot remain so long
If we but do our duty.

Startling, too, sustained into approaching old age, is the prophetic
vision directly still generated in the ancient, organised "delight in innocence before the face of the Lamb". Blake knew from his Wimbledon
years, and from his revelation in the vale of Feltham, and he wrote it
into *Jerusalem*, that

He who would see the Divinity must see him in his Children
In friendship & love; then a Divine family, & in the midst
Jesus will appear; so he who wishes to see a Vision; a perfect Whole
Must see it in its Minute Particulars; Organized.[14]

While Blake began writing *Jerusalem* soon after he arrived in South
Molton Street, it may have been 1820 before he finished the etching.
Throughout these years, with total consistency "he kept the Divine
Vision", not only in times of fulfilment, but also "in time of trouble".
While it is unremarkable that *Experience* should be reflected so widely
in the epic, as a reaction to unrelenting oppression, the sustaining
influence of *Innocence*, given its tragic brevity, is another matter. The
early eventualities of no other writer retained such tenacious compul-
sion over his thinking, across thirty or more years, and into old age. The
people of St James's parish Blake had known so closely, whose undertaking he had immortalised, were long since departed. But their true charity, organised "in its Minute Particulars" survived as the focus for
Jerusalem. Meanwhile a sequence of patrons and friends kept *Innocence*
and *Experience* under his eyes all his working life, as he coloured copy
after copy to meet their inexorably changing wishes.

In the difficult years after he arrived in South Molton Street, he was
kept in food and rent unfailingly by Thomas Butts "of the war office",
who also had mining interests. Butts filled "his house to overflowing
with pictures and books", employed Blake to teach his son drawing, and
had sacks of coal delivered to South Molton Street.

But even in this period of depression, copies of the *Songs* still sold;
and even in the dark year of 1807 Southey "knew not whether most to
admire the genius of Mr William Blake or of Mr William Hayley": praise
indeed. Even Ozias Humphrey, the expensive miniature painter, conde-
scendingly used his royal connections for permission for his friend,
William Blake, to dedicate his designs for *The Grave* to Her Majesty.[15]

There was little or no trade for Blake among booksellers, and it was

14. See *Jerusalem*, plates 20, 55, 91,
and 95.

15. For biographical details, see
Bentley, *Blake Records*, by dates.

his continuing acceptance among "the better sort" that was crucial to the sustained demand for copies of the *Songs*. Misgivings and uncertainty among readers about the uncompromising tone of *Experience*, as years went by, meant it was the illustrations rather than the script which attracted commissions. Indeed patrons came to demand plates so richly coloured, that at times the text lost the clarity of the earlier, more gentle tinting. There were even requests for the designs uncluttered with words. Blake severely disapproved, since this would be "to the Loss of some of the best things For they when Printed perfect to accompany Poetical Personifications & Acts without which Poems they never could have been Executed".[16] Nonetheless, it is this discriminating patronage that has left us with twenty-seven copies of the combined *Songs*, and twenty-one of *Innocence* alone still surviving, each uniquely coloured.

At the beginning of 1818 Blake joined a dinner party given by Lady Caroline Lamb, where he made such a clear impression on Lady Charlotte Bury, that she wrote one of the most perceptive contemporary account we have of him.[17] It was the year life changed for Blake; and his best chance, by far, in that year was his first meeting with John Linnell, through "the younger Mr Cumberland". Linnell saw Blake through the last years of his life, and sustained the social connections which kept him working on the *Songs*. It was at this time also that he was "discovered" by a group of young artists known as the Ancients, whose enthusiasm and admiration carried him into the future.

Blake had been forced to sell his stock of prints, and by 1821 a move from South Molton Street had become financially unavoidable. The Blakes moved to 3 Fountain Court, a "house kept by Mr Banes whose wife was sister to Mrs Blake", and occupied two rooms on the first floor.[18] Blake installed his workplace in a corner and covered the walls with pictures.

It is a misleading truism among biographers that Blake in later life "laboured for his bread, eccentric dirty and obscure". Labour and eccentricity, yes. But that Blake was far from obscure or dirty is evident in his unbroken and recorded sequence of visits and dinner parties, in affluent and delicate society. Moreover, Blake received more friends and admirers in 3 Fountain Court, than he did in any of his previous homes. Not one reports squalor. All report Blake's indifference to poverty, and go on to stress the pleasure of the company they enjoyed in the clean rooms, though a chair might be too fragile for safety.

Even more assuredly that Blake was not "dirty" is demonstrated in the spontaneous welcome the young Linnell children gave him to Collins Farm in his last years; and then climbed on to his knee. Young children do not cosy up to ageing, dirty men.

16. Ibid., 20 January 1818.

17. Letter to Dawson Turner, 8 June 1818.

18. So John Linnell, in Bentley, *Blake Records*, p. 564.

Blake's eccentricity, especially in old age, put him in constant touch with the illustrious dead. Their opinions and advice (not all taken kindly by Blake) were reported factually to his friends. But, against this, a happy normality possessed his days especially when he was in the company of children, about whom he loved to talk. "That is heaven", he once said to a friend, "leading him to the window, and pointing to a group of them at play".[19]

Though enclosed by warehouses, the rooms in Fountain Court had compensations. The Coal Hole Tavern along the street kept Blake supplied with porter, and a window in the back room gave a narrow view of the Surrey hills across the Thames. Best of all, "lying a little off the Strand, between it and the river", Fountain Court was handy for the stage-coach, which carried Blake from the Strand to John Linnell and the children in Hampstead.

The Linnells had moved for the Summer to Collins Farm, North End, the "country-ward side" of Hampstead.[20] While Blake was over-coming his "wilful dislike to Hampstead", for the sake of "the many happy hours he had spent there", forebearance never came easily. On one occasion, when Mrs Linnell ventured to express her humble opin-ion that Hampstead was a healthy place, Blake startled her by saying, "It is a lie! It is no such thing!"

From his time closer to Blake, Alexander Gilchrist tried to ratio-nalise this intense aversion to the "mountainous places" north of London. "Perhaps from early associations", he suggested, Blake

could only tolerate the southern suburbs. They who are accustomed to the varied loveliness of Surrey, Sussex, and Kent, with their delightful mixture of arable, pasture, woodland, waste, and down, one shading off into the other, cannot but find the unvaried pastures and gentle hills of Middlesex and Hertfordshire wearisomely monotonous.[21]

It is a measure of Linnell's support, that on 14 July 1826, Blake was able to send him a receipt for the very considerable "Sum of One Hundred & fifty Pounds for the Copy-right & Plates (Twenty-two in number) of the Book of Job". It was the major gesture in a summation of generosity. Seven years earlier, Blake had prepared a special copy of the *Songs* at a special price, for an incomparable friend. Six guineas, ten guineas, were the going prices, but the receipt shows Linnell paid £1 19 6 for this copy on 27 August 1819.[22] It was the copy which his children later shared so memorably with their visitor.

At a pre-Christmas dinner party in 1825, which Linnell also attended, Blake gave Mrs Elizabeth Aders and Crabb Robinson each a copy of the

19. So Samuel Palmer, in Gilchrist, *Life of Blake*, p. 319.

20. See Jones and Woodward, *Architecture of London*, R3, for location. The house, now Wylde's Farm, still stands, less its farmland, the only surviving farmhouse in Hampstead. It was known to Blake and Linnell as Collins Farm, after the farmer then resident, to whom Linnell paid rent for four rooms. Linnell and Blake were first of a line of eminent sub-tenants and visitors to the farm. For its history and associations see the monograph by Philip Venning, *Wyldes: A New History* (London, 1977).

21. Gilchrist, *Life of Blake*, pp. 372–73.

22. Copy R, in the Fitzwilliam Museum. About 1818 Blake transferred 'The School-Boy' conclusively from *Innocence* to *Experience*, and apparently soon after that began the practice of putting framing lines round his plates. Since 'The School-Boy' does not appear in *Experience* in this copy, but the framing lines are there, we may speculate that *Experience* in copy R was printed after 1818 to publish alongside an earlier *Innocence* set, 'The School-Boy' being omitted, since it already appeared in the latter. It looks like a special arrangement, and it is the copy that went to Linnell. I guess the small fee was pressed upon Blake.

Songs. The next month, Mrs Aders embarrassingly explained that it had "been by no means either Mr Robinsons intention or mine, to beg the books, when ask'd for them of that most interesting Man". Six months later John Linnell characteristically eased five guineas out of Mrs Aders for Blake.

In these last months he was now "Printing a Set of the Songs of Innocence & Experience for a Friend at Ten Guineas". The unlikely "friend" is identified by Gilchrist as Thomas Wainewright, credibly suspected of poisoning his relatives. He was transported years later for the more serious offence of forgery, committed while he was manoevering to make capital out of Blake during his early years in Fountain Court. The forger became much in demand as a portrait painter in Tasmania. Though Blake now worked "shut up in a Corner", his hand lost none of its skill. Gilchrist considered this last copy Blake finished to be "one among the best of the *Songs of Innocence and Experience* I have seen".[23]

In February the next year, concerned for his friend's health, Linnell spoke to Blake about moving into, or close to, his studio in Cirencester Place. Blake was too ill to face it, and two months further into his last year, on 12 April 1827, he returned from "very near the Gates of Death". But there was still the "Mental Fight". Writing to George Cumberland, his friend from the days of the Gordon Riots so long ago, about subservient conformity took his mind back: "Since the French Revolution Englishmen are all Intermeasurable One by Another Certainly a happy state of Agreement to which I for One do not Agree".

In his last hours, Blake worked with clear delight on a little "calling card" for George Cumberland, which became a design of Innocence recalled from "ancient time". It "would have been more finished if WB had lived" beyond the evening of 12 August 1827.

Nearly forty years later Gilchrist learnt how the Linnell children anticipated Blake's approach to Collins Farm over Hampstead Heath:

The children, whenever he was expected, were on the qui vive to catch the first glimpse of him from afar. One of them, who has now children of her own, but still cherishes the old reverence for 'Mr Blake', remembers thus watching for him when a little girl of five or six; and how, as he walked over the brow of the hill and came within sight of the young ones, he would make a particular signal . . . She remembers how Blake would take her on his knee, and recite children's stories to them all; recollects his kind manner; his putting her in the way of drawing.

At this same time, into her declining years "Mrs. Collins of the Farm" still remembered Blake as "that most delightful gentleman!"[24]

23. Gilchrist, *Life of Blake*, p. 295.
24. Ibid., pp. 312, 373

Figure 9. 'Mr Cumberland's calling card' by Blake (1827).
Reprinted with permission of the Pierpont Morgan Library, New York (PML 9948).

Some Sales and Early Reactions

Critical reaction to *Songs of Innocence and of Experience* in Blake's lifetime was almost invariably superficial. It can be followed through to the years soon after Blake's death in the pages of *Blake Records*, and for later years in *William Blake: The Critical Heritage* (1975), also edited by G. E. Bentley.

By far the most remarkable and effective early appreciation of Blake's work appeared anonymously in the *London University Magazine* for March, 1830. The writer not only knew "the noble Songs of Innocence and Experience" and *Thel*, from both of which he quotes at some length, but also *Jerusalem*. With an insight refreshing and alert among much contemporary condescending denigration, he acknowledges the "extraordinary power developed" in Blake's art and poetry, and writes enthusiastically in justification of poems and designs as challenging as 'Hear the voice of the Bard!', 'A Poison Tree' and 'The Garden of Love' ("a curious and mystical poem, which as yet can be but partially understood"). It is a pity that we cannot identify the critic who was so uniquely responsive to Blake so early.

In 1807, Wordsworth was pleased to have copies of 'Laughing Song' and 'Holy Thursday' from *Innocence* in a commonplace book, together with 'The Tyger'. However he thought most of the *Songs*, while pleasant, to be of questionable sanity. When, in 1818, Coleridge listed some of the *Songs* in an elaborate order of merit, in tune with his times, he preferred those which expressed a moral orthodoxy; and if he discussed a poem, he did so from a doctrinal viewpoint, and was solicitous for Blake's readers. He would have omitted 'A Little Girl Lost', "not for the want of innocence in the poem, but for the too probable want of it in many readers". We can see what he meant, but not why the poem should be exempted. It was a reaction to Blake that lasted through a century.

Moral tone was most missed in Blake. As we have seen, J. G. Wilkinson hoped that the *Songs* would help along the "New Spiritualism" he optimistically sensed to be dawning by 1839. But, it is clear, on the basis of the editorial exclusion of 'The Little Vagabond', that 'Newton's Pantocrator' was still marshalling his stars. Then the prerogatives of the Pantocrator were protected through the century by the relegation of the *Songs* to the nursery floor, until Alexander Gilchrist, almost literally, rescued Blake from oblivion.

Throughout his life, for the most part Blake was his own publisher and bookseller. In his prospectus of October 1793 he priced *Innocence* and *Experience* at five shillings each, when, as we know, three shillings paid to nurses at Wimbledon was reckoned good money, to foster a child for a week. The price Blake asked through the years varied greatly. In 1806 Butts paid six guineas for the complete *Songs*. On 9 June 1818, Blake quoted three guineas a set to Mr Dawson Turner, of Yarmouth. Crabb Robinson and Mrs Elizabeth Aders, the wife of a collector, seem voluntarily to have paid five guineas for the complete *Songs* in 1826. In April 1827, Blake quoted ten guineas for the set to George Cumberland, and was at work on a copy "for a Friend", probably Thomas Wainewright, the painter who poisoned his relatives. Wainewright was later transported for life for the more serious offence of forgery, and profitably took up portrait painting in Tasmania.

G. E. Bentley's reasonable estimate is that Blake's yearly income seems "never to have gone much above £100", and was probably often nearer £50. Then there were the deliveries of coal which Butts, who owned mines, sent at times, instead of, or as well as, money. Given the labour and time each copy involved, and the general unacceptability of the sentiments, especially in *Experience*, Blake was bound to rely for a living on commissions rather than on booksellers. As years went by, he found that it was the illustrations rather than the poems that attracted customers for the *Songs*. Indeed friends and patrons clearly came to demand plates so richly coloured, that at times the text lost the clarity of the earlier, more gentle tinting. The priority was not Blake's. When he replied to Dawson Turner's enquiry, mentioning a list of books he had "printed for Mr Humphry ... such as could be Printed without the Writing", he was clearly not including the *Songs* in the list. He had brief dealings with the bookseller Humphry in 1802, and this sounds like a reference to a later enquiry. These intimations of rare commercial transactions suggest that the booksellers shared with most of Blake's patrons an indifference to the poetry. Certainly the tone of his reply to Dawson Turner makes it plain that the approach from Great Yarmouth was for designs untroubled by words. Blake severely disapproves, since this is "to the Loss of some of the best things For they when Printed perfect accompany Poetical Personifications & Acts without which Poems they never could have been Executed".

PART 2

SONGS OF INNOCENCE AND OF EXPERIENCE

Facsimiles of two copies

Plate 1 Combined Title-page

Plate 2 Frontispiece to *Songs of Innocence*

Plate 3 Title-page for *Songs of Innocence*

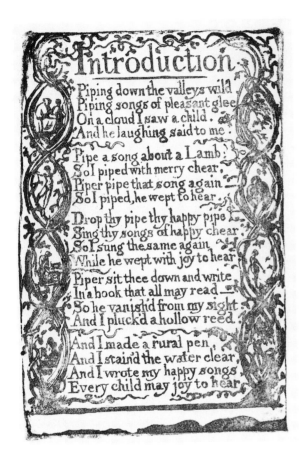

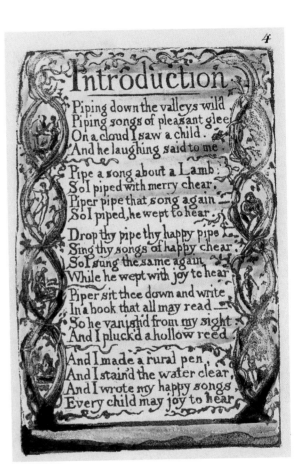

Plate 4   Introduction

Plate 5   The Shepherd

Plate 6   The Ecchoing Green I

Plate 7 The Ecchoing Green II

Plate 8   The Lamb

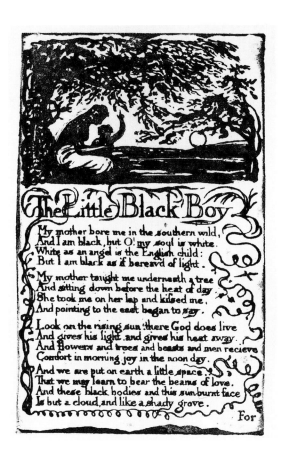

Plate 9   The Little Black Boy I

Plate 10   The Little Black Boy II

Plate 11 The Blossom

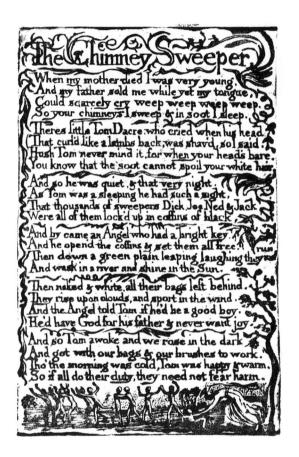

Plate 12 The Chimney Sweeper

Plate 13 The Little Boy Lost

Plate 14   The Little Boy Found

Plate 15   Laughing Song

Plate 16   A Cradle Song I

Plate 17   A Cradle Song II

Plate 18 The Divine Image

Plate 19   Holy Thursday

Plate 20   Night I

Plate 21 Night II

Plate 22   Spring I

Plate 23 Spring II

Plate 24 Nurse's Song

Plate 25   Infant Joy

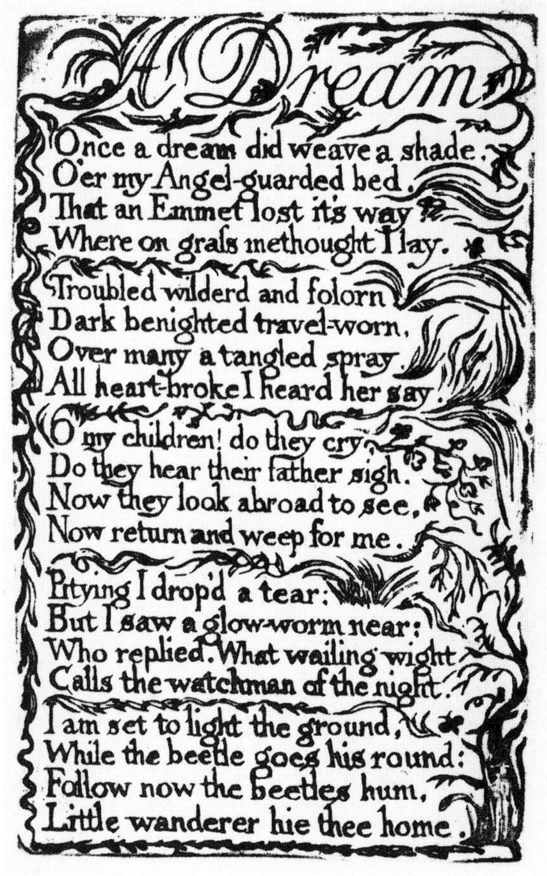

A Dream

Once a dream did weave a shade,
O'er my Angel-guarded bed,
That an Emmet lost it's way
Where on grass methought I lay.

Troubled wilderd and folorn
Dark benighted travel-worn,
Over many a tangled spray,
All heart-broke I heard her say.

O my children! do they cry
Do they hear their father sigh.
Now they look abroad to see,
Now return and weep for me.

Pitying I drop'd a tear:
But I saw a glow-worm near:
Who replied. What wailing wight
Calls the watchman of the night.

I am set to light the ground,
While the beetle goes his round:
Follow now the beetles hum,
Little wanderer hie thee home.

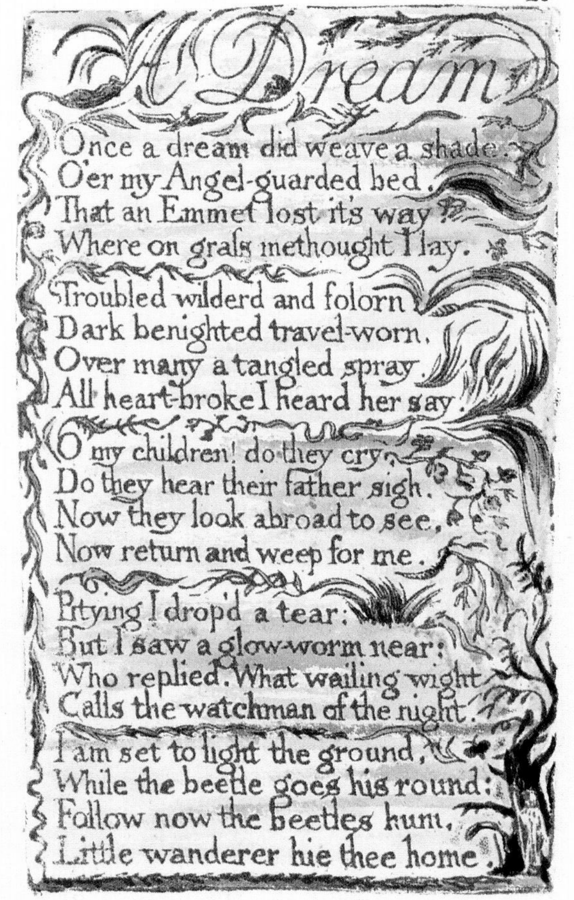

20

A Dream

Once a dream did weave a shade,
O'er my Angel-guarded bed,
That an Emmet lost it's way
Where on grass methought I lay.

Troubled wilderd and folorn
Dark benighted travel-worn,
Over many a tangled spray,
All heart-broke I heard her say.

O my children! do they cry
Do they hear their father sigh.
Now they look abroad to see,
Now return and weep for me.

Pitying I drop'd a tear:
But I saw a glow-worm near:
Who replied. What wailing wight
Calls the watchman of the night.

I am set to light the ground,
While the beetle goes his round:
Follow now the beetles hum,
Little wanderer hie thee home.

Plate 26 A Dream

Plate 27 On Anothers Sorrow

Plate 28 Frontispiece to *Songs of Experience*

Plate 29   Title-page to *Songs of Experience*

Plate 30   Introduction

Plate 31 Earth's Answer

Plate 32   The Clod & the Pebble

Plate 33   Holy Thursday

Plate 34   The Little Girl Lost I

Plate 35 The Little Girl Lost II, The Little Girl Found I

Plate 36   The Little Girl Found II

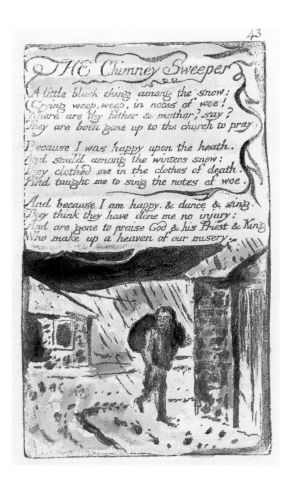

Plate 37   The Chimney Sweeper

Plate 38 Nurses Song

Plate 39 The Sick Rose

Plate 40   The Fly

Plate 41 The Angel

Plate 42 The Tyger

Plate 43   My Pretty Rose Tree, Ah! Sun Flower, The Lilly

Plate 44   The Garden of Love

Plate 45 The Little Vagabond

Plate 46   London

Plate 47 The Human Abstract

Plate 48   Infant Sorrow

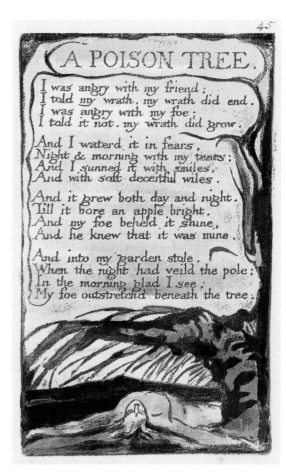

Plate 49   A Poison Tree

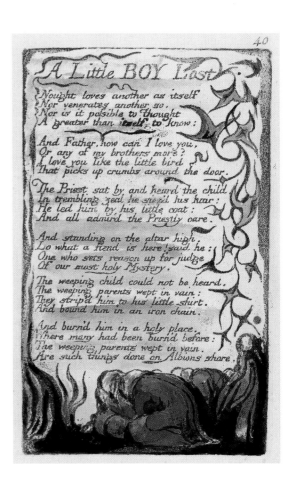

Plate 50   A Little Boy Lost

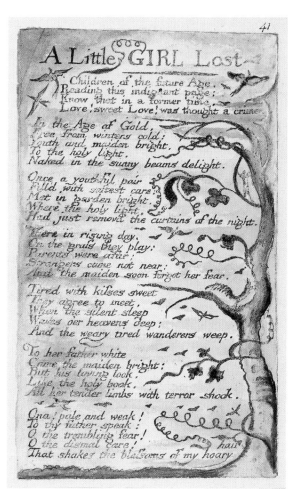

Plate 51 A Little Girl Lost

Plate 52   To Tirzah

Plate 53   The School Boy

Plate 54 The Voice of the Ancient Bard

COMMENTARY

The Songs of Innocence and of Experience

 As far as we know, twenty seven copies of *Songs of Innocence and of Experience* still exist, and twenty one of *Innocence* alone. The colouring varies in every copy, while the text is uniform. 'The Little Girl Lost' and 'The Little Girl Found' were included in *Innocence* when it appeared in 1789, but transferred permanently to *Experience* as soon as the latter was printed. 'The School Boy' left *Innocence* for *Experience* by 1818. 'The Voice of the Ancient Bard' appears, from time to time, in either. The evidence is that 'To Tirzah' was added to *Experience* sometime after 1802.

Note: Plate numbers are given in parantheses after the title.

¶ 1 Combined title-page

In this combined title-page of 1794, the year of the Treason Trials and intrusive oppression in London, Innocence is only briefly acknowledged. The violent flames encompassing the figures of distressful sexuality give way tentatively to the opening of the sky at the top left of the plate, to which the bird is escaping.

Birds, of various shapes and sometimes indeterminate identity, fly through many of the illustrations, at times it seems for decorative reasons, at other times to more purpose. A bird with forked or elongated tail is often associated with Innocence. Three fly up through the title-page of *Innocence*. One appears in a panel of the 'Introduction', while another is on the wing in 'The Shepherd' (5), in a dawn of unbroken clarity. It glides to the ground in 'The Ecchoing Green' (6). In *Experience* the bird seems to typify the loss of natural, unconstrained emotion. Lyca lifts her arm to its flight in 34, and a flock offsets the spiritual desolation of 'A Little Girl Lost' (51) against an "Age of Gold", and "futurity".

In the loop of the initial 'S' of the title-page a small figure stands beckoning with arm upraised, while another sits reading beneath the open sky, an evocative recollection of Innocence. At the bottom of the plate the man leans over the woman with a gesture of frustration or wrath, or both. The woman lies in a posture of dread or seduction, or both. The complex, indeterminate tension Blake draws into the relationship typifies sexuality in Experience, and the flames which engulf them aggrandise the desolation which we see generated there so often. The wisps of smoke and foliage embroider nakedness with a prurience bred, we are to learn later, in the nurseries and gardens of Experience.

The figures are often identified as post-lapsarian Adam and Eve. But this seems to me difficult to relate to the contemporary immediacy of the *Songs*. The scant tendrils conceal the woman in the unconvincing propriety of Experience.

Songs of Innocence

¶ *2 Frontispiece*
The shepherd, sheep and lamb enter Blake's thinking with *Songs of Innocence*, where his 'pastoral' poetry owes little or nothing to literary fashion, much to Christian tradition, and most, it seems, to a familiar undertaking in actual care. In it and the related engravings he sets out his vision of the nurture of children as exemplifying Christian charity, untarnished by the condescension of good breeding.

The overwhelming impression of the frontispiece to *Innocence* is of true pastoral care and communication. The trees are in full leaf, sheltering the flock, the paradigm for children, in a grove of light. The child is wingless; no angel, but mortal, an idea of inspired alertness. Communication is instinctive, immediate. The shepherd's arms are flung wide, and the picture seems to carry his voice. The frontispiece conducts us towards the lines in the 'Introduction'.

¶ *3 Title-page*
In the rising trepidation of 1789, Blake set these quiet figures at the head of the poems he had gathered over the preceding six or so years. In so doing, he surely exemplified "organised Innocence" as the recollected reality he was determined to record, and eventually immortalised.

While the conceptions subsumed under Blake's Experience are readily understood, at times even today Innocence is taken to mean no more than "unacqaintance with evil, especially exemplified in early childhood". This hardly measures up to the loaded transgressions of *Experience*. The primary, more potent, definition of 'innocence', as 'freedom from sin, guilt or moral wrong', more closely identifies the substance of *Innocence*: especially adult freedom from moral wrong.

On only three plates of *Innocence* are children shown unaccompanied by an adult: two 'pastoral' scenes exemplifying communication, and a third where, being alone, the little boy is lost. The book's sustained presentation of relationships among children and their seniors, "free from moral wrong" (in the way Blake seemingly alone saw it) is overwhelming; and, of course, the activity is graced with the tranquillity and rejoicing of the same adults. This is the effective 'contrary' to Experience. This is Innocence. Years later, Blake spelt it out:

He who would do good to another, must do it in Minute Particulars
General Good is the plea of the scoundrel hypocrite & flatterer.

That plea of 'General Good' was philanthropy, defined at the start of Blake's century almost in his words, and judiciously advocated throughout, as "an Inclination to Promote Publick Good". It was anathema to him, belonging to Experience, where it is fixed in the philanthropic wrists of the lady in 'Holy Thursday' (33).

In *Innocence*, with no philanthropic inclination, nurse, teacher and visitor "Labour well the Minute Particulars, attend to the Little-ones", "and those who are in misery" do not "remain so long".[1] A vision is realised—an Arcadian one perhaps, since we are stumbling for it yet. But it recollects the documented "Minute Particulars" with which the foundlings Blake knew were briefly rescued by his neighbours, in an unprecedented, even revolutionary, commitment. Until, that is, philanthropy relentlessly prevailed again, and "an Inclination to Promote Publick Good" dispatched the children unlettered to "Manufactories near Manchester", as Blake turned to engrave *Innocence*.

On this title-page a "fit and proper nurse", reassuring and composed, shares a substantial book with children absorbed and at ease. Her hold on the volume constitutes an offering; the boy's eye follows the girl's hand. The togetherness of Blake's "sweet instruction" is exemplified: the concord of *Innocence*.

Around and above the group, nature rejoices. Small figures use the flourishing lettering as seats and swings and leaning posts. Perhaps Blake sets himself among them, since in the initial letter of *Innocence*, sits "a man in a wide hat, such as Blake wore".[2]

At the bottom of the plate, the fields behind the nurse and her pupils spread out to the river, a life enhancing symbol. In this landscape of Innocence the children and nurse react with composed acceptance to the exuberance of nature around them. Nature and nurture are complementary in this vision.

¶ *4 Introduction*

Reading the 'Introduction', we recollect the frontispiece; and these two plates, with the title-page, comprise a complex and illuminating insight into the concept of *Innocence*.

In the 'Introduction' the piper reaches us as a traveller, "Piping down the valleys wild"; but from the frontispiece we recollect him as the guardian of the flock and the child, a recollection which is confirmed when the lamb now is called to the piper's mind and ours by the laughter and command of the child. This seems to change the piper's journey of

1. *Jerusalem*, plate 55.
2. Geoffrey Keynes, ed., *Songs of Innocence and of Experience* (Oxford: Oxford University Press, 1970), p. 132.

"pleasant glee" into a special relationship. The initiative is the child's. It is a relationship and an initiative which pervade *Innocence*. And we are meeting it here already in the interaction of poetry and illustrations unique to Blake.

If the frontispiece is not "a literal illustration" of the 'Introduction', neither is its border simply decoration. The interweaving panels are occupied by figures from everyday living: a flying bird; a seated nurse teaching a standing child (recollecting the title-page); a printer, like Blake, at his press; a woman sowing seed. Nothing of the action or location of the text is here, except in the copies where a stream flows along the foot of the illustration.

We shall get used to this dissociation. Here it seems Blake is fixing the inspired meeting in a framework of everyday existence. Then, in these lines, we are introduced to the peerless race of common speech (epitomised in that colloquial repetition of "so") with which Blake released English poetry from the self-regard of contemporary versified diction.

℘ 5 *The Shepherd*

In the first line of the poem, the apparently (only apparently) careless repetition of "sweet" acts as a Blake signature. The epithet is spontaneously transferred from the shepherd's state of being to the onlooker's appreciation of it, by the deceptive, easy run of the verse. And this shepherd's tongue is to "be filled with praise", not for a Divinity, but down-to-earth, for the symbolic community of care which he and the flock comprise. Christianity is literally grounded in Innocence. Then in the last line that little word "when", not "that", brings in the tremble of uncertainty. The state of Innocence is not inevitable.

The illustration comes nearer than most to being an emblem for the text. The flock is at peace in a field enclosed by a hedge in full leaf, beneath the delicate tree, flecked with light. The shepherd's glance affirms his care

℘ 6 & 7 *The Ecchoing Green*

The poem and its illustrations report related circumstances of exemplary child care in a community: recreative play, attentive control, affection, togetherness, an unspoken sense of "belonging". In the poem, even sunrise is given a social purpose—to make skies "happy" for the villagers. The birds' song is a mounting accompaniment to the open-air ringing of church bells, in a daylight of rejoicing.

In the second verse, Old John sits "among the old folk", moved by laughter to recollect his youth. In the last verse, it as if the sun goes down because the little ones "No more can be merry", with that implied priority of human need over natural forces which characterises the poem. And the children are not dismissed for sleep, but brought together into a calm, protective assurance for the night. It is the direction of the emphasis throughout Innocence—a direction abandoned among the vagabond fires and tendentious nurseries of Experience.

On the first plate, a cricket match (the most organised of games except when Joe Bradley joined in) completes a circle of the community, with the children, nurses and neighbours round the oak. On the left an old man in breeches and hose contemplates the game. Behind him a villager has his arm round a child: a social entity.

The two illustrations pursue complementary themes. Some children are already "weary" round the tree, anticipating the next illustration, which extends the poem, until the graceful symbolism of the adolescents and the grape-vines intimates a natural maturing. But above all the illustration represents the adult control, considerate and sure, that underpins the relationships of the text. It is this caring firmness, which now responds to their weariness, and visually brings the children to rest. Innocence becomes a combination of awareness and selfless concern: again, precisely the accord which is lost in the nannying of Experience.

The young "mother" carrying an infant, a weary child at her skirt, can hardly be the natural mother of all the cricketers and kite flyers being shepherded home. She is a foster-mother or, to give her the official title in the minutes of the King Street Governors, a nurse. And it seems she gets help with the children either from Blake himself, or from someone who has borrowed his hat.[3] It is evident that, when Blake illustrated the poem for *Songs of* Innocence in the dismaying circumstances around 1789, he recollected Wimbledon Common, where "five or six children" were "placed in one house" with a "suitable" nurse, and became in a domiciliary sense, "Round the laps of their mothers/Many sisters and brothers". It is not blood, but the bond of nurture, which makes these children siblings in the historical reality of Innocence.

¶ *8 The Lamb*

This text, with the Child Saviour, lamb and child sharing a common identity, is the most clearly religious pastoral poem in the *Songs*. And, as so often in Blake's writing, the faith is related to every-day affairs, by the unself-conscious use of a simple word or phrase. Here by calling the lamb's fleece "clothing of delight,/Softest clothing wooly bright", Blake turns the imagination to the garments of children, "multitudes of lambs".

In the poem "all the vales rejoice" at the "tender voice" of the Lamb,

3. The man helping with the children in the second plate is wearing the "broad-rimmed, but not quakerish [tricorne], hat", which his friends always associated with Blake. He was wearing it when the military detained him on the Medway. He wore it among "the dressed-up, swelling people" at the Academy, and was still wearing it to visit the Linnells at Hampstead in his old age. G. E. Bentley, *Blake Records* (London: Oxford University Press, 1969), pp. 280–281; Stanley Gardner, *Blake's Innocence & Experience Retraced* (London: Athlone, 1986), pp. 48–50.

which in the second verse becomes the voice of the Saviour. The illustration brings both voices home to the village location, to a pasture beside the river, where the emphasis is protective care. The flock is gathered before the shelter with an open door, the doves of peace on the roof, near the village oak. The recollection of true pastoral care could hardly be more effectively conveyed.

¶ *9 & 10 The Little Black Boy*

Exceptionally in *Innocence* the little black boy receives a religious upbringing from his natural mother. Both maternal teaching and the child's response are as alien to Innocence on Thameside, as is the heat of the tropical sun.

In a land known only from books to Londoners "of the better sort", the mother gives her son a lesson something like those same Londoners might have heard (less its direct humility) in the church of St James, Piccadilly. Yet, if they were honest, they would concede that the mother's lesson is as implausible in its setting as the rest of the cant of the "noble savage", under the "base laws of servitude" the century had heaped on such alien races;[4] except that in the end Blake gives the cant an underplayed validity.

In those pages of *Innocence*, "where laughter sat beneath the Oaks", no rescued child was seen as angelic, none conscious of "bearing the beams of love", none given a lesson in salvation, and none required to acknowledge Divine love, as is the black boy here. Except, that is, for Tom Dacre and his chimney sweeping friends, who, with "the little black boy", were alone deprived of the blessing of rescue by the nurses. It seems that God's promise was the last reliance of those excluded from the society of Innocence. So, at first, it seems that the little black boy, bred by his mother to spiritual genuflexion, well away from Westminster, faces us with the assurance of Christian salvation, in the absence of Christian intervention. However there is more, as there turns out to be also for Tom Dacre: reconciliation here and now. And presently release from both black and white clouds of enmity.

If the black boy's words were put into the mouth of a foundling at a nurse's knee, Innocence would be degraded to a philanthropic gesture. Reaching us from this unsophisticated distance, the expression of faith is curiously disturbing.

In the second illustration the little black boy brings his white friend to pray at God's knee. Christ, gowned, appears elsewhere in *Innocence*, but nowhere so prominently as here. Here uniquely is Christ the shepherd, with his crook, with an emphatic halo of light coloured into some copies, and his flock safely grazing. He leans forward, arms ready to

4. Gardner, *Retraced*, pp. 62–63. Working on the engravings for J. G. Stedman's *Narrative of a five years' expedition against the Revolted Natives of Surinam*, Blake would have found many of Stedman's designs harrowing. Stedman himself wrote of the natives: "a happy people ... whose errors ... are of ignorance, and not the rooted depravity of a pretended civilisation, and a spurious and mock Christianity". *Narrative* (1796), I, p. 381.

accept the white boy from his companion. This measures the reality of faith to which the black boy is able to conduct the "little English boy". On the lips of a child born in the "the southern wild", the message acquires a sentient truth, seldom to be learnt in a nursery in Golden Square.

❡ 11 The Blossom

Neither robin nor sparrow figures widely in Blake's developing use of symbolic language. In nursery rhymes, there may be a hint of the traditional association of the sparrow with merriment and the robin with grief. If so, the hint is soon subsumed under an affirmation of nurture realised in nature. The poem is a tenuous semantic loop, where plant and birds, and the nurture of infants, comprise a single strand of sense in which the twin expectations of joy and sorrow converge towards solace. The response to both joy and sorrow is "happy", since in Innocence neither is self-absorbed.

Though the flames are coloured differently from copy to copy, the illustration is always a spectacular celebration. The figure in the loop of flame above the title, angelically winged and clad as a nurse, takes a child to her bosom. Behind her a winged child sits reading, others frolic among the colours of gold against an azure background. The illustration in its glory relates the poem's symbolism to its explication in 'The Divine Image', and to the complementary theme in 'Infant Joy'.

❡ 12 The Chimney Sweeper

Chimney sweeping was an apprenticeship the Governors of the King Street school rejected during the 1780s, since they thought it dehumanising, even for workhouse children. It was a view few people but Blake would bother to share. Yet there is no notice of this in the poem.

Alongside all the seemingly essential miseries facing the children of eighteenth century adversity, sweeping was not the instant emotional trigger it is for us. If we read the poem through spectacles two hundred years old, its effect is the more disturbing; especially against its 'contrary' in Experience. On the way to propositions even more perilous in Experience, we may accept the sweepers' condition as commonplace.

Tom Dacre and his friends lack the care of Blake's neighbours. They are sold from parental necessity into commercial custody—Tom Dacre, himself, by an inmate of the Lady Dacre Almshouses, who had been allowed by the almshouse rules to foster then "apprentice" him. The boys inevitably finish sleeping "in soot".[5] Being "very young", they are set to clear the narrow horizontal box flues: "coffins of black".

Most readily noticed is the change in rhythm at the fifth line of the

5. The chimney boys in Innocence suffer personal conditions worse than the boy in Experience. Sleeping in cellars between bags of soot marks the boys as employed by the worst "class of chimney sweepers, recently journeymen".

poem. The first four lines speak in quiet resignation of the inevitable consequences of disadvantaged birth. And then the jaunty run of the verse discounts adversity. A divine assurance becomes a refuge for childhood when all else fails, precisely as Isaac Watts and all his disciples taught. Irony asks us if this ultimate reality of faith justifies exploitation, and even its indoctrination for commercial ends.

The illustration, where the children are released by Christ from their "coffins of black" to "wash in a river", seems to relate the climax of the text to a recollected actuality. Though many climbing boys went five years without water reaching the soot ingrained in their flesh, lucky ones were taken by their masters on a summer Sunday morning each year to wash in the New River. Tom Dacre's dream could be real.

¶ *13 & 14 The Little Boy Lost, The Little Boy Found*
With a lilt of sentimental mockery in the first four lines, a version of the 'The Little Boy Lost' appears in *An Island in the Moon*, among the other poems later associated with *Innocence*.[6] Then Blake wrote the exclamatory concern out of the first verse, added the sequel, and in 1789 linked the two parts with illustrations that anticipate the arboreal symbolism, which runs so profoundly into *Experience*, and through his later books.

The early Islanders were creditably touched by the verse. At the end of the piece, for a while "nobody could sing any longer". They heard that the little boy wept; "and away the vapour flew". Tears meant deliverance. In *An Island*, nothing suggests to us that the troublesome vapour is other than "an exhalation arising by natural causes", as the dictionary defines it, "from some damp place", such as the "marshy bottoms" around Battersea and Lambeth. In *Songs of Innocence* the "vapour" becomes "the wand'ring light", not simply confusing, but misleading; and the boy is now lost and rescued in a forest of Urizenic gloom.

This is no longer familiar Thameside. These trees are rooted in Blake's symbolic landscape, and the illustrative extension of the text is a technique which soon becomes familiar. The illustrated "wand'ring light", on which the sequel is built, may suggest that Blake recalls the "vapour" to have had an inflammatory sense in *An Island*; understandable in an age when electricity was still "a subtil effluvia or vapour", and given the Islanders' combustible sensitivities.

The birds and angels framing the poems celebrate a past and passing delight, offsetting "the dun forest" above them. The figure of the boy's rescuer is haloed with varying intensity in different issues, and the boy is given a halo, as if he is a child of Christ. The rescuer anticipates Christ sitting before the little black boy, and rescues the lost child into the care of the "mother". The salvation of Innocence is typified.

6. See Gardner, *Retraced*, pp. 68–70.

❡ *15 Laughing Song*

When someone copied an early draft of the poem into *Poetical Sketches*, the girls were Edessa, Lyca and Emilie. By changing the names, and dropping the early title, 'Song 2nd by a Young Shepherd', Blake recovered the verses from the sophistication of pastoral romance. With their seemingly unrevised repetition the lines become a run of epithets transferred between the revellers and nature so readily, that we accept the brilliant artifact of "the painted birds" in the shade as a natural triumph of laughter. The chorus of the last line takes us into the illustration.

None of the revellers is anything like as young as "Mary and Susan and Emily" out among the hills and streams. The run of the text, lively with the voices of children, is bordered by innumerable "painted birds" against the vivid sky. Then the illustration extends the celebration of Innocence into adult conviviality round the table under the evening oak. Again the scene seems to be an idealised recollection of a local occasion. Here are no fewer than six young women (off duty nurses?), being saluted by a visitor with a plumed hat, and his companion. In the years of peace, between defeat in America and revolution in France, the Governors of the Poor in Blake's parish frequently travelled to dine with "the nurses and children at Wimbledon".[7]

❡ *16 & 17 A Cradle Song*

If Blake developed 'A Cradle Song' from Isaac Watts's 'A Cradle Hymn', he found there neither theme nor language.

Watts begins predictably with an admonition: "Hush! my dear, lie still and slumber", includes a roll-call of adult open-handedness:

> *Sleep, my babe; thy food and raiment,*
> *House and home, thy friends provide;*
> *All without thy care or payment:*
> *All thy wants are well supplied,*

and, having used the lullaby to confirm how much better off his reader's infant is than the Christ child was, finishes with an admonition even more predictable: "Then go dwell for ever near Him,/See His face, and sing His praise!" If it is in *Innocence* at all, Watts's 'Hymn' is unrecognisably transformed.

On the first plate, an inconsequential interlacing of invocations brings us to a child suffused with protective slumber—"all creation slept and smil'd". Among the drowsy repetition, in the moonlight of doves and angels, the sustaining presence is the Christian empathy of the mother. The statutory moral directive is missing.

7. See Gardner, *Retraced*, pp. 50–51.

Even when Blake turns the theme towards the Nativity in the sixth
verse, the powerful historic pull towards a judicious reminder such as
Watts favoured ("Soft and easy is they cradle;/Coarse and hard thy
Saviour lay") counts for nothing. On the contrary, the closer Blake brings
the infant to the Nativity, the more uncompromisingly he sees Christianity as simple caring, and Christ in the lineaments of the cradled child:

> *Infant smiles are his own smiles*
> *Heaven & earth to peace beguiles.*

The leafy curtaining which borders the first page is alive with
human forms. Occupying the space of the title, the piper leans against
the letter 'A', while another figure (perhaps reading a book) sits in the
loop of the 'C'. Most intriguing of all, a solid citizen brings his authority
to the space of the letter 'D'. The evocations of the poem are already well
attended. Even so, the transition to the uncompromising care of the
next plate is startling.

The recollection of the Nativity is heightened by the tent-like,
screen and the nurse's substantial, old-fashioned head-rail.[8] The dream,
slumber and the maternal religious sensuousness are brought to terms
with the practice of assiduous child care. The 'mother's' guardianship,
with its reflections of the Nativity, makes "fit and proper" nurture an
exemplification of pristine Christianity. In cradling the living child, the
nurse is cradling Christ:

> *Sweet babe in thy face,*
> *Holy image I can trace.*

Moreover the child is wrapped in the correct loose covering Dr
William Buchan approved. The substantial cradle and chair will stay
put, and the nurse with them. The infant and the vision are safe. As
Blake relief-etched the scene, it is as if his imagination was clenched on
a reality grounded on an insight, which he desperately refuses to relin-
quish against the rising doubts of Experience, where vanity swaddles
the child to a disfiguring purpose.

❡ *18 The Divine Image*
When the eye arrives at the second line of the second verse, it looks as if
we have here a genuflection to conformity. Everything changes when
"God, our father dear" is identified in "the human form divine", and the
"virtues of delight" are shaped in mankind. It is the basic philosophy of
Innocence, especially the cohesion of delight and virtue in that electrify-

8. Blake put a reflection of this
screen in his drawing of 'The
Virgin Mary Hushing the Young
Baptist' some ten years later.

ing phrase. The Almighty, in Innocence, is "pleasant". It is these "virtues of delight" that the little vagabond in *Experience* so shamelessly and unacceptably attempts to reclaim, from the intensity of his family's distress.

The text provides an explication of 'The Blossom', the two poems being related visually in their illustrations. Here the flames of enlightenment exemplify the power implicit in the four pleasant, realised virtues of the poem.

In the right hand bottom corner of the plate, the gowned Christ of *Innocence* conveys his nature to mankind in a gesture. At the top of the illustration, in the loop of flame which crowns the title, two children "pray in their distress". They are answered across the sky by a gesture, which brings, not simply the reassurance so commonplace, but rescue, in the presence of a woman carrying what look like a loaf of bread and a jug. The circumstance illustrated is Innocence.

§ *19 Holy Thursday*
The essential facts are:
1. Blake attended one of the earliest services for charity school children held in St Paul's.
2. Neither the children nor their parents were intimidated.
3. These children were not rescued from destitution.
4. Parents were commonly not "of the lowest order of poverty", but the "deserving poor".
5. Competition for places was keen.
6. The uniforms were appreciated, as was being washed.
7. The schools were locally administered, and (at least the London day schools) well supervised.
8. The procession to St Paul's was not a march, but a festival, and is so illustrated: a crocodile of children chatting. When Blake's procession was copied for *City Scenes* in 1818 (reproduced in Bentley, *Blake Records*, plate 36), the children were still shown casually disciplined. It seems no-one, even then, expected a school crocodile to march.
9. The Guardians of the Poor had nothing to do either with the charity schools, or with the service in St Paul's. They were responsible for rescuing foundlings.
10. The beadles had no status as Guardians. The white wands make them officials at St Paul's (*OED*, 'wand', 13).
11. The service never took place in a church on Holy Thursday. If Blake borrowed the title from someone like Joe Bradley, it links to the contrary in *Experience*.
12. Blake is not satirising the occasion. He erased a topical satirical godsend, by excluding the Grey Coat children.

♪ *20 & 21 Night*

The first four lines of 'Night' lead on, as it were, from the conclusions of 'Nurse's Song' and 'The Ecchoing Green'. The initial echo is of a child's voice—"The birds are silent in their nest./And I must seek for mine"—which persists through the references to leaving the "green fields and happy groves", where the flocks, so strongly associated with childhood, "have took delight". The ideal of nurture is extended to all nature, when the night time angelic watch takes over from the shepherds and nurses, and a recollection of the cradle is heard in the curious use of "cover'd warm".

On the way to the triumphant conclusion there are further reflective impressions of the assurances in 'The Chimney Sweeper', and 'The Little Black Boy', until the lion, "with tears of gold", is converted to "cherish pity". This transformation identifies the lion-Saviour's intervention in *Innocence*:

> *wrath by his meekness*
> *And by his health sickness,*
> *Is driven away*
> *From our immortal day.*

On the first plate, the lion sleeps in a green and comfortable "cave", at the foot of the most resplendent tree in *Innocence*. It rises from the banks of the river of life resplendent with angels and the doves of peace, to encompass the light offsetting the title. Across the page a "Glorification of Angels"[9] hovers in the sketched heavens, sun, moon, stars, above what I take to be the gowned and watching figure of Christ.

On the second plate the five girls, their gowns blown by the breeze, come together beside the soaring branches of a sketched oak, set against a starry sky, and opened to make space for the song. The light around them gives them a celestial air, and illuminates the landscape they grace. Angels once more adorn the tree on the left, to which the girl with her back turned draws attention. The girl nearest the angels appears to cradle an infant in her arms. The restful togetherness of these figures complements the friendly revellers we meet in 'Laughing Song'.

♪ *22 & 23 Spring*

The infant in 'Spring' is held on a lap which has the substance to match the cradle in 'Cradle Song'. The nurse, so prominently painted, does not appear in the text. Again we meet Blake's technique of using an illustration to extend a literary theme. The poem generates the etching, as Blake visually relates the religious association of lamb and child to

9. *A Vision of the Last Judgment*, p. 85.

objective child care. And the transition follows from the least sophisticated text.

Beneath the familiar oak, the nurse supports and "tumbles" the
infant in line with the best medical advice, and at the same time
encourages the gesture symbolising the joy of communication, which
pervades Innocence. On the next plate, the grown child in turn cherishes the lamb, in text and illustration. The poetic and visual themes
come together. Whatever is left of commonplace pastoral has come
through a powerful catalysis close to Blake, to bring us this inimitable
rejuvenation of ideas; and it is made to look simple.

❡ 24 Nurse's Song

When Blake first slipped the lines into *An Island*, he took four attempts
to decide their singer. They landed with mother, where they served well
to satirise the vogue for maternal rhyming. To capitalise this vogue,
Blake might have left the poem with a mother in *Innocence*. Instead,
conclusively, since eighteenth-century nurses were rarely versified, he
returned the poem to its begetter, and fixed its matrix with his etching-
needle: seven children *of the same age* at their evening pastime, unobtru-
sively supervised by their "mother".

The poem exemplifies the nature of discipline in Innocence. The
nurse's admonition "*Then* come home my children" is a sequel to the
concord of happiness in the first verse. She bases it on her sensitivity to
nature, and on the responsibility she owes her charges. In the last verse
she yields not only to the children's importunity, but to her own second
thoughts. Her "heart is at rest" in the stillness enclosing the fields,
which clearly echoed for Blake to the voices of children.

The nurse's shoulders catch the evening light, which suffuses the
company, drawing shadows along the grass. Her reading brings the
discipline of composure and civility to the scene. The symbolic ampli-
tude Blake always gives to a nurse's lap and gown completes the ring of
children; then her figure is diminished in perspective to include her in
the circle. So many children, all of an age, identify the fostering.

In *An Island*, Mrs Nannicantipot's mother was lent, for a time, a song
about a "fit and proper nurse", here uniquely and immortally acclaimed.

❡ 25 Infant Joy

As we know too well, in Blake's lifetime infants commonly died. So
when Mrs Thrale, a devoted mother, lost a daughter in 1772, her reaction
was defensive emotional reserve: "one cannot grieve after her much, and
I have just now other things to think of". The child, ten hours old, was
already christened Penelope. Though one meets, from time to time,

versified laments for the mortality of infants of Mrs Thrale's social standing, her preoccupation with "other things" was more commonplace.

Alongside this, the century's reaction to the birth of a foundling was severely pragmatic. Sensitivity, if it existed, was curtailed in the priority of assigning the cost of the infant's rearing to the home parish: above all, to forestall cross-boundary transfer. Indifference to the survival of a foundling, "but two days old", was substantiated in the rates. Yet it is just such a survival that Blake uniquely celebrates here. In the terms of its underplayed, delighted resolution, the poem is astringent, the illustration a triumph of love. Together, this is almost incredible against the odds and prudence of the times.

For Blake, nurture and joy, those gifts of a "pleasant" God, were the birthright of every child, not least of this foundling, incomparably named Joy. It was a vision beyond the reach of the century. It remains unmatched today. In the illustration Blake acclaimed the principle, which drew the angel down to earth, and which he called Innocence.

¶ 26 A Dream

Blake temporarily transferred 'A Dream' to *Songs of Experience* when he brought out the combined edition in 1794. It is not difficult to understand his hesitation. Just as the sombre trees of 'The Little Boy Lost' and 'Found' anticipate the forests of affliction and superstition planted in the Prophetic Books, so the imagery of 'A Dream' holds intimations of another range of symbols.

In 'A Cradle Song' the dream, woven by sleep "with soft down", was a protective, reassuring solace. Now the speaker reports the recollection of a dream weaving "a shade", turning the image towards ominous intimations of the "curtains of darkness" under the "Web of Religion", where the solace of dreams will become illusory.

Dreamlike, the participants in the poem shift and evade identity. The speaker is a voice without substance. The "angel guarded bed" in woven shadow suggests all the ineffectual reassurance official religion affords in Experience.

In the second verse, through broken syntax, we move from the suspicion that the dreamer is "Troubled wilderd and forlorn", to the knowledge that this is the state, not of the dreamer, but of the insect in the dream; and then that the dream is not of a lost child, but of a benighted mother, an idea alien to Innocence.

The "sigh" of the father here diminishes even the limited effectuality of the male in *Innocence*. The "children" wander away in tearful distress, and, uniquely in Innocence, are welcomed with no better than tears, and a transference to official oversight.

Identities are blurred, voices blend, speakers become difficult to distinguish. Consideration becomes implausible. A kind of initial rescue arrives in nothing more tangible than an admonition. At the voice of the "wailing wight", perception wavers, as in dreams it will, from the whirl of inconsequential associations to pavement poverty, with the abandoned child calling to the watchman, as it were outside the drawn curtains of Golden Square. Only the self-sufficing deception of a dream suggests the watchman is obeyed, wherever "home" is for the lost child. It is a near thing.

The flourish and reassurance of the illustration retrieves the dream for *Innocence*. The light and the foliage in full flower take us into Summer. The dreamer sleeps in the loop of the 'A' of the title, under a tangle of grass, while a figure sits bent over a book, enclosed in the 'D'. The eagle of inspiration soars between them.

An angel guards the first line. The emmet, the glow-worm and the beetle inhabit the leaves and tendrils at the right of their respective lines. And at the foot, outlined against the base which supports the border, the admonitory watchman waits.

¶ *27 On Anothers Sorrow*

Here, for the only time in *Innocence*, Blake speaks as it were with his own voice; and, it seems to me, with a rising misgiving. The reader is faced with a personal reaction at the outset: "Can I see anothers woe / And not be in sorrow too" followed by a series of rhetorical questions and exclamatory assertions, which breed more uncertainty than reassurance.

In the first six lines the speaker asks how he can consider the sorrow of another and not share it, or "seek for kind relief". Elsewhere in *Innocence* the sharing is spontaneous, not reflective, and the "relief" substantially brought, not sought. The whole poem reflects the secondary, comparatively ineffectual nature of paternal intervention in Innocence. The questions are transferred to the father, then, in a kind of ascending order of expectation, to the mother and (through the familiar analogy of cradle and nest) to the Deity. Redemption from grief (the reiterated theme of the poem) rests here to the end. The poem has found its way, as it were, from the perturbed acknowledgement of empathy, to the rescue of Divine solace. But in the last line, even this takes us back full circle to the start of the poem, God doing what the initial speaker asked if he must do; and no more. No effective intervention disturbs this elegiac farewell to Innocence.

Only the illustration rejoices at the recollection of Innocence achieved. On the left, at the foot of the vine, the piper stands playing to a creature, maybe a lamb, at his feet. The vine itself is entwined with figures, less formal than the presentation in the 'Introduction'. Above the piper's head, a climber begins his ascent towards a grander figure alongside the third and fifth verses. Then above, the little black boy lifts his hands in prayer, and a gowned figure raises his arms towards the title.

Songs of Experience

❡ *28 Frontispiece*

An ominous change has come over the shepherd and child introduced to us in the frontispiece to *Songs of Innocence*, and to their relationship. The shepherd no longer holds his pipe, and no longer looks up at the exultant child. The child is refashioned as a cherub for adoration astride an adult intelligence. We shall soon meet more intimately the kind of child "guidance" prefigured here.

At the outset of the tragic journey through Experience, we see the child is constrained, and conveyed past the sheltering oak, away from the fields and hills of Innocence. The flock is being deserted. The man is neither shepherd nor piper. The inspirational child is potently angelic. He is to be the darling of the priest and the nanny.

❡ *29 Title-page*

The dead, who are effigies of death, are mourned by the adolescents in the stylised manner of *Experience*. They are barred from the living by the featureless panelling, with its heavy coping of EXPERIENCE. Above and beyond this, the dancing, flying figures celebrate a lost and contrary state "of the Human Soul".

❡ *30 & 31 Introduction, Earth's Answer*

"Hear the voice of the Bard!" leads into the reply, 'Earth's Answer'. While he changed the order of other texts, Blake kept these two songs invariably together.

Blake had written 'Earth's Answer' (complete with title) in the Notebook a year or more before he prefaced it with the 'Introduction'.[10] Together the texts compose an enigmatic lead into *Experience*, based on the symbolic use of language Blake developed from the late 1780s, and into the Lambeth Books.

In directing the reader's imagination to discard preconceptions, Blake of necessity had to break old and pre-set verbal associations. Reconsider the sea: for Blake it was impressive as the ocean into which Britannia's merchantmen dumped slaves as sickness, retribution and ballast required. It was the element which separated Albion from the impulse towards liberty generated in America, overwhelming and

10. David V. Erdman, ed., *The Notebook of William Blake, A Photographic and Typographic Facsimile*, (London: Oxford University Press, 1973), N. 111.

dividing mankind. The verbal associations Blake reiterates may be unexpected; but history hardly invalidates them.

As we have seen, for Blake the stars rarely, if ever, shed a gentle and romantic light. "Tis the Bloody Shrine of War/Pinnd around from Star to Star" were the last words on the night sky he wrote at the foot of the last page of his Notebook. And if it is not war, Urizen's "overflowing stars rain down prolific pains" and pestilence, "scattering death Thro' the red fev'rous night". It was something every sailor knew, who battened down the hatches against the influence of tropical stars.

Then the forest became a symbol of deeply rooted oppression; and the illusions of "veiled evening", and the promise of a false dawn, became two specious consolations of life under the constraints of Experience. By creative repetition of such ideographic recusancy, Blake challenges the validity of "authority" and its crippling of true Christian relationships.

We may hear in the voice of the Bard an echo of the poet himself in *Experience*. 'The Holy Word', set prophetically among the "ancient trees", might, if it were transformed ("fallen"), both refashion the universe, and lighten the dark. But we are faced with the emphasis of self-persuasion, rather than hope, and solace is the illusion of a false dawn, soon named for what it is: "starry Jealousy", and a prison on "the wat'ry shore".

The cry for "free love" here is still misconstrued. The phrase was unknown in its present sense until the 1850s. This love is neither explicitly sexual nor intimate; the freedom is not self-will. The cry is tragic. In Blake's day, marriage, which bound a woman as a chattel (sic "a moveable possession") in body, mind and "duty", was an irreplaceable bedrock for social bondage. "Free love" is a cry, two centuries before its time, for release into humanity, open-hearted fulfilment, a breaking of the shackles. From this, it becomes a general cry for release from subservience in an empire of spiritual and social inertia. The nature of compliance, required in one way from the poor, in another from "the better sort", is delineated in the book which follows this 'Introduction' and 'Answer'.

Maybe the cosmic nature of these two texts made illustration difficult even for Blake, as it did in 'The Tyger'. To my eye, the illustration to the 'Introduction' pictures humanity among Urizen's stars, couched in self-indulgence and looking towards the deceptive dawn. In the illustration to 'Earth's Answer', every movement and stroke descends to meet the serpent, upon which the poem rests, its menacing head lit by a pallid sun.

Aspects of these two texts are developed less symbolically in several later plates.[11]

11. In 'The Clod & the Pebble', 'The Little Girl Lost' and 'Found', 'Nurses Song', 'The Sick Rose', 'The Fly', 'The Angel', 'My Pretty Rose-Tree', 'Ah! Sun-Flower', 'The Garden of Love', 'A Little Girl Lost', and maybe even 'The Tyger'. See Gardner, *Retraced*, pp. 91–98, for a discussion of these plates, and Blake's symbolic use of language. A valuable insight comes from the commonest references in David V. Erdman, ed., *A Concordance to the Writings of William Blake* (Ithaca: Cornell University Press, 1967), 2 vols.

¶ 32. *The Clod & the Pebble*

Fictional biographies of inanimate objects were highly profitable from the 1780s into the next century. Inevitably it was John Marshall who set the fashion, with Mary Ann Kilner's *The Adventures of a Pincushion* in 1783, "designed chiefly for the use of young Ladies", and followed the same year with rougher stuff for boys, *Memoirs of a Peg-Top*, where a meal consists of custard and cow dung.

As ever, Blake transforms a hackneyed notion. The "moral" "for the use of young Ladies", boys or us, becomes incisive; and instead of a cosy answer, we are left with disturbing questions, sharpened by the illustration. The sheep and cattle are supported in the togetherness by the Clod of Clay: "love seeketh not Itself to please". The Pebble does what? Below the text, the frolicsome water creatures enliven a kind of nursery frieze, a fiction in which self-interest becomes a splashabout, and a parody.

¶ 33 *Holy Thursday*

The title has no relevance except to identify the plate as a 'contrary' to 'Holy Thursday' in Innocence, where "Babe can never hunger there". The title is the link which pulls together the tragedy. And if Blake took the title from the lips of children, the irony in it is sharpened.

Every Londoner knew the story of Captain Thomas Coram, who worked for seventeen years to establish the Foundling Hospital in the fields near Tottenham Court, as a refuge for children "dropped" by the roadside. Equally familiar to Londoners was the engraving called 'The Foundlings', from a design made by Hogarth in 1739. The Hospital used it as a head-piece to its appeals for subscriptions well into the next century, so frequently that a blank space was left for the date as each issue went out.[12] Hogarth's engraving contrasts the well dressed children of the Hospital, with the condition of the just rescued foundlings. A mother weeps, having parted with her infant. A dropped child is rescued from the hedge in the distance. Catching the eye, in the foreground another foundling lies cruciform, naked and soon saved.

It is this foundling, from the focal point of an ubiquitous design, that Blake transfers to the bottom of 'Holy Thursday'. Only the angle of the body is made more telling. The mother has placed a white cloth under the head of her dropped child—the last comfort of starvation. Blake adds the deliberate gesture of dignity and love to a signal everyone knew from the Foundling Hospital flyer. The family sits in its underground foliage of loss before moving away. The indigent mother fends off another naked infant: the next of necessity to be dropped? Her eldest child stands in tears. He is the one left she can afford to keep because by now, being weaned, he earns his keep. He alone is clothed.

12. Reproduced on page 139 above. See Gardner, *Retraced*, pp. 120–125. A child abandoned by destitute parents was said, in the jargon of the day, to be "dropped".

Above ground, in a landscape of "eternal winter", a woman regards a
dropped child. The woman is not the child's mother. No gracious lady,
gowned and groomed as she is, would be driven to drop her child, with
a prayer that the rider with the basket, not death, would be the finder.
The lady is distressed, horror stylised in her wrists, superseding both
compassion and intervention: "Is this a holy thing to see?".

The appalling illustration, in its day so familiar in its reflections,
transfixes us with the consequences of the "usurous hand" of philanthropy. Set it, the title tells us, against the "red & blue & green" excitement of those children on another Holy Thursday in the hopeful years;
set it against "cherish pity". And set it, the last verse says, against the
landscape of Innocence.

¶ *34, 35 & 36 The Little Girl Lost, The Little Girl Found*
Blake first included these three plates in *Innocence*. They were too good
to leave out; but once the combined *Songs* was ready he transferred
them to *Experience*, where he left them permanently. This is clearly
where he felt "lovely Lyca" belonged, her narrative being a symbolic
exposure of so many consequences of sophisticated and tendentious
aspirations. However, despite Blake's unambiguous re-allocation, the
plates have at times been returned to *Innocence* by editors. This, it seems
to me, re-introduces concepts quite alien there, such as chastity, deference, royalty, fear, awe, loneliness, and separation.

In 'Night' the lion's eyes flowed "with tears of gold", as he lay down to
guard the lamb. Sovereignty was transformed in those stately cadences,
to sustain the concord of Innocence. To read these 'Little Girl' poems
alongside 'Night' is a revelation in symbolism. Lyca's solicitous beast
takes on a menacingly effete characteristic, as Blake turns the symbol
contextually towards Experience. Arriving from "caverns deep" (a most
ominous association), this "kingly lion" "view'd" the seven year old
"virgin", "gambold round" her and wept "ruby tears", before "the lioness"

> *Loos'd her slender dress*
> *And naked they convey'd*
> *To caves the sleeping maid.*[13]

The providence of Innocence has become lubricious attention. We
follow a child to a questionable retreat, in language modulated with the
formality of sexual deference. The movement of the verse facilitates its
equivocal propositions, until at the end of the first poem Lyca is
"found", not by her parents, but by an authority which moves with the
prurience of a masque. It is a measure irreconcilable with *Innocence*.

13. See Gardner, *Retraced*, pp.
96–102, and 'cave' and 'cavern' in
Erdman, ed., *Concordance*.

The parents' search persists through tribulation, grief and weariness, with an insistence on the adjective "deep", so inevitably associated by Blake with unrelenting oppression.[14] The search ends in condolence, and a reunion (if this happens at all) in loneliness. Lyca's parents are told in distancing terms that "the maid" is "asleep" in the "palace deep"; it turns out, among "tygers wild". Some reassurance this, as the paradox redrafts the playful tigers, and gives the ominously deferential lion a growl.

Then in the last verse, if "they" refers to the parents alone, the family remains separated. On the other hand, if "they" means all three (Lyca and her parents), they protract their sunless lives confined "in a lonely dell": by definition a "deep natural hollow", its banks "clothed with trees and foliage". Home is a place of buried isolation for the submissive.[15]

The most obvious aspect of the illustrations is how little of the text they reflect. Instead they take us through its corollary. At the outset we meet a mature Lyca, sometimes in a diaphanous gown, which she later changes. Her raised arm points us to the bird of Innocence soaring towards the word "Lost". Lost: the willow which shades the couple was universally "taken as a symbol of grief for unrequited love or loss of a mate".[16] The poem's conclusion, the loss of Innocence in a parentally contrived, royal intervention, is predicated.

On the next plate, grown to womanhood, Lyca is alone and alert in a forest of massive trees, with one lifeless stump in the foreground. She reclines unrelaxed, pointedly beneath this tree. Its dead limbs carry the text of the disrobing and "deliverance" of her younger days. She gathers her dress around her, as she looks up to see her childhood recollected. Under this formidable head-piece, 'The Little Girl Found' opens against the sky beneath the leafless arch of a tree familiar in *Experience*.

Lyca's unfulfilled expectation and the subsequent restless anxiety are resolved in the retreat with the "kingly lion" and attentive lioness: no "tygers wild" around her here, no "lonely dell", no "lions growl", but a conclusive reception into custodial luxury. Two naked children dally with the consorting lioness, while another fondles the lion, presently the symbol of prerogative and power—a prerogative that has surely been questionably exercised in this text. The adult Lyca lies naked, cradling her face against the earth, under the interlocked trees. It is a sorry consummation of the promise for humankind in the first illustration.

The themes of the text and its relief-etchings are distinct but related, in a presentation unique in its effect.

¶ *37 The Chimney Sweeper*
Chimney boys who served Blake's neighbourhood endured one degradation among many sustaining the city around it: a social delinquency

14. See 'deep' in Erdman, ed., *Concordance*.

15. The one impressive dell in or near London was the ravine on Wimbledon Common, running to the south west of the windmill. It drops some thirty feet in its first 150 yards. Richard Milward tells me it was known as Glen Albyn in the last century; but Blake would not know it as such, since the word "glen" was not then current in England. For him, its enclosing trees and shrubs comprised a unique and "lonely dell". It suggests that Wimbledon was the matrix of 'The Little Girl' lines, alongside the rest of *Innocence*. Until Blake thought about it, Lyca "belonged" there?

16. See *OED*, 'willow', 1, d.

such as any age can somehow muster. The 'contrary' which Blake points lies not in conditions, but in relationships. The "little black thing" is profiting his father, who is conniving at a trick of the law, when he chances his son's life in the flue.[17] By law, the father's only offence was the boy's cry for custom, with which he disturbs the silence of sabbath snow.

Mere indigence would keep Tom Dacre out of church; the chimney sweeper here is excluded by an even more corrosive evil. Condoning the boy's compliance is the trinity of "God & his Priest & King", to which the parents "are both gone up to the church to pray", having broken the family. Blake exposes the nerve in the fist of self-righteous paternal cupidity.

The illustration is unusually direct in its representation of the text. The boy, humping his bag home to an empty house under the blizzard, is in rags and bare-foot, because shoes made climbing chimneys difficult. Again it seems Blake is observing a common practice (that master sweeps equipped their offspring fully into the part), while symbolising the totality of deprivation procured by avarice across the barriers of class.

For all that the boy belongs to a family whose standing admits them to church, the sweep in *Experience* is denied both Christ and the rough fellowship that Tom Dacre knew.

¶ *38 Nurses Song*

Innocence, recollected briefly, is lost. The present is telescoped into the past, as neighbour whispers of neighbour among the nurses "in the dale". The children are now called to "come home" on the grounds of sickening regret and waste, by a speaker who dissociates herself from them, and whose good-night reproof is the cynical verity of Experience.

The "green and pale" anguish of the memory of her youth refers us to the nurse's complexion in 'The Fly'. The two plates comprise a single condemnation. Even the movements of the two nurses' hands have a continuity. Each illustration develops its own impetus from the text.

Here the green and the dale, so bitterly misrepresented in cynical recollection, go undepicted. Instead the community of nurture has become a nursery for mis-shaping the soul. The nurse leans over the youth, coaxing him into (or out of) puberty in a posture of assiduous nannying. The repose which was the basis of care in Innocence is lost in self-regard. Blushing from brow to bosom, the sophisticating female, a sexually alert pink, is provocatively dressed for the part.

The sister, withdrawn into her book, brings to the solicitude in the

17. 28 Geo. III, chap. 48. The practice was legal till 1817.

foreground the indifference of familiarity. The boy's posture of inviting self-protection and the nurse's delicately working hands depict the breeding of seductive withdrawal, framed in the sensual implications of the vines.

The contrast with 'Nurse's Song' in *Innocence* is total. The community of children there, spared the excesses of polite tutelage, immune from "whisprings", unvisited by dame Lurch, have the living advantage over this precious privacy.[18] The illustration takes us from the irremediable loss of the poem into the nurseries and parlours of Albany and Golden Square. It depicts the other side of desolation, unimaginable to the vagrants round their night fires among the brick-kilns.

℩ 39 *The Sick Rose*

In 1747 the *Gentleman's Magazine* had printed the opinion that "the plague itself is caused by the air's being full of invisible *animalcula* to which it owes its infection". The word 'germ' is first recorded in its modern sense of 'microbe' in a medical journal fifty years later. So Blake was left with his poetically loaded translation, "the invisible worm", and its imperceptible cargo of spiritual decay. Then the phrase collects to itself all the secondary associations of the words. The worm typified "a grief or passion that preys stealthily on a man's heart or troubles his conscience, especially the gnawing pain of remorse . . . "the worm that never dies".[19]

Moreover, particularly during the early 1790s, it brought to Blake's lines the implication of sinister, unspoken intrusion abroad in the air. All this, together with invisibility, and progress through darkness and storm, fetches the influence of Urizen and his "secrets of dark contemplation" spiralling into our imagination, through the garden rose of Experience.

The intimate, intimidating message of these lines depends on a sequence of swift and transitional associations, to the exclusion of any precise visual recollection. Since any illustrative recapitulation would diminish, or even unsay, the poem, we are faced with a visual consequence, fetching the imagination down with the "invisible worm", from the elements of night into a ring-fence of briar.

The menacing thorns and serrated leaves loop down to the overblown, cultivated rose, with its ferreting worm and distraught woman at the base of the picture. Two victims, prostrate or crouching, are impaled on the thorns overhead, while above them "the Catterpiller and Fly/Feed on the Mystery".[20] The illustration reinforces the grip of the poem, trapped in a garden, with all the sorrows of jealousy and fear this means in Experience.[21]

18. "Whisprings" sound more menacing than mere gossip. See 'The Little Vagabond' below.

19. See *OED*: 'worm', 11; 'infection', 2; and Erdman, ed., *Concordance*: 'disease', 'infection', 'pestilence', 'plague'.

20. 'The Human Abstract'.

21. See Gardner, *Retraced*, pp. 141–8, and index under 'garden'.

¶ *40 The Fly*

"The want/Of thought is death." It is one definition of Experience, and the speaker comes to identify himself with the "happiness" of this deadly unconcern. Blake gets him there by the most unlikely, least portentous and most difficult route: a nursery form of verse, and a nursery theme—Innocence turned topsy-turvy. And, at the same time, again we have a swift and satirical pastiche of tales for children of "the divine nature of the meanest creatures"—how they have "affection, and impulse ... in them ... like our inferior emotions".[22]

Sometimes this was taken even further, beyond "inferior emotions". So in 1803 Sarah Trimmer looked back disapprovingly at *The Life and Adventures of a Fly*, which came out in 1789. "In this book", she wrote, "as in many others of modern date, humanity towards animals is carried to an excess. [They are] elevated to the ranks of human beings, they are our fellow creatures, our equals, if not our superiors in virtue."[23] Blake elevates the speaker, the voice of *Experience*, at least to the rank of the fly. It could be said that in *Innocence* every action was "thoughtful"; that is, considerate, sensitive to the needs of others. As the speaker acknowledges,

> *thought is life*
> *And strength & breath.*

So, from the speaker's own lips, the "thoughtless hand" of the first verse is not simply chance, but negligent killing, a moral and manual gesture commonplace in *Experience*, where "the want Of thought is death". The speaker, trapped in his own self-pleasuring, happily and fatally accepts this condition of "thought-lessness". Speaker and fly are pals in facile indifference; except that the fly is, with Sarah Trimmer's emphasis, "*superior in virtue*". It is the speaker from *Experience* who does the offhand killing.

In the illustrated extrapolation, the girl turns away absorbed in her companionless play. What spectral partner delivers the shuttlecock to her racket from the unpeopled wash of cloud and sky? Nanny and children are caged by the dead trees, with a desert for foothold, beneath a blank horizon.

This "summers play" and its location are the antithesis to the sociable cricket and skipping ring in the fields. The nanny leans over her toddler with the same histrionic care we saw in 'Nurses Song'. Her face is tinted "green and pale", not yet blush-pink, beneath her nurse's cap. The child barefoot, like the chimney sweep, is fastidiously taught to walk a different, equally dispiriting landscape. In years to come, nanny will change her dress for his adolescent education in "want Of thought".

22. Mary Wollstonecraft, *Original Stories from Real Life* (London: J. Johnson, 1791), p. 15.
23. *Guardian of Education* (1803), pp. 184–85.

❡ *41 The Angel*

In Blake's writing, angels are primarily the divine servants of God, the spiritual guardians of human kind; but not always. Satan has his angels too; and Blake also used them with satirical reversal. In *The Marriage of Heaven and Hell*, which Blake advertised for sale the year before he brought out the combined *Songs*, the inspired revolutionaries are demonic, and the submissive are angelic. In *America*, brilliantly printed by Blake, again in 1793, both the revolutionary leaders and the effete officers of imperial oppression are angelic. The context distinguishes them.

While the benign identity of the angel in 'A Dream' in *Innocence* is in no doubt, the angelic cupid here is suspect, as the Queen reveals in confessing her dream of Experience; and although she is her own deceiver she ironically and sadly concedes that her guardian was beguiling: "Witless woe, was ne'er beguil'd".

The incipient dream was of maiden royalty, angelically guarded. As the years of dream pass by, it is as if the image of the angel changes. His loss becomes a deeper regret. The maiden "wishes but acts not", and prudently arming herself against the angel's return, finds too late that her years are spent.[24] It is the introspective rejection of self-fulfilment. The blush-red morning confirms the frustration which the dreamer's gesture makes explicit, as she fends off the importunate cupid with his impressive wings.

❡ *42 The Tyger*

The least effective illustration accompanies the most familiar and famous poem. A tiger walking, bewildered or benign, beneath the leafless tree neither represents the poem, nor extends its meaning. Any attempt to depict the intensity and scope of the lines seems bound to fall short.

The tyger, Blake's unique poetic symbol of spiritual and physical insurrection, burns in the "forests of eternal death".[25] The primeval Urizen comes down the ages from the "forests of the night" to arrive in Westminster as the "Satanic Holiness",[26] whom the rulers of Church and State require their subjects to worship "in moral gratitude & submission".[27]

The text refers the history of oppression to its cosmic origins. In primordial "distant deeps and skies", mankind's sentence to "eternal dying" is challenged, not only by the incandescent tyger, but also by the labour which tempers the questions. Intransigent resolution was for Blake the only counter to the operators of Experience.

Then in the incomparable after-thought of the fifth verse,[28] when

24. *A Song of Liberty* (1793). Much there is relevant to *Experience*.

25. References to the forest are legion. See Erdman, ed., *Concordance*.

26. *Jerusalem*, plate 60. The epithets Blake applies to holiness—selfish, hypocrite, secret, cruel, false, among others—express his revulsion at the tyrannous misuse of religion.

27. *Milton*, plate 11.

28. Blake's re-writing in the Notebook, N. 108–9, is illuminating.

the starry cohorts of oppression "threw down their spears", the question "Did he who made the Lamb make thee?" has the ring of a startled revelation, as it echoes that earlier rhetorical question, "Little Lamb who made thee?" Blake's technique of loading a commonplace phrase with a poetic charge is familiar. Here the underplayed mention of the Lamb is the climax, carrying the weight of a staccato, enigmatic interrogation.

The immortal Creator of the tyger in mankind is now one Being with the Creator of the pastoral Lamb, not in dismissible rhetoric, but mortally relevant to us in the phrases remembered from Innocence: "gave it clothing", and "bid it feed". So the impulse behind the intensity of 'The Tyger' lies, not only in reaction to the time-worn atrocities of Experience, but in recollection also of those transient years when children, "multitudes of lambs", were fed a benediction, truly, if briefly, Christian. We come to find that both Innocence and the challenge of the tyger are subsumed under Christ himself.[29]

¶ *43 My Pretty Rose Tree, Ah! SunFlower, The Lilly*

'My Pretty Rose Tree'—We are shown three flowers on the page for three aspects of living in Experience. While down the centuries the rose had come to represent immaculate virtue in woman, much more powerful for Blake, it seems, was the familiar circumstance of his move to Lambeth.[30] His reaction to immediate influence was always intense. There has been no mention of the garden and its rose in his work before *Songs of Experience*. Perhaps unexpectedly for us, the garden is not a necessary solace in *Innocence*. It becomes the solace of jealousy in *Experience*, where a neighbour excludes his neighbour, cultivating introspective preoccupations, and where suspicion of intruders invites intrusion. The garden develops into a symbol of apprehensive vigilance. In it grows the rose of secretive desire, disguised in "hypocrite modesty". "Modesty", sensually charged since its first appearance in *Poetical Sketches*, is now invariably suspect.[31]

Autobiographical allusions are frequently read into 'My Pretty Rose Tree', with no more justification than surmise based on the poem itself. Given the contextual symbolism, the 'I' in these verses is quite different from the 'I' of 'London', where Blake himself walks the streets. Here he objectively excludes autobiography from both text and illustration, where we move out of the garden to the barren ground of Experience.

Here one woman, her "modest tresses . . . bound up", reclines beneath the skeleton tree; another, her "locks of shadowing modesty shining" loose, sits slumped in dejection.[32] The speaker of the poem has satisfied neither wife nor lover, and makes no appearance in the landscape.

29. See Gardner, *Retraced*, pp. 149–58. For a persuasive reading of the poem relating it to Blake's reaction (albeit some fifteen years late) to the American Revolution, see David V. Erdman, *Blake: Prophet Against Empire* (New York: Dover, 1977, 3rd edn.), 'tyger' indexed. Certainly the everyday application of the name to other feline beasts, especially the jaguar, in America ("the tigers in the woods", "spotted tigers"), can only have sustained a ready association in Blake's mind. See *OED*, 'tiger', 2a.

30. See Gardner, *Retraced*, pp. 141–42.

31. In 'To Spring', 'To Autumn'. See Erdman, ed., *Concordance*, 'modest', 'modesty'.

32. *Jerusalem*, plate 70.

℣ 'Ah! SunFlower'—The sunflower, turning its face to the sun as the hours are counted, typifies man's aspirations beyond the gardens of Experience. But the hope is no better than the diminished fulfilment promised to "the virgins of youth and morning" in 'Earth's Answer'. The fulfilment will not be a vision of "eternity's sun rise".[33] The best release the youth and the virgin may expect from spiritual debility in these gardens is the consolation of something like "The lost Traveller's dream under the Hill".[34]

℣ 'The Lilly'—The lily traditionally represented "persons or things of exceptional whiteness, fairness or purity".[35] To illustrate the irony of the immaculate impossibility of the poem, Blake shows the flower on the left of the plate as a day-lily, which draws together its petals against the night, and opens with the sunrise. A serpent trails implications down from the sunflower.

We may watch Blake arriving at the disturbing effect of these four lines in the changes he made to his early ideas. The discarded associations are revealing.[36] So the "lustful rose" became the "modest rose", and the "coward sheep" became "humble". A challenge generated in lust or cowardice is ordinary. But to make "modesty subtil modesty" draw blood, and humility threaten, is a different matter.

℣ *44. The Garden of Love*
"On January 9, 1793", as Blake's mind was on *Songs of Experience*, John and Sarah Bond were granted a lease of land fronting South Lambeth Road, "for the erection of a proprietary chapel". So "a Chapel was built" on a green a short walk from Blake's house, where fee-paying communicants were submitted to the Divinity, while against the inadmissibly poor "the gates of the Chapel were shut". The local initiative brings a bitter double sense to "Thou shalt not, writ over the door".

Whether this speculative provision directly motivated the poem matters little. Such closed doors were commonplace. Blake sees the excluded parishioners turning for solace to the "sweet flowers" in "the Garden of Love", only to find it supervised by the Priests with harsh prohibitions. The symbols of rose and thorn in the gardens of jealousy are given a more general emphasis.

The illustration compounds the loss. The garden becomes a graveyard annexed to the chapel. The young, who "used to play on the green", kneel in obedience behind the priest. His hand directs their prayers and their vision down into a burial which is bound in briars. Blake's symbolic journey, which started, as so often, from some ordinary, socially divisive contract not worth a second thought, finishes with minds and eyes on the grave.

33. See Erdman, ed., *Notebook*, N. 105.
34. 'The Gates of Paradise', Epilogue.
35. See *OED*: 'lily', 3.
36. See Erdman, ed., *Notebook*, N. 109.

¶ *45 The Little Vagabond*

The little vagabond who speaks the words, and the mother he add-resses, must be a cut above the illustrated family round the night fire. They at least to have risen to a place in a cold, if separate, congregation. The speaker is both the vagabond round the fire, and simply the "spir-ited rascal" one sense of the title implies. His suggested improvements come out with an insolence no more acceptable to Sarah Trimmer and her readers than the proposals themselves. Blake took the language from the lips of the knock-about children he knew. It is vagabond verse. And in it the speaker basically proposes a return to something like the circumstances of Innocence.

A full belly and lodging "healthy & pleasant & warm" are the prereq-uisites of prayer; make the church as congenial as the ale house, and God, in that presumptuous, incredible phrase, would rejoice that His children were "as pleasant and happy as he".[37] The proposition, in its assumptions about the nature of the Divinity, is subversive of all the social advantages necessitous obedience was required to serve.

But more directly subversive still, the little vagabond is given a swipe at the security service set up by the Home Office. Besides thrashing her children and punishing them sick with starvation, "modest dame Lurch" was engaged to inform on her neighbours.[38]

In the headpiece the youth kneels to the Lord among "the forests of affliction". It looks at first as if his supplication is received with the light of redemption. The light has a different sheen after we have read down to the family round the night-fire at the foot of the page, where their state is the consequence of all that the precocious speaker condemns.

With the children already rejected, the family can be no more than a day-break away from dropping a child in a field some Holy Thursday. It would take the unlikely transformation of Sarah Trimmer's Church and its deity, as the little vagabond proposes, to rescue this family; and to return the boy, naked in destitution, to the arms of the Redeemer in the head-piece; and then prepared to kneel.

¶ *46 London*

We hear Blake's own voice as he "wanders" (such a gentlemanly word) through "all this dreadful ruin"[39]. His restraint never falters as he passes by the dead-living which the text reports. The rejection of either anger or indignation mounts an unanswerable indictment of the forgers of those intangible manacles.[40] We sense that Experience, of which this poem is a walking summary, is no fresh dispensation, but an old and chartered alienation, refashioned for the latest oppression. The poem's quiet, colloquial voice pronounces that the contemporary manipulators,

37. 'Pleasant':Blake loaded the word with much more weight than it carries for us— closer to "blessed".

38. Dame Lurch, as her title declares, kept a Dame school for young children. This was both profitable and useful as a cover for the other undertakings her name spells out. See *OED*, 'lurch', v, 1: "To remain in or about a place furtively or secretly, esp. with evil design. 1790." And Potter, *Dict. Cant.* (1793), 'lurch': "to lay by, to sneak, to hang on". Ironically the Dame's modesty could be taken to imply decorum and even clemency at the time. Her pupils were bandy owing to rickets ("the English disease") brought on by under feeding. Fasting was an economically advantageous corporal punishment.

39. *The Four Zoas*, plate 79. *OED*, "charter'd": "Charters are dona-tions of the sovereign; and not laws, but exemptions from law" (Hobbes). So privilege is set against "every ban", that is an "interdiction which curses" the poor.

40. "Mind-forg'd". In Erdman, ed., *Notebook*, N. 109, Blake first wrote "german forged links", referring to the Hanoverian monarchy. The scare over Hessian mercen-aries increased after the defeats of 1793 in the war of the Vendée.

having the past in their hands, have no need for dexterity of mind. It is the poem's continuity from past into present (then and now) which is appalling, driven home by the insistent repetition of "mark".[41]

Its termination is in the illustration. The young vagabond leads the cripple beside a workhouse door. The door is shut. The boy's shadow falls against it. Its substantial crudity both imprisons and excludes. The old man is directed across the relentless cobbles to the vagabond fire in the field; but he never arrives. For the first time, the street boy is without a family; and for the first time, thrown on his own devices, he warms himself at the fire. For old and young, the excluding charters of London streets come down to this.

¶ *47 The Human Abstract*
Originally entitled 'The Human Image',[42] the plate is specifically a 'contrary' to 'The Divine Image' in *Innocence*. Beyond that, the "mind-forg'd manacles" of 'London' are shaped from the base matter of these shifting, discomforting assertions.

Initially the "we" of the second line, the "Opressors of Albion in every City & Village", cynically resent the state of loss they have induced.[43] The "he" then reported in the third verse identifies a generalisation in a singular ambiguity: the hypocrite fear, regret and humility feed an extortionate and parasitic officialdom. The condition is nourished on the fruit of "the tree of mystery", rooted in the "mutual fear" in the mind of man.[44] The vain search through times past of "The Gods of earth and sea" lends this abstract of Experience a revered antiquity.

The illustration fixes the 'contrary' state. In a Surrey village, beneath a protecting oak, the old folk sat in harmony during those interim years before "the Opressors" once more prevailed. Now, the grace of age becomes a nodulated senility in which the "tree of mystery" is rooted. The brain is roped to earth by a tension we read in the text to be at once socially imposed and self-inflicted. The hand hangs on to the mental guy-ropes, for assurance rather than release it seems, while a rib-cage of shadows extrudes from the captive. The tree of Experience rising from this mortal stock has its branches desiccated to filaments.

¶ *48 Infant Sorrow*
Both poem and illustration express the perversion in luxury of the matchless charity in 'Infant Joy'. The repose of that 'contrary' state gives way to this infant's post-natal report of parental anguish and grief, as she leaps into a world of dangerous affluence. And the couch she struggles across, the obstacle of privilege, is 'contrary' to the substantial protection of 'A Cradle Song'.

41. In the Notebook, lines 3–4, Blake first wrote: "And see in every face I meet/Marks of weakness marks of woe". He deliberately altered "see" to "mark", despite the solecism of the repetition. The apparently unpolished address, so effective throughout the *Songs*, was deliberate. All the main meanings of "mark" carry physical implications. "Weakness", that is, debility, is not merely visible, but marked in the minds of poverty.

42. Erdman, ed., *Notebook*, N. 107.

43. *Jerusalem*, plate 44. The passage may be read as an explication of 'The Human Abstract'.

44. See *Ahania* (1795), chapter III, verses 3–6, for Blake's account of the origin and effect of the 'mystery'. 'The Catterpiller and Fly' are often mistaken to be the priesthood. Both cannot be. Matters go deeper. In the eighteenth century, a 'caterpillar' commonly meant an extortioner, "one who preys on society"; and a 'fly' a spy. *OED*: 'caterpillar', 2. 'fly', 5b. Dame Lurch was both a genteel 'caterpillar' and a modest 'fly'.

The well-born infant is bred to the sulks in a carpeted and curtained affluence, yet threatened at birth with the constraints of status. Blake transforms a time-worn, discredited coercion into an intimate transgression against nature. The nannying and bracing, in a claustrophobic bedroom of good breeding, raise questions which again come awkward and timely across the centuries.

49 A Poison Tree

The "poison tree", seeded "in the human brain", is planted and "sunned" in the garden of possessive enmity. The mind shifts through animosity, dread and suspicion to the gladness murder brings to the soul.

The design, it has been said, "is a literal illustration of the last stanza". But the words keep us threatened in the garden, moving inwards, while the illustration takes the murderous consequence of the last two lines away to the barren landscape of Experience. The garden is the nursery of a radiating malice. The corpse is vast in perspective, a symbolic groundbase under the caging trunk and branches, which spread mortality to the bleak hills. Beyond them, we may imagine, a dropped child is dying.

50 A Little Boy Lost

"A little boy" is much more surely lost here than "the little boy" among the trees in *Innocence* ever was. And the totality of his loss charges his claim in the first two verses with an effrontery which authority can only erase with iron and fire. Addressing the Deity from his lost existence, the boy effectively appeals for the reality of Innocence, when a "lost" child shared with "the little bird", not freedom merely, but a birthright of sustenance; and was no more obliged than the birds, to gratify God, Priest or King.

The first two verses are a reminder of Innocence accomplished. It is having to outface this that dements the Priest. Customary supplication he could have dealt with. But the boy's impudent "reason" goes straight for a notion of charity which had been circumspectly abandoned. The response lies in the "holy" virtue of keeping "somebody poor". Livelihood, status, even social order under the Priest's "most holy Mystery", are threatened by the boy's cocky heresy: and so the terrifying, mounting retribution of "Priestly care", and another broken family.

In the illustration, the fields of Innocence become the brickfields of north London. This is the "holy place" of vagabond fires, "where many had been burn'd before". The congregation of paupers kneels behind the supplicant parents. At the bottom right hand corner, the boy turns away, hands over his eyes and ears, towards the column of flame. He is unconsumed. If Blake intends to point the survival of his challenge, this is a lamb-like corollary to the fury of 'The Tyger'.

¶ *51 A Little Girl Lost*

"A little boy" on the previous plate suffered a loss spiritually no more destructive than this "little girl's". If she is indeed "little", she is precociously reared; and we recollect the mood of mind and hands, which the nannies in Experience brought to their responsibilities. It was an upbringing others than Blake had noticed without anger.[45]

From their emancipated "future Age", children will read in disbelief this quietly underplayed account of the spiritual consequence of "systems of seduction and education"[46]—the evasive guilt in the "youthful pair", and the repression of the "father white". But this is no simplistic confrontation between youthful fulfilment and moral authority; and the indignation is conveyed with a restraint which withholds any condemnation.

The femininity typified by Ona, "the maiden bright", and identified in the poem's consistently suspect imagery, implies a nurtured acceptance of paternal authority, which survives far beyond puberty. Blake's account of the relationship between the lovers, through the required privacy, the formality of "agreement", the convenient parental withdrawal, the intrusion, the "little girl's" return to her father—all this prepares apprehensively for the outcome.

That "love was thought a crime" is not simply a lesson imposed by age on the young, but inbred. Moreover, the paternal repression is accepted as "loving", and the poem concludes with a proper priority of regret—for the father in his fear and "dismal care".

There are hints of desolation among the birds and windblown tendrils traced across the sky, painting an ironic commentary on the frustrations of the poem. The tree spirals ineffectually. A squirrel climbs towards a figure perched high and insecure, the word "fear" underlined by its tail. If we are to read a message into the squirrel's unique appearance, it is that the "little girl's" emotional journey in embarrassed sexuality and trepidation has been forlorn.[47]

¶ *52 To Tirzah*

'To Tirzah' was added as an afterthought to the *Songs*, in copies Blake relief-etched later than 1803.

Tirzah is one of the multitude of mythological figures with which Blake populated his later epics. There she represents the repressive laws and the manipulative influence of "false self-deceiving tears". Tirzah, the temptress and prude, is the daughter of Rahab, "the great

45. "Children are taught revenge and lies in their very cradles... strange prejudices and vain fears". They "would play harmlessly together, if the distinction of sex was not inculcated long before nature makes any difference". So, Mary Wollstonecraft, *Thoughts on the Education of Daughters* (1787), p. 9, and *Vindication of the Rights of Woman* (1792), p. 87.

46. See Gardner, *Retraced*, p. 131.

47. See *OED*, 'squirrel', 7: shallow-minded and purposeless.

Whore". Both serve Urizen, and she is matriarch to all that is mortal in humanity: "Whate'er is Born of Mortal Birth". With the soul confined within the body, mortality becomes an affliction.

Perhaps the two women in the illustration represent the two aspects of Tirzah, demure and seductive. As the mother of his "Mortal part", she hears mankind's last breath echo the question as his mortality runs into the earth, and his soul is anointed with the blessing of resurrection.

Underplaying the mythology, we may relate the plate directly to *Experience*. We may understand the female addressed, as representative of all we have learnt of sexually alert "modesty" in the manners of Experience. The words of Jesus to Mary, quoted in the last line, then become Blake's fierce and retrospective irony.

¶ 53 *The School-Boy*
It is difficult to name another book of poems which matches the linguistic versatility of the *Songs*. Then in all the modulations of metre and tone, and among the many voices Blake uses from poem to poem, the schoolboy's educated prosody is unique and just right. The educated manner never wavers, starting when the "huntsman winds his horn" in high summer, and progressing line by line into "the blasts of winter". The "cruel eye outworn" had schooled the lad well. His timeless grumble runs in an accomplished stream of poesy, on a theme that might have been set for the class: 'Lines upon a Breaking Up for Summer'.

But here is prosody of such elegance, by a poet untutored in the skill, that an incredulous Dr Samuel Johnson himself would have applauded. And, for once, Blake is turning out poetry "editorially acceptable in theme and presentation". This is so good that it has to appear in the *Songs* somewhere.

If we set about slotting it seriously in, it is no more about Innocence or Experience than anything a magazine would take. In their recreation, the pupils become self-absorbed. Their resentment of authority is unknown in *Innocence*, and the game of marbles, which turns their vision to the ground, is no longer a recreation bringing together a community. The fronds, which loop over the girl by the root of the vine, cage her to the ground, bending her over the game. The children climbing the trellis of branches escape to the relief of their separate devices. When the children climb the branches in 'The Ecchoing Green', where "the grapes of desire ripen in sunshine", it is to reach them down in relaxed accord to their companions walking home in "organized Innocence".

On the other hand, the teacher who delivers "the dreary shower" to the schoolboy may be a stranger to Innocence, but he is no Dame Lurch. He is an anonymous labourer whose weary state earns predictable regret.

Blake left this plate in *Innocence* until the turn of the century, when he moved it into *Experience*. His hesitation is understandable, but it is our pleasure that he did not simply drop it from the *Songs*.

¶ *54 The Voice of the Ancient Bard*
This plate was first included in *Innocence*, and then transferred to *Experience*. But Blake never seemed certain where it belonged, even in later copies.

The italic script and the design suggest that it was the last plate Blake etched for *Innocence*. The listeners still have the grace and composure of that community, though the bard is a newcomer, hardly expected.

From its style, it seems that the poem was written at the end of the 1780s, most likely reflecting in its sanguine proclamations the optimism generated in the earliest days of the French Revolution. The last line of the poem is then an injunction to political leaders, which was to prove forlorn.

List of Sources

WORKS BY BLAKE

Wilkinson, J. J. G., ed. *Songs of Innocence and of Experience*. London: Pickering, 1839.
Keynes, Geoffrey, ed. *Songs of Innocence and of Experience*. Oxford: Oxford University Press, 1970.
Erdman, David V., ed. *The Complete Poetry and Prose of William Blake*. New York: Doubleday, 1988.
———. *The Notebook of William Blake, A Photographic and Typographic Facsimile*. London: Oxford University Press, 1973.
———. *The Illuminated Blake*. London: Oxford University Press, 1975.
Phillips, Michael, ed. *An Island in the Moon*. Cambridge: Cambridge University Press, 1986.

OTHER WORKS CITED

Barbauld, Anna. *Hymns in Prose for Children*. 1781.
Barksdale, Clem. *Noctes Hibernae*. 1653. Bodleian Library, Oxford [Wood 84(5)].
Bentley, G. E. *Blake Records*. London: Oxford University Press, 1969.
———. *Blake Books: Annotated Catalogues of William Blake's Writings . . .* Oxford: Clarendon Press, 1977.
Bindman, David. *Blake as an Artist*. New York: E. P. Dutton, 1977.
Blackmore, Sir Richard. *Creation. A Philosophical Poem*. 1712.
Chambers, E. *Cyclopaedia: or, an Universal dictionary of arts and sciences*. 2 vols. London, 1753.
Cromwell, Thomas Kitson. *History and Description of the Ancient Town and Borough of Colchester*. 2 vols. London: Robert Jennings, 1825.
Cunnington, C. W. & P. *A Dictionary of English Costume*. London: A. & C. Black, 1965.
Day, Thomas. *The History of Sandford and Merton*. 3 vols., 1783–7.
Domestic Medicine. 1786 ed.
Dyer, John. *The Fleece*. 1757.
Erdman, David V. *Blake: Prophet Against Empire*. New York: Dover, 1977, 3rd ed.
———. *Commerce des Lumières: John Oswald and the British in Paris, 1790–1793*. Columbia: University of Missouri Press, 1986.
———, ed. *A Concordance to the Writings of William Blake*. 2 vols. Ithaca: Cornell University Press, 1967.
Essick, Robert. *William Blake: Printmaker*. Princeton: Princeton University Press, 1980.
Gardner, Stanley. *Blake*. London: Evans Bros., 1962 [Literature in Perspective series].
———. *Blake's Innocence and Experience Retraced*. London: Athlone, 1986.
George, M. Dorothy. *London Life in the Eighteenth Century*. Harmondsworth: Penguin Books, 1987, 1st. ed. 1925.
Gilchrist, Alexander. *The Life of William Blake*, edited by W. Graham Robertson. London: The Bodley Head, 1907.
Gloucester Journal.
Goodwin, Albert A. *The Friends of Liberty*. London: Hutchinson, 1979.
Guardian of Education. 1803.
Hanway, Jonas. *An Earnest Appeal for Mercy for the Children of the Poor*. 1766.
———. *Sentimental History of Chimney Sweepers*. 1785.
Hoole, Charles. *A New Discovery of the Old Art of Teaching Schoole*. 1660. Bodleian Library, Oxford [8°. A 6(2) Med.BS].
Jennings, Humphrey, *Pandæmonium 1660–1866*. London: André Deutsch, 1985.
Jones, Edward, and Christopher Woodward. *A Guide to the Architecture of London*. London: Weidenfeld & Nicholson, 1983.
Jones, Mary G. *The Charity School Movement: a Study of Eighteenth-Century Puritanism in Action*. Cambridge: Cambridge University Press, 1938.

Leader, Zachary. *Reading Blake's Songs*. Boston: Routledge & Kegan Paul, 1981.

Lonsdale, Roger, ed. *Eighteenth Century Women Poets*. Oxford: Oxford University Press, 1989.

Lowery, M. R. *Windows of the Morning*. Yale: Yale University Press, 1940.

Mason, William. *Works*. 1811.

More, Hannah. *Strictures On The Modern System Of Female Education*. 1799.

Mss. Rawl. Poet. Bodleian Library, Oxford.

Newton, Isaac. *Opera*, vol. IV.

Opie, Iona and Peter, eds. *The Oxford Nursery Rhyme Book*. Oxford: Clarendon Press, 1955.

Pafford, J. H. P., ed. *Isaac Watts: Divine Songs Attempted in Easy Language for the Use of Children*. London: Oxford University Press, 1971.

Paine, Tom. *The Rights of Man*. 1792.

———. *The Age of Reason*. 1794.

Paley, Morton and Michael Phillips, eds. *William Blake, Essays in Honour of Sir Geoffrey Keynes*. London: Oxford University Press, 1973.

Pepys, Samuel. *The Diary of Samuel Pepys*. Edited by R. C. Latham and W. Matthews. 11 vols. London: G. Bell & Sons, 1970–83.

Phillips, Michael. 'The Printing of Poetical Sketches'. *Bulletin of The New York Public Library*, LXXX (1976).

———. 'From Manuscript Draft to Illuminated Book'. *The Book Collector* (Spring, 1979).

Pickering, Jr, Samuel F. *John Locke and Children's Books in Eighteenth Century England*. Knoxville: University of Tennessee, 1981.

Plumb, J. H. *The First Four Georges*. London: Batsford, 1956.

Raven, James R. *English Popular Literature, and the Image of Business 1760–1790*. Unpublished thesis (Cambridge, 1985).

Shroyer, R. J. 'Mr Jacko knows what riding is'. *Blake: An Illustrated Quarterly* (Spring 1979).

Sitwell, Edith. *English Eccentrics*. London: Faber & Faber, 1933.

The Spectator, no. 10 (12 March 1710), no. 404 (13 June 1712).

The Survey of London. Various publishers, for London County Council. 1900–.

Thomson, James. *The Seasons*. 1730. Reprint.

Townsend, John Rowe. *Written for Children*. London: Bodley Head, 1990, rev. ed.

Trimmer, Sarah. *Reflections upon the Education of Children in Charity Schools*. 1792.

Turbeville, A. S., ed. *Johnson's England*. Oxford: Clarendon Press, 1933.

Venning, Philip. *Wyldes: A New History*. London, 1977.

Victoria History of the Counties of England: Kent. 1908. Reprint, London: Dawson, 1974.

Victoria History of the Counties of England: Surrey. 1902. Reprint, Folkestone: Dawson, 1967.

Williams, Gwyn A. *Artisans and Sans-Culottes*. 1968. Reprint, London: Libris, 1989.

Winny, James, ed. *The Frame of Order*. London: Allen & Unwin, 1957.

Wollstonecraft, Mary. *Thoughts on the Education of Daughters*. 1787.

———. *Vindication of the Rights of Woman*. 1792.

———. *Original Stories from Real Life*. London: J. Johnson, 1791.

Index of Plates

Page numbers in parentheses refer to the Commentary.

General Index